THE WORLD'S COMMON SENSE CHALLENGES

WHY IS COMMON SENSE NOT COMMON?

DEVON S J MORGAN

First published 2019 by TruthSeekers Publishing

Every effort has been made to trace copyright holders. If there have been any omissions, please contact us at:

ISBN: 978-0-9569191-5-1

CONTENTS

CHAPTER TWELVE
The tenth major life issue to apply Aristotelian syllogistic reasoning
**   to is understanding common sense about the core issues in**
**   politics, including government, economic policies, the role of**
**   the media, and how to select politicians**

CHAPTER THIRTEEN
The eleventh major life issue to which Aristotelian syllogistic

CHAPTER FOURTEEN

FOREWORD

Philosophies are the ideas that provide the framework for how we should live. They can be empowering, disempowering, effective, or ineffective. It is intended that the philosophies discussed here should serve as an effective guidance system.

PREFACE: HOW THIS BOOK CAME TO BE WRITTEN

Truth is singular; there cannot be a version!

If you watch movies, you've probably seen a scene where a person and their family are threatened with death by an assailant armed with a gun, who is eventually knocked down. However, instead of doing what instinctively makes sense, at least ensuring the assailant is incapacitated, they run. The assailant quickly recovers and shoots them before they can get away. Even if someone isn't inclined to inflict severe injury just for the sake of it, common sense suggests they should at least get rid of the gun. What about those moments in horror films when, in a haunted house, the characters don't do what seems obvious, that is, to leave? Do you sit back and enjoy the drama, or scream at them to run? After the film, do you complain about how silly it is that people don't flee from obvious danger, only to be reminded that it's just a film? Some of us might prefer the writer had found a creative way to justify why people remain in a house filled with danger, rather than situations where it's clear they could have opened a door and escaped, but choose not to. This attitude can be seen as an instinct for wanting people to act logically. If these scenarios happened in real life, would they indicate a lack of 'instinctive survival common sense'? So, what exactly is this thing called common sense? To what extent do we understand it?

Reason is not automatic. Those who deny it cannot be conquered by it. Do not count on them. Leave them alone. – Ayn Rand

My journey to understand what we call common sense did not begin with the intention of writing a book about the subject. It started with a discussion on social media about the origins of common sense, which then grew into a personal quest to examine, question, and validate this often overused and misunderstood concept. Human beings have a unique trait called consciousness, which can develop into awareness and understanding of ourselves, other living things, and our environment. This consciousness facilitates complex emotions but does not come fully equipped with knowledge. Therefore, we need to study both formally and informally to survive and perform at our best. Our uniquely complex human nature has led to disciplines such as psychiatry and psychology, which exist to help us better understand ourselves and each other. Yet, despite this self-awareness, we observe behaviour that is both baffling and fascinating, seemingly contradicting our supposed logic, intelligence, and reason. The fact that we often recognise a habit or behaviour as harmful but persist in it reveals an aspect of our complex nature related to our emotional traits. From these emotional traits, perhaps our most profound behaviour emerges: that we often consciously harm ourselves. To say we are complicated beings is obvious. Among our many contradictions is the notion of "common sense"—an expression referring to a quality we all supposedly possess, despite most agreeing it's anything but common. In conversations with and surveys of several hundred people, only a few attempted to define what it means. The most common response? "Common sense is not common."

So, if it's not common, why do we call it "common"? Is common sense, then, a myth—or a misunderstood reality?

PROLOGUE

> **Life is and will always be an ongoing pursuit to gain knowledge and enhance our human experience.**

Common sense is not a myth—it is real, and it plays a vital role in making human relationships effective and mutually beneficial. This applies to our relationship with nature as well. However, common sense is often misunderstood, misrepresented, and consequently underdeveloped and underused. While it can be taught to some degree, it is mainly the result of a deeper process involving the growth of both the mind and emotions. This mental and emotional development—often called personal development—follows a methodology that can be explained and practised.

> **Human psychology is profoundly complex and varied. The intricacy of our thoughts and emotions means our mind can be segmented into areas like child psychology and gender psychology. We are also sensitive to various stimuli such as child comedy, sophisticated humour, toilet humour, reverse psychology, sports psychology, and more.**

There is a saying that goes, "An accurate diagnosis is half the cure." So, keeping this in mind, let's begin this journey of understanding by examining the historical context in which the principle of common sense was first informally and *consciously* promoted, and dissect one of its standard definitions.

> **Using accurate information can be the most challenging part of the common-sense formula because it involves knowing which information is most relevant and carries the most weight in terms of importance to a given subject.**

Common sense, at its core, is accurate knowledge applied logically and practically.

Syllogistic reasoning, a form of deductive logic, underpins much of what we consider common sense. Essentially, common sense is often rooted in simple logic and straightforward truth. Once we develop the habit of applying syllogistic reasoning, we become more capable of evaluating arguments based on their merits rather than being influenced by the reputation or qualifications of the speaker. When we let ourselves be influenced by such factors, we often respond emotionally, which is usually unhelpful, especially with complex issues. Common sense is in line with truth, and ideally, truth should also be in line with common sense.

According to writer David Reynolds, the eminent philosopher Aristotle was the one who originated or at least formalised syllogistic logic. This system of reasoning profoundly influenced not only philosophy and scientific inquiry but also the very way we think about the world. One classic example of syllogistic reasoning is: "All men are mortal. Socrates is a man. Therefore, Socrates is mortal."

The **European Age of Enlightenment, or Age of Reason** (of the 17th and 18th centuries), marked the emergence of conscious awareness of syllogistic logic, which forms the foundation upon which we can reliably understand the realities of life and people. Essentially, it is a formula. The extent of Aristotle's influence is demonstrated by the fact that, more than two thousand years after his death, he was credited as the source of many doctrines that shaped the American Constitution. America's Founding Fathers confirmed this. Fathers. One such common-sense doctrine is, "Government should govern for the good of the people, not for the good of those in power." Pakaluk suggests that "the teaching of Aristotle that the Founders most admired was his insistence upon the rule of law, especially as stated in a passage from the *Politics*, where law is said to be reason or intelligence (*nous*), free from passion…"

Our emotions, although vital to the human experience, are the least effective of our faculties in resolving complex problems. The Age of Reason arose as a response to an era ruled by dogma, superstition, and irrationality. It is within this context that the Founders conceived a constitution guided by reason, intentionally crafted to be shielded from the influence of passion.

Philosopher René Descartes (31st March 1596 – 11th February 1650) was influenced by Aristotle. He, in turn, was highly influential during the Age of Reason, or the Enlightenment, and is often regarded as the father of modern Western philosophy. René Descartes is credited with establishing the foundation for rationalism: the view that opinions and actions should be based on reason and knowledge rather than religious belief or emotional impulse. Rationalism was often contrasted with empiricism, which asserts that knowledge and belief mainly arise from sensory experience. However, upon closer examination, both principles form essential parts of the basic framework that underpins common sense.

Descartes is also believed to have shaped the most recognised modern meaning of *common sense* when he stated that everyone possesses a similar and adequate amount of it (*bonsens*), but that it is seldom used effectively. This remark may have hinted at the idea that, as intelligent beings, we all have the potential to develop and utilise a sound understanding of life and human nature. However, if everyone genuinely had the *correct* understanding of life's issues, it would be unlikely for common sense to be so inconsistently applied.

The Age of Reason introduced the idea that human affairs are best guided by reason, rationalism, and logic, rooted in the principles of Aristotle's syllogistic reasoning. This principle remains valid, and it will be demonstrated here that it underpins all of our sound judgements. The principle of syllogistic or logical reasoning will be applied to offer better solutions to **eleven** *critical life issues* discussed in this work. These issues include: childbirth and nurturing children; health and nutrition; pharmaceutical medicines and the medical system; old age, culture, and lasting happiness; caring for Mother Earth, the environment, and our food; money, teamwork, and success; sex and relationships; women's rights and sexism; education; politics, government, economic policies, the role of the media, and how to select politicians; and, finally, the illegality and criminalisation of drugs.

The enlightening power of common sense will be focused on these eleven key issues of life, as they greatly influence our success, survival, and happiness—arguably the three most vital elements of human existence. Common sense is suitable for addressing these essential issues of life because, by nature, it functions as life's most effective emotional and intellectual 'navigation system'. These eleven issues are not an exhaustive list of all significant life challenges that affect most or all of us. They are included in this book because of their unavoidable nature and the considerable difficulties they cause if we lack sufficient knowledge, understanding, and control over them. Moreover, by gaining the knowledge and the common sense to approach life's challenges better and manage them, our lives can be significantly improved.

Our rational mind is meant to gradually reduce and eliminate the problems we create in our interactions with each other and with Nature. You will notice that the solutions to some of the significant challenges we face are not as evident as others. Hence, they are referred to as 'that which ***ought*** to be common sense' because they relate to answers to problems that affect most or all of us.

This definition of common sense by Wikipedia is somewhat flawed, as will be explained shortly.

Wikipedia definition:

> ***"Common sense is a basic ability to perceive, understand, and judge things that are shared by ("common to") nearly all people and can reasonably be expected of nearly all people without the need for debate."***

Common sense = accurate knowledge and understanding that should be common among most or all people.

An example of accurate knowledge or common sense, as earlier defined by Aristotle's syllogistic reasoning, concludes that 'Socrates is mortal because he is a man'. Regarding the Wikipedia definition just quoted, if we say 'common knowledge' instead of 'common sense', it is clear that it is not 'ability', but knowledge and understanding that should be common. Therefore, the more precise part of Wikipedia's definition of common sense is its reference to knowledge and experience that can reasonably be expected to be known and accepted by almost everyone, without the need for debate.

However, in many cases, it is unreasonable to expect that most people would possess specific knowledge and understanding. This is because some knowledge that concerns all of us needs to be taught or deliberately sought. Often, there is no awareness that certain things are necessary. For example, knowledge about the science of nutrition should be common knowledge or common sense, yet many people do not consider or adopt this understanding.

Based on the Aristotelian syllogistic reasoning mentioned earlier, common sense is the correct *conclusion* that derives from a logical, deductive process of reasoning rooted in truth and accuracy. Thus, in essence, common sense represents the accurate knowledge or understanding of issues related to life and human behaviour. Therefore, defining common sense as "the ability to perceive, understand, and judge things" can be seen as the capacity to process information and impressions accurately. However, the *ability to judge* is not, in itself, common sense, as suggested by Wikipedia; rather, it is the outcome or conclusion that stems from our capacity to apply an accurate understanding to life and people.

The process of living involves solving minor and major problems. Our ability to accurately assess life's challenges is vital in today's complex world.

We may have named the output of our ability to perceive and make sense of life and things 'common sense' because of an unconscious desire for a universal understanding – a universal "language" that everyone speaks. Perhaps we expect each other to be accurate in every situation we consider essential. The mind needs to be developed to correctly interpret and **understand things** and issues (information and activities) that are shared by, or common to, nearly all people. When this occurs, information becomes knowledge/understanding, and this can lead to wisdom.

Electricity has always existed on Earth. However, it had to be discovered and understood before we could harness it for purposes such as lighting, machinery, and other applications. Similarly, common sense, the correct knowledge and understanding of things that are familiar to nearly all of us, is always available. However, we must discover it; then use it to understand and relate to each other; we must use it to understand and relate to Nature and our artificial environment; we must use it to navigate life's ups and downs, and we must use it to interpret life's events accurately. The possible exception to the rule that common sense is always here pertains to knowledge related to new customs or societal advancements. In this reality, many of us find that we need to learn new things, such as modern technology that is common sense to a younger generation.

From the correct definition of common sense, the 'ingredients' of common sense are in two parts:

1.   Relevant information and accurate knowledge, which lead to correct solutions (common sense) to realities that are shared by nearly all of us, and,
2.   The ability to perceive, understand, interpret, judge, and use this information to provide correct solutions (common sense).

According to the definition of common sense, most of us have the potential to understand, interpret, and judge things—or to process information and impressions—that are broadly shared across human experience. How fully this potential is realised depends on our willingness to broaden our knowledge by taking a greater interest in life and other people.

We acquire such knowledge through both formal and informal study and by enhancing our ability in logical thinking, especially relating to human behaviour and everyday life. Equally crucial is the accuracy of the information we absorb, as this directly affects the quality of our judgement—what we call common sense.

Another obstacle to developing common sense is a narrow focus. If we are primarily concerned only with what directly affects us and show little interest in the broader human experience, our overall understanding of life will remain limited.

So, what is an example of a shared reality that everyone should recognise, if not for themselves, then at least to guide others? One such example is this: in a relationship breakup involving children, neither parent should poison the minds of the children against the other. Doing so can seriously harm their mental and emotional well-being. Children are far better served when they are supported in maintaining healthy relationships with both parents. This should be common knowledge—common sense.

To genuinely become a person guided by common sense, we must practise *active thinking*. This process involves observing, listening, reading, and, most importantly, questioning everything rather than accepting things at face value.

Becoming a keen observer is essential for developing common sense. A fundamental lesson we learn from being a keen observer is this: if an action consistently yields poor or no results, it is not based on truth, so we should stop performing it. This should be obvious. Persistently engaging in a redundant action would equate to repeatedly banging our head against a brick wall and expecting a different outcome.

Many of us limit active thinking to certain areas of life. As a result, our fundamental ability to perceive, understand, and judge is underutilised in many situations, which leads to a limited amount of common sense. This is **part** of the reason why people often say that common sense is not so common. Even some individuals with a highly developed ability to perceive and understand tend to focus on only specific areas of interest. Consequently, their acquisition of common sense becomes very selective. A limited understanding can stem from a lack of intellectual curiosity or having a narrow range of curiosity. Dr John Sklare describes intellectual curiosity as a desire to invest time and energy into learning more about a person, place, thing or concept. Such curiosity provides us with enough information, ideas, and impressions to process through our logical mind, and this knowledge, in turn, influences our attitude, which shapes our actions.

Many people have never developed the ability to perceive, understand, and judge things that are shared by ("common to") nearly all people because they have been busy "minding their own business."

When syllogistic reasoning is rooted in truth, it shapes our ability to discern what is accurate and relevant. Our capacity to use such knowledge constructively and effectively fosters common sense. The closer our thinking process aligns with the precision of maths and science, the more accurate our conclusions will be, and this is when we are at our most effective. As emotional beings, in practice, this 'precision thinking' represents where emotions and intellect merge in an ideal 'balanced marriage', with 'logical-truth' as the dominant and guiding force.

We do not live in societies where there is a constant and urgent need for individuals to be wise or deeply knowledgeable about issues that affect everyone. In reality, developing or enhancing our fundamental ability to perceive, understand, and judge shared human experiences is not crucial for survival—or even, in many cases, for happiness. Psychologists have observed that most people tend to follow the path of least resistance, often doing only what is necessary to get by or to achieve a certain level of success.

You can achieve success without being aware of essential information that should be common knowledge but isn't. A typical example of taking the easiest path is choosing to watch television instead of reading, or favouring sensational stories in tabloids over well-informed articles in broadsheet newspapers and a wider variety of books.

Much of what is **considered** common sense is much more than just basic understanding on how to manage in life or succeed in business or a profession. Common sense is **supposed to include** knowledge that some of us regard as higher learning, yet remains unknown to most. This advanced knowledge should be common sense for nearly everyone because it relates to issues that affect almost all people. These are aspects of life that we cannot 'perceive' or understand without being taught or actively seeking knowledge of. For example, the science of proper nutrition is not common knowledge, even though it is relevant to everyone, and can therefore be considered 'higher' or 'exclusive' knowledge. It is somewhat 'exclusive' because it isn't an understanding we can 'perceive' without study or instruction. Mainly, we cannot simply 'perceive' it because it involves an invisible science. Similarly, you cannot just 'perceive' or understand how a car works by looking at it.

Most people are unfamiliar with the science of adequately caring for our body and mind because it has never been widely taught. Moreover, many have not made the effort to acquire this understanding, which is why it has not become 'common sense'. It is possible to be regarded as successful while lacking the knowledge to care for one's health correctly.

All knowledge about our well-being and survival must be actively sought, so it becomes common sense. This is essential because no instruction manual for practical living was embedded within us at birth.

Wisdom is often regarded as a synonym for common sense, which might explain why both are widely and accurately seen as rare. After all, how many of us can genuinely claim to be wise?

We should not judge truth based on sincerity, because it's possible to be sincerely wrong. So, we should weigh truth on truth scales and sincerity on sincerity scales. –Jim Rohn

---

Being perceptive is also a trait of having common sense. However, it is not a vital necessity for survival. This lack of necessity ensures that common sense is not applied across all aspects of life that it aims to address. We called it 'common sense' because we intended that all knowledge influencing our interactions with each other, our environment, and Nature should become a shared understanding for everyone. This has not happened, as reflected by widespread disharmony and our strained relationship with Nature.

As syllogistic reasoning becomes a familiar and instinctive way of understanding and solving life's problems, the claim that 'common sense is not common' will become less frequent.

A lot more than 'sense' for dummies

Common sense should be our default response when interpreting life's issues. However, most of the actions needed to be effective in life are not hardwired into our conscious or unconscious minds. In this context, common sense is not about a focus on "'sense' for dummies". Every individual must acquire a certain level of common sense because, without it, they would struggle to survive or face very severe difficulties. We all know how to cross the road safely, how to handle sharp objects in the kitchen, how to work, and many other everyday skills.

However, while common sense includes basic knowledge about how to live safely and avoid danger, it also aims to encapsulate a deeper understanding of life, one that guides us towards realising our highest potential.

Gaining a profound sense of common sense requires the development of both our minds and emotions through logical thinking, bringing us closer to fully living up to our nature as conscious, thinking, and reasoning beings. To become above average, we should all actively study life and people. Once we acquire an understanding that goes beyond surface knowledge, we will have common sense – an effective guidance system. An effective guidance system (common sense) is produced through a syllogistic and deductive method of thinking. When this kind of logical reasoning is grounded in a rational and balanced philosophy, it can significantly influence the way we feel, shaping our emotions in constructive ways. When our emotions are guided by clear reasoning, we are better equipped to pursue the core objectives of life, which common sense tells us are health, happiness, success, and survival.

Isn't it fascinating that common sense reveals the purpose of life, and that similar principles are also enshrined in the American Declaration of Independence? It states: *We hold these truths to be self-evident, that all men are created equal, and that they are endowed by their Creator with certain unalienable Rights, among which are* **Life, Liberty and the pursuit of Happiness.**

Common sense = knowledge that is of varying degrees of importance but applies to some or all of us.

Does the following story of Dave Jones illustrate a life guided by intelligent emotions or logical reasoning? Dave Jones is a keen fan of *rap music*, especially 'gangsta rap'. This brief story shows how powerful suggestion can be. Dave weighs 125 pounds and is about 5 feet 7 inches tall. The music had a

substantial impact on his personality. He adopted an unusual walking style, which he believed suited a street gangster. In his mind, he was a gangster. His intimidating behaviour had made many people step back. Confident, he attempted to threaten a security guard who was 6 feet 2 inches and at least 220 pounds. He was knocked to the ground.

The film *'Stupidity'* explores the nature and history of stupidity. In it, the narrator explains how, every two to three months, someone uses a lighter or another naked flame to check the fuel level in their car's petrol tank, often leading to disastrous results. YouTube videos show numerous similar cases; the internet displays many more incidents of extreme human behaviour. However, some understandings do not need formal or informal teaching; these are things we are expected to pick up from our environment, much like the process of osmosis. When someone then acts against this understanding, it can be very shocking. Yet, as this book progresses, you will see that common sense is much more than that. This is because much of what this book discusses is not as simple as the above examples, but since they influence nearly all people, they should be regarded as common sense.

The extensive research, mainly inspired by the Oscar Pistorius murder trial, has uncovered some intriguing and fascinating findings about key aspects of common sense that are not widely recognised or fully understood. These include:

- The origin/history, and reason for common sense
- Some critical areas of life, such as food and medicine, are where common sense is not widely applied. It is not commonly used because societies have never considered the need to develop a philosophy that can be universally applied to them.
- The reason why there is a widespread belief that common sense is not truly 'common'
- The reason why it is called 'common' sense, even though everyone appears to agree that it's not 'common'
- That common sense can be specific to time and place.
- That common sense can be founded on science or customs.
- Common sense is vital to the duration and quality of our survival, happiness, health, and prosperity.

Specific knowledge that should be common sense because it applies to everyone may not be considered critically important for living an effective life. For example, people won't accuse you of lacking common sense if you say that the sun rose and set today, even though in reality the sun doesn't move and it is always a case of the Earth rotating around the sun.

People are unlikely to accuse you of lacking common sense if you say that 'up' is above your head or 'down' is below your feet, even though there is no absolute 'up' or 'down', as demonstrated by the Earth being round. In reality, up can also be down from a different point on Earth. We now consider this information trivia because no sensible person believes the world is flat anymore; therefore, there is no fear of 'falling off the earth', nor can we walk to the 'end of the earth'. Another phrase that may be connected to the old belief in a flat Earth is "the four corners of the earth." While it is often explained as a reference to the four cardinal compass points, whatever its original meaning, the critical point is this: the world has advanced because it is now common knowledge, and common sense, that the Earth is not flat. We are at our best when our thinking is rooted in common sense.

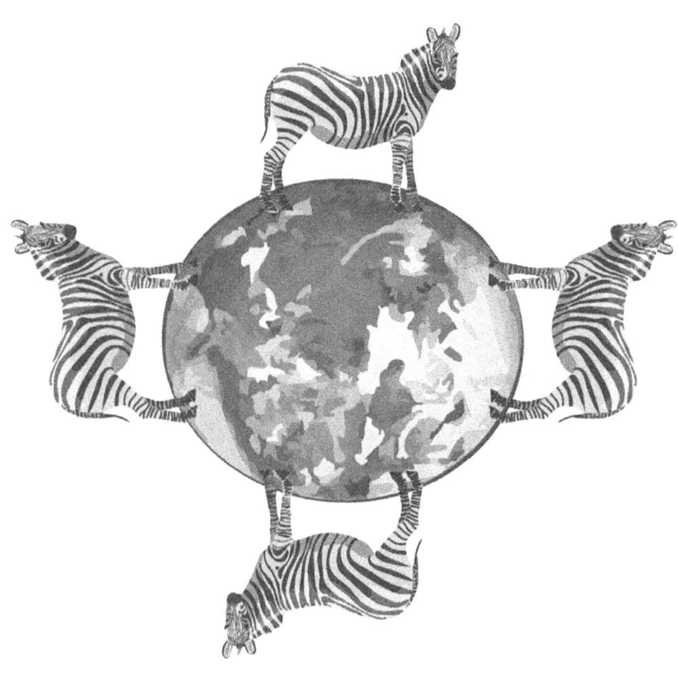

Which way is up?

CHAPTER ONE

The context and fundamental basics of common sense:
The challenge of being human

We are the most complex creatures on this planet. Just observe our various artificial body modifications, including some extreme alterations to resemble animals, our numerous sexual preferences, and our diverse cultures. This complexity is also driven by our ability to think and believe anything we choose, regardless of its truth or falsity. This is evident in the countless religious beliefs that divide us, with each group following its principles with equal conviction. We also hold many political and social ideologies that oppose one another and create divisions, each group adhering to its beliefs with similar certainty. To manage our diversity and intricacies, it is clear that a logical way of thinking is essential to help us understand life. All of this stems from our unique trait of lacking a fixed programme to follow, since we possess free will. As a result, we can think and feel however we wish, and we do so every day.

The whole world is written down in books, but, like eggs, you have to crack them open to get anything out of them. – Clifton Taulbert

---

The significance of our logical mind is apparent in how it guides and influences our understanding of science, technology, architecture, agriculture, and more. As a result, it allows us to meet our fundamental needs for societal progress, food, clothing, shelter, survival, and happiness. We are social beings – we require one another to survive, flourish, and find happiness. Nevertheless, this is not easy to accomplish due to our complex nature.

This complication requires that we have sufficient knowledge and understanding of how to communicate effectively, please each other, or at least avoid conflicts and coexist. None of this is easy to achieve because we all exist at different levels of understanding and emotional development.

We notice that those we consider wise and full of common sense are individuals who have enriched themselves with a detailed understanding of life. They tend to be very practical and have a talent for understanding how things function in practice. They also benefit from possessing a sense of historical perspective, which helps them interpret the present more accurately; today becomes clearer when viewed through the lens of yesterday or any other previous time. The wise gain their insight partly by acting as amateur sociologists and psychologists, developing an ability to understand and anticipate human behaviour. This wisdom is acquired through careful observation of life and people, as well as through extensive and thoughtful reading.

Understandings about being human that should be common sense

A mind, like a home, is furnished by its owner, so if one's life is cold and bare, he can blame none but himself. – Louis L'Amour

---

Our mental home is infinitely more important than our physical home, so develop and guard it carefully.

- Physical brain =hardware.
- Physical brain's software = mind.
- Our mind's **best food/tools** = ideas and accurate (and relevant) knowledge = common sense.

Our life did not start with us having thoughts. It began with us possessing *basic* emotional intelligence. We cried when we needed food, when we felt discomfort, and when we desired affection or felt 'abandoned'. This bundle of emotions was shaped and developed through a process of feeling, touching, hearing, smelling, tasting, and seeing, until we reached our current capacity to think and reason. We now have the opportunity to continually refine our philosophy based on accurate knowledge, which in turn enhances our emotional intelligence—the foundation of sound decision-making.

Much of our daily activities do not require careful, analytical, or deep thinking. We perform them in 'autopilot' mode – in unconscious competence. So, if we spend eight hours working in a job that doesn't demand much thinking or new ideas, eight hours sleeping, an hour or more eating, and a few hours watching television, we are unlikely to do much thinking. Therefore, our minds and imaginations do not get adequate exercise. Without proper exercise, our minds and imagination could atrophy, leading to failures in achieving good health, happiness, and prosperity. Our mental and emotional faculties need regular exercise to stay sharp and precise. Limited thinking results in limited outcomes.

Your thoughts become the blueprint for your life, dictating what you do and expect from life. – Nightingale Conant

---

If we don't take the time to plan our own lives, we're likely to end up following someone else's, and their plan may not serve our best interests.

We are born with an instinct to survive. However, like a computer, human beings need a programme or philosophy to function. The key is to have a programme or philosophy that aligns with our self-interest, and the best self-interest is enlightened self-interest, which also benefits others. The fact that many have a programme that causes them to act against their self-interest reveals something about the nature of our mind and emotions – like soil, they do not care what we plant in them. They will grow weeds, poisonous plants, and flowers in equal measure. The fact that a person can be programmed to commit suicide, based on a promise that cannot be proved, confirms this about our minds and feelings.

The fact that many of us act in self-destructive ways, despite being born with a drive to survive, clearly shows that our minds and emotions can be conditioned to go against our self-interest. We must learn to nurture thoughts and feelings that lead us to happiness, survival, and prosperity. The more diverse and positive information we feed into our minds, the more powerful we become. This is because everything in life is interconnected like a giant jigsaw puzzle. Once we put the pieces together, life becomes clearer; much fear is alleviated, and our place in the grand scheme of things becomes evident. A knowledge of history reveals that life on Earth has varied dramatically across different periods. What caused these differences? The driving force was knowledge. Each era was shaped by the knowledge people held, and by how that knowledge influenced their mindset and temperament. The outcomes of their actions, in turn, depended on whether their understanding was guided by wisdom, common sense, or logical thinking.

Today, we have made mechanical technology one of the main driving forces of our world. This might have been ideal if it had come from an environmentally conscious viewpoint. Logic indicates that any technology that damages life is fundamentally flawed—or at least, not optimal. The effects of our current technological progress include environmental pollution and numerous other adverse effects.

Fortunately, common sense motivates some of us to choose environmentally friendly options. Since modern transport and energy production are major sources of pollution, the growing adoption of electric vehicles and cleaner energy should be supported and promoted.

Technological innovations that curb air pollution should be recognised as genuine advancements, owing to their direct effect on reducing respiratory illnesses. They will also contribute to a preferable decrease in another pollution consequence, severe environmental harm to our groundwater and soil.

Common sense, not just a human necessity?

Despite having a stronger innate instinct for survival, animals are still capable of error, and such mistakes are often detrimental. In a David Attenborough nature programme, orca whales (killer whales) were on the verge of killing a baby blue whale when two other adult blue whales arrived. The tide turned, and the orcas fled. However, instead of doing the instinctive and sensible thing—staying behind to protect the baby whale—the adults continued chasing the orcas. Eventually, they were drawn too far away to defend the calf. The orcas, being much faster, seized the opportunity, doubled back, and killed the baby whale.

Logical, syllogistic reasoning would begin with the premise that the main goal is to protect the baby whale. The second premise would be that the orcas are much faster; therefore, pursuing them would be counterproductive and futile. In their actions, we can see that the whales lacked syllogistic reasoning, which led to the disastrous result.

The unique human and common sense

In a world of complex individuals, the basis of common sense starts with recognising how we fit into the broader scheme of life on Earth. The first lesson must be recognising the contrasts that exist in life and what they are meant to teach us about our unique capacity and potential. This fundamental understanding of the self should be common knowledge—what we call common sense.

Characteristics of one-half of life on earth – human life

- We have free will.

- We possess a remarkable capacity for thought and imagination, yet there is no urgent, universal force compelling us to utilise this power entirely.

- The direction and scope of our lives are mainly determined and controlled by our ability to think.

- We can enhance our intelligence, knowledge, reasoning ability, and wisdom—all of which contribute to common sense, even in complex situations—but this development is neither automatic nor compulsory.

- However, our complex world requires us to think and utilise all of our abilities, as mentioned earlier, or we may face severe consequences for not doing so.

- In effect, free will has led to vastly different ways of using our ability to think and imagine – some of us engage in much more thinking and imagining than others. Free will has shaped a broad spectrum of emotions – some motivate us to act in our best interest, while others do not.

- Our full potential remains unknown.

- Due to the significant difference in how we use our capacity to think and imagine, many people often do not live life to the fullest – they fail to maximise their potential.

Characteristics of the other half of life on Earth – animals and other living creatures

- All animal species possess an instinct unique to them. The use of this instinct is generally automatic and necessary unless disrupted by humans.

- The direction and scope of their lives are dictated and controlled by instinct and adaptability.

- They do not have the **conscious ability** to increase or alter their instinct; change occurs gradually through an evolutionary process whereby they adapt to their environment.

- Their potential is usually maximised (lived to the full). Unlike humans, who may halt their mental development, a tree will not grow only halfway to its maximum height, and other living beings tend to be fully functional in all their abilities.

Our conscious, reasoning mind makes us uniquely human, but it also puts us at a disadvantage compared to other creatures in a simple yet profound way. A beaver, for example, usually lives up to its full potential; as far as we know, all beavers instinctively understand how to build dams and are not lacking in any vital aspect of their lives. In contrast, human beings must choose to pursue their potential. This is the nature and consequence of what we call free will. Because of free will—and thus not being forced by Nature to maximise our potential—many of us opt to limit our understanding of life, people, the Earth, and the universe we inhabit. How we experience life and what we gain from it largely depend on our interest in and understanding of it. The varying degrees of intellectual curiosity and the depth of one's interest and knowledge of life distinguish people from one another and ensure that equality in achievement, happiness, and even survival will never be fully realised. Since babies are naturally curious, isn't it astonishing that many adults are incurious about many aspects of life? How did so many of us adults lose our curiosity?

Generally, animals have an instinctive understanding of how to respond to everything that affects them in their environment. In contrast, human beings need to be taught about many of the factors that influence us or choose to learn about them. And because we are often not compelled to gain a complete understanding, we tend to settle for a superficial or surface-level grasp of things.

Our uniqueness lies in being born without knowledge and understanding, needing to learn about life. This often contrasts sharply with other life forms. We frequently unknowingly consume substances that can ultimately cause our premature death. In the nature series, Swarm – Nature's Incredible Invasions, the narrator, David Tennant, said of African driver ants: "…the soil millipede is killed quickly, but the soldiers' highly sensitive antennae immediately reveal that it's poisonous. The message soon reaches nearby ants. They know exactly what to do. They gather lumps of mud and bury the problem. With the millipede out of harm's way, the trail can safely continue its journey."

Life in the natural world is a clear and observable aspect of our reality. Simply observing it can prompt the two most powerful questions that drive our pursuit of knowledge and discovery: *Why?* and *How?* If we study our co-inhabitants on Earth, it can spark contemplation about the nature and differences between intelligence, reason, and instinct. For example, what lesson(s) can we learn from studying the botfly? The botfly's young feed on the blood and tissue of living cows. The mother is such a large insect that the cows would notice if she landed on them and flick her off. Solution: Find a lightweight courier. She captures a housefly and attaches her eggs to it. The fly eventually lands on a cow to drink its sweat. The warmth of the cow causes the botfly eggs to hatch. They fall from the housefly, land on the cow, bore into the cow's skin and feed. After a few months, they emerge and fall to the ground to continue their life cycle.

How does the botfly know about this? How does it consistently solve this problem? Is it through deductive reasoning or instinct? Its solution involves a systematic three-step process or 'planning'. Does this seem like an extraordinary level of sense for a fly to possess?

Since we possess far greater intelligence than a botfly, we must also have the ability to develop a consistent, systematic approach to solving our challenges. **It is called syllogistic deductive reasoning, and it produces common sense with practical solutions more reliably than emotions ever will. When infused with accurate knowledge, deductive reasoning can provide the foundation for solving even our most complex problems. We will only be less consistent than a botfly in reaching correct conclusions and solving our problems if our knowledge is insufficient, or our emotions dominate our thought processes.**

Suppose we combine curiosity about life in the natural world with a curiosity about the 'why' of human behaviour, our understanding of life expands. Even with this curiosity and the pursuit of knowledge, our deep and complex nature means we have a subconscious mind that we don't fully understand. This further highlights our depth and complexity. Have you ever been reprimanded for asking too many questions, or told that you delve into matters too deeply? Isn't this strange, considering that everything about us is deep and complex? The fact that some of us are even unaware of the existence of our subconscious speaks loudly about our profound nature. This is further emphasised by the fact that we don't understand madness well enough to cure it, and that our dreams remain largely a mystery to us.

The complexity of human nature necessitates that we develop a shared understanding of how reality works, particularly in our relationships with one another. An absence of this understanding underpins many of the world's issues, starting within the most basic social unit: the family. Often, conflicts between family members emerge not from intentional harm but from a lack of mental and emotional skills.

Since we are driven by emotions, to be sophisticated, we have to educate our emotions.

What knowledge or abilities were we born with?

Innate behaviour is that which does not need to be learnt or practised. It is governed by genetics. How much innate behaviour do we possess regarding the knowledge we call common sense? If you see broken glass on the floor, common sense advises you to walk around it. Would a baby naturally know this and behave accordingly? No.

Syllogistic and deductive reasoning is the thread that runs through actions as basic as 'instinctively' walking around broken glass. We naturally develop this understanding through our ability to identify and categorise objects, and recognise the cause-and-effect consequences that arise from interacting with them. *The following elements of syllogistic reasoning are used to arrive at this 'instinctive' common-sense decision.*

- Human flesh is soft
- Broken glass is sharp and hard; therefore, it will cut human flesh if stepped on. This will cause pain and bleeding.
- Therefore, avoid stepping on broken glass; walk around it.

This pattern of reasoning applies to all our sound judgements and common-sense decisions, even in seemingly complex issues. It identifies the natural and more probable causes and effects of our actions.

Because the science of cause and effect is not like magic, where there is an instant correlation between our thoughts, our actions, and the result, many people cannot examine their undesirable result and retrace their steps back to their philosophy, and thus accept responsibility.

What becomes clear in this discussion is that much of what should be common sense stems from a mental and emotional development process that we, generally, must nurture. If a baby had never heard words, would it be able to speak? Evidence suggests it would not. We know that a larger vocabulary enhances our thinking, so if we had no words, how much thinking could we do? While not absolute, evidence indicates it wouldn't be much. Therefore, demonstrating common sense would be challenging. If a child never interacted with others, would they know how to maintain a good relationship? The answer is no. This is shown by the fact that the rules of relationships vary across cultures. As social beings, we learn this skill through various processes of interaction, observation, and gathering impressions, ideas, and knowledge.

Helen Keller was a testament to the importance of words in our development. Although she was not blind and deaf at birth, she became so at 19 months old, and she never learnt to speak clearly; words still acted as the catalyst for her growth. After this tragedy, she was violent and difficult to control. Her transformation began after her parents hired Ann Sullivan to help her. Sullivan taught her a 'finger language'. However, this did not have an immediate effect until one day, when Sullivan was trying to teach her that everything has a name. During one lesson, she pumped water onto her hand while using the finger technique to spell " water ". The cascading water on her hand evoked a 'lost' memory, and she suddenly tried to enunciate the word. Once she could assign names and meanings to things, her life was changed. The simple experience of learning the name and meaning of things sparked her personal growth, and that process continued until she became an accomplished and renowned figure. She became the first deaf-blind person to earn a Bachelor of Arts degree. She was an author, political activist, and lecturer. Her birthplace in West Tuscumbia, Alabama, USA, is now a museum, and it sponsors an annual Helen Keller Day.

How much common sense do children have? One day at school during the 1970s, I was about to drink some water when I had a negative interaction with a girl. It was a time when every boy, including me, practised karate and believed he was Bruce Lee. So, when the conflict arose with this girl over who should drink first, I lacked the sense to recognise that even though I was supposed to have an advantage, being male, she was almost a foot taller than I; therefore, my perception of karate greatness was of no value. If I had common sense, I would have walked away, but I didn't. We didn't have a 'fight', in the strict sense of the word. She grabbed me by my shirt collar with one of her long arms. Her strength and her arm length enabled her to hold me at bay and made it impossible for me to make contact with her. She then reached for a stone with her other hand and proceeded to rain 'stone-in-fist' blows on my head.

We then went into a sort of pirouette while I tried to get away. At this point, she seemed much taller than she was. When she finally released me, half-dazed and spinning, with a bruise on my pride and my head, I felt glad that the first stone I threw struck her head, because it stopped her in her tracks and spared me from her fury. Yet, I hadn't learnt the lesson from this about the danger of clashing with girls taller or bigger than myself. Years later, at the same school, there was a very tall girl whom the boys and I called 'Crane'. She didn't like it, and considering that she was much bigger than the girl who hit me with the stone, I was lucky she wasn't violent, or I might not be here writing this book. My behaviour was that of an immature child lacking common sense.

Our mature and logical mind tells us that a woman's height should not be the basis for mockery.

We are born with an innate instinct for walking. This is one aspect of our makeup that Nature urges us to develop. That's why, eventually, everyone learns how to walk. However, much of what we become is not instinctive. We must choose to learn and grow, or we become who we are by default, because Nature does not tolerate a vacuum in our emotions. Helen Keller's early life experiences demonstrate our innate curiosity. In her case, when she was unable to understand her surroundings, she often became frustrated and lashed out, sometimes by breaking things. She was also unable to relate appropriately to other children; they were frightened by her curious attempts to push her hand into their mouths. She was even violent and resistant to something as simple as sitting at a table to eat. Her emotional capacity, especially her curiosity and anger, continued to develop, even without words. Her early life showed that no matter how limited our intellectual growth, our emotions will still grow and change. However, they only become refined and sophisticated once we have words and ideas to guide them. Yet, even without guidance, our emotions do not stay those of a toddler or child. That is why even an adult who never faced Helen Keller's limitations would be unlikely to throw a tantrum by lying on the ground, crying, and rolling around. In terms of our sophistication and intellectual development, we need words and ideas. Words and concepts form the basis of how we think. In this sense, we are like blank slates waiting to be written on, or like computers that cannot operate without software. Just as a computer's performance depends on the quality of its software, the quality of our thinking depends on the ideas we are exposed to and adopt. Common sense can become part of that software if we choose to develop perceptiveness.

Common sense =perceptiveness

We also have a built-in drive to be intimate and have sex. This explains how the first humans learned to do it without a teacher. However, the consequence of their actions was not something they would have understood instinctively, and this can still be true today. Imagine a boy and a girl shipwrecked on an isolated island with no knowledge of the birth of babies. If they matured and engaged in sex, they would not anticipate that the outcome could be pregnancy, and so they would have to 'learn on the job'.

When it comes to life on Earth, humans take the longest time to develop, whether in terms of walking, running, reaching maturity, acquiring survival skills, realising full potential, or achieving social progress. These abilities often require years of growth via both formal and informal education, as well as life experience. However, this developmental timeline could be shortened if syllogistic and deductive reasoning were formalised and integrated into school curricula, equipping students early on with tools for clearer thinking and improved decision-making.

It would become an instinctive process of reaching conclusions at every level of our school systems, and common sense would flow and transform societies. The very nature of human beings dictates that we must develop our senses (knowledge) to be effective in the art and science of living well. Currently, the overwhelming emphasis of our formal education is on preparing us for employment. Common sense is both the basic level and the pinnacle of the development of our senses and abilities in understanding and dealing with life and people.

The status of common sense

If you believe that academic brilliance, intelligence, and a high IQ are the ultimate markers of human development and essential for success in life, consider this:

According to Brian Tracy, the life coach, "Gallup, Inc., [an American research-based, global performance-management consulting company] did a study by surveying 1,500 of the most respected people in America to find out what the single most important quality for success is. They agreed almost unanimously that it was common sense."

Many of the wealthiest self-made millionaires and billionaires did not achieve a degree.

It is worth noting that these successful individuals place greater value on common sense than on academic qualifications, a high IQ, or raw intelligence.

These top achievers likely recognise from experience that academic abilities do not prepare a person for life's peaks and troughs, or its vicissitudes. Since psychologists agree that emotions influence us, we improve our chances of success in life by actively developing our emotional intelligence. Mary C Lamia, Ph.D., explains: "Your emotions will drive the decisions you make today, and your success may depend upon your ability to understand and interpret them." It is from this emotional competence that our insights and perceptiveness grow. As you examine the dictionary definition of common sense below, you will see that insight and perceptiveness are part of the common-sense formula. These skills help

us deal effectively with people, which is a key aspect of common sense. Undoubtedly, one reason why high achievers might place common sense at the top of the list of competencies is that it involves the ability to resolve or avoid conflicts. In a world where conflicts are common, such a skill is highly valuable. However, it's not possible to be proficient at conflict resolution or avoidance without a good understanding of life and people.

In his book, Emotional Intelligence: Why It Can Matter More Than IQ, Daniel Goleman wrote, *"People who are emotionally adept – who know and manage their own feelings well, and who read and deal effectively with other people's feelings – are at an advantage in any domain of life, whether romance and intimate relationships or picking up the unspoken rules that govern success in organizational politics...People with well-developed emotional skills are also more likely to be content and effective in their lives, mastering the habits of mind that foster their own productivity; people who cannot marshal some control over their emotional life fight inner battles that sabotage their ability for focused work and clear thought."*

You do not want to be an intellectual heavyweight but an emotional lightweight.

Scientists have confirmed that living in a concrete jungle (urban cities) makes us more vulnerable to stress. ***This is something everyone should know—and it should become common sense.*** Studies have shown (and many people know this instinctively) that exposure to green space reduces stress, improves health, and makes us less vulnerable to depression.

The village lifestyle contrasts sharply with urban living, fostering a different mentality. Here are two examples of the village mindset that promote practical living, which is the aim of common sense: The song, 'Lean on Me,' contains lyrics that say, "Lean on me, when you're not strong, and I'll be your friend, I'll help you carry on, for it won't be long, 'til I'm gonna need somebody to lean on..." The songwriter, Bill Withers, explained the story behind these lyrics as follows: "My socialisation was, it was very likely and very practical to expect a Lean On Me circumstance to exist. My experience was trying to adjust to a world where that circumstance was not the rule (rather than) but the exception." According to Withers, in the Deep South (USA), where he was born, it was usual for the community to share an individual's sorrow. If a person's house were destroyed, community members would help to rebuild it. Secondly, Miriam Makeba, a once-famous South African singer, made this profound statement: "In my culture, we do not have a word for 'alone', it simply does not exist. Everyone in the community is family, which means everyone is responsible for everyone else."

Dolly Parton, married for 50 years, is a musician, singer-songwriter, record producer, actress, author, and businesswoman who demonstrates the connection between emotional intelligence and common sense or wisdom. The Ricky Gervais character, David Brent, in the sitcom The Office, quoted Dolly Parton as describing life like this: "Life is just a series of peaks and troughs, and you don't know whether you're in a trough until you're climbing out, or on a peak until you're coming down. And that's it, you know, you never know what's around the corner. But it's all good." If you want the rainbow, you've got to put up with the rain." This is wisdom, a synonym for common sense. Is such a person less likely to be frustrated by life's experiences and events? Yes, wisdom is accessible to everyone, regardless of whether they have only completed a high school education. It's a potent reminder that wisdom is not limited to the formally educated. It often surpasses academic learning in its relevance to real life.

If you accept the definition of common sense and its interpretation as given in the introduction, you will see that it is not the same as being well-educated. Nor is it the same as being intelligent or having a high IQ. However, education, intelligence, and a high IQ can help develop common sense. Someone may have exceptional intelligence in areas like mathematics, physics, or economics, yet still lack a good deal of common sense. A person could become a prime minister or president and not be known for having much common sense. Common sense is built through broad, deep, and consistent engagement with both life and people. However, many of us choose not to engage deeply with either, and as a result, our understanding of common sense remains limited. This limitation, in turn, influences how often and how effectively we use it in our daily lives.

Part of our engagement with life and others involves "borrowing" other people's brains through reading, listening, and analysing. A mix of information from these sources, together with your own experiences (e.g., things that happened to you), would then be combined with your observations of life, people, and the environment to improve your common sense in navigating daily life.

Understanding people is quite straightforward, but it cannot be grasped instantly. We notice what we regularly do, and when we understand why, it brings us wisdom or common sense.

> **The average person has an enormous amount of common sense because they have not used any of it yet. -- Brian Tracy (life coach –humour)**

We know for certain that we are not born with common sense, so it is not a standard prerequisite for being human. I trust you agree that this has already been established. Nonetheless, having common sense is essential for a good quality of life, so how do we acquire it?

Common sense can be taught

Syllogistic or deductive reasoning naturally occurs when an active logical mind faces a basic problem. The outcome of such reasoning is what we understand as common sense. It will be shown in the discourse on the birth of common sense (chapter two) that this is likely how it first began. If this type of reasoning becomes instinctive, the logical mind-muscle will develop.

Since syllogistic reasoning can be taught, it makes sense to prioritise teaching it because it serves as the 'factory' that produces common sense. While it's possible to compile a basic list of what should be considered common sense (as in the shortlist that follows), developing the ability to reason syllogistically is far more empowering than merely memorising a list.

When this reasoning ability is applied to meaningful knowledge, gained through studying life, human behaviour, and the environment, it naturally produces a practical body of common sense, much like what is outlined below. The following points are taken from Dale Carnegie's *How to Win Friends and Influence People*, a book based on keen observation and experience. Although these actions may seem instinctive, the fact that many people fail to practise them suggests otherwise. The book remains popular today because people recognise that its lessons are not universally known or consistently applied, and many realise they still have room to grow. The following common-sense lessons, sampled from the book, relate to people and can be taught, as can the syllogistic reasoning (imbued with truth) that produces them.

- **Treating people with respect**. You will get more from others by showing respect than by not doing so. (Syllogism: people have a deep need to be respected – if treated with respect, their response is usually positive; therefore, if treated with disrespect, their response is generally negative).

- **Getting along with people.** Most people dislike being criticised, even if it is done constructively. So, if you want to make friends or influence people, praise the good in them and use criticism sparingly, if at all.

- **Avoiding Arguments and Seeking Agreement.** I once joked with someone, "We don't need to argue, just agree with everything I say!" The truth is, arguments are rarely, if ever, genuinely won. Why? Because of something called ego, our natural reluctance to lose face or feel embarrassed. Think about it: how many arguments have you "won" where the other person sincerely thanked you or congratulated you for being right?

Other truths that can be tested, widely understood, and therefore qualify as common sense will be presented throughout this discourse. Can there be a long list of common sense? It is possible. Suppose we accept the points above, along with others offered for your consideration, and combine them with your insights and contributions from other scholars and great thinkers. In that case, we might be able to compile a comprehensive list of common sense. This book will also include various quotes to examine, and you can decide if the ideas they present should be common knowledge that makes it onto the list of common sense. However, in general, common sense is not a fixed list of ideas or facts that can be learned and memorised. It emerges from a way of thinking underpinned by accurate knowledge. Accurate knowledge is its 'tool', and this 'tool' is used to interpret complex life issues. The process of acquiring precise knowledge follows a method.

Here are some of the fundamental subjects we need to study, along with the methods and processes through which we can gain accurate knowledge, which is the 'tool' necessary to go beyond basic common sense.

- Acquiring extensive and accurate knowledge about life and human behaviour, and learning from experience, will cause syllogistic common-sense reasoning to become an instinctive mental-emotional process when addressing any of life's issues.

- You must build a broad and in-depth knowledge of major life issues. Since cultures worldwide often hold polarised views on topics such as religion, history, politics, relationships, medicine, and nutrition, gaining an accurate understanding requires looking beyond the surface. To achieve this, aim to consider multiple perspectives on any given issue or experience. For example, in a war, don't be content

with only the viewpoint of the victor or the defeated. As the saying goes, "Until lions have their historians, tales of the hunt will always glorify the hunters."

- To gain accurate knowledge about religion, examine the history of religion in general and the specific religion that interests you. This is based on the principle, "If you know what happened yesterday, today will make a lot more sense to you."

- To gain a precise understanding of history, explore the histories of various peoples from their viewpoints.

- We should all have a broad understanding of the fundamental differences between the two leading political ideologies: capitalism and communism. In communism, the government mainly controls capital and the means of production, whereas in capitalism, these are primarily controlled by individuals.

- It is essential to understand the difference between greed and ambition. Greed is when you want to achieve at the expense of others. Ambition is when you aim to achieve in the service of others. – Jim Rohn.

- There are two main types of medicines in the world today. The oldest is called **naturopathic**, and the other is called **allopathic**. Learn as much as you can about both so you can make an informed decision about which is most effective for your well-being.

- There are various viewpoints on what makes up good nutrition or a 'balanced diet'. Ignorance in this area poses a clear and immediate risk because it is well known that diet, lifestyle, and illnesses are directly connected. This risk is even greater because we often eat multiple times each day. Study it carefully because, as the saying goes, you are what you eat. Therefore, understanding this aspect of life is essential, and you cannot afford to get it wrong. In today's world, acquiring accurate knowledge about this subject is crucial for protecting your health.

- Become a keen observer. Being a keen observer is not just about looking; it involves observing with a keen desire to understand and learn truths.

- Enhance your listening skills. A keen listener is an active listener, which means you listen with an attitude of not just memorising what was said. In situations where you can interact with the speaker, confirm with them that your understanding is correct. If you cannot interact, listen, remember what was said, review it in your mind, and question what was said. If possible, debate it with others. There is a good reason why we have two ears and only one mouth: we are meant to do more listening and learning than talking.

- Understand the purpose of experience. Experience can be extremely valuable for gaining knowledge because it takes time and involvement to grasp some subtleties and nuances of life. However, experience and involvement will only enhance your knowledge and wisdom if you gain insight and understanding. A person might have ten years of 'experience', but effectively, they may have one year's experience repeated ten times. In such cases, they have not *actively* sought to improve through learning valuable lessons from their experiences. The experiences did not enhance them in terms of knowledge, understanding, and ability. Essentially, they were not engaged in a ***deliberate personal development journey.*** A powerful habit that increases the value of our experiences is regular reflection.

- Develop the ability to engage in different methods of thinking, such as syllogism, which uses **deductive reasoning** to reach conclusions. It's also helpful to learn about **inductive reasoning.** These reasoning methods can be almost scientific in uncovering the truth in many situations. This is especially true of deductive reasoning.

  - **Deductive reasoning** is a logical process based on a general theory about a topic, which is then gradually narrowed down into a more specific *conclusion* that **can be tested**. The example of deductive reasoning by the Greek philosopher Aristotle: *All men are mortal. > Socrates is a man. > Therefore, Socrates is mortal,* just as 2 plus 2 equals four.

  - **Inductive reasoning** is also a logical process, but it relies on a weaker and less reliable method of reasoning. It takes specific observations and draws general conclusions from them, which are assumed to be true or are generally true most of the time. In other words, it provides, at best, a 'probable' conclusion. It suggests truth but does not guarantee it. For example, Amy and Jane are best friends from school. Amy loves dancing, language, and drama. Jane also loves dancing and language, so it is reasonable to assume that she also loves drama. Another example is: "All biological life forms that we know of depend on liquid water to exist. Therefore, if we discover a new biological life form, it will probably depend on liquid water to exist.' This argument could have been made every time a new biological life form was found, and it would have been correct each time. However, it remains possible that in the future a biological life form not requiring liquid water could be discovered." – Wikipedia. This method of reasoning, of course, does not always lead to the truth.

- Learn from everyone! This includes those who have succeeded and those who have failed. From one, you learn what to do; from the other, what not to do. The benefit will give a clear understanding of how reality works and enhance your ability to judge situations and make sound decisions. A person's life can act as a warning or an example.

Belief – accepting something without proof. Essentially, it is a feeling rather than a certainty, which is why it is not recognised in a court of law. A valuable lesson that makes sense is that we should not convict or liberate someone based on a belief!

The method of acquiring common sense can be taught because it is not based on random 'non-principles'. It relies on solid principles, and in some cases, scientific principles like the principle of addition and multiplication. But before you become incredulous, this is about mental science. Ultimately, if you study life and people, you will recognise the natural or common ways in which different individuals behave in various situations. After gaining extensive knowledge, experience, and understanding, you will be able to analyse many of life's scenarios and reach accurate conclusions.

We can teach common sense because every part of life follows certain principles. Once we understand these principles, we can create effective methods to learn and apply them. For human beings, our 'principles' of how we 'work' are the mind and emotions. Once you have even a basic understanding of how the mind and emotions operate, a thinking method can make the reasons for a person's actions or activities very clear. In other words, whatever aspect of life we want to understand, we can seek information about it; we can learn how to analyse it, and thus develop the ability to relate to it and reach accurate conclusions. After we understand it, we can teach it to others.

One of the 'senses' that is 'common' and almost universally understood and applied in our modern societies is the knowledge of how to cross the street safely. This is widespread common sense because it is almost always taught to children. This seemingly simple act involves visual maths because it requires visually measuring and gauging distance. If done incorrectly, it could be deadly. While you cannot teach a child exactly how to judge how soon a vehicle will become a threat based on its distance and speed, you can teach them the method that helps them spot the 'danger car' and thus avoid being run over. If cars drive on the left side of the road, we teach children to look right, then left, then right again before crossing. That final glance to the right is crucial for safety. As they looked left, a vehicle could have approached from the right, making the situation dangerous.

This final part of this simple syllogistic reasoning is the critical element we call common sense. The fact that if children are not taught how to cross the road safely, there is a high risk that they will be injured or killed, demonstrates that we are not born with what we call common sense. This is further highlighted by the fact that we often do not allow children of a certain age to cross the road on their own.

Syllogistic logic in the safe method of crossing the road

- If the speed of an oncoming vehicle exceeds our crossing speed, it would be unsafe to cross at that moment.

- We would be at risk if the driver could not brake in time. Therefore, for safety, looking in the direction of oncoming vehicles should be the last thing to check before crossing.

Common sense can be straightforward knowledge that does not need syllogistic reasoning, like 'the sun is hot.'

No one wants to acquire common sense for all aspects of life. What is useful is developing a method of thinking that can be used to discover the truth about most subjects. We can then apply this method to the topics and issues of life that impact us as individuals and collectively. As shown above, there is a way of thinking (syllogistic reasoning) that resembles a mathematical formula and can be used to solve problems. Methods of thinking, such as deductive (and inductive) reasoning, can help uncover many truths, including historical truths, health truths, and other human realities.

Understanding ourselves, others, and life as a whole is vital for developing common sense. Therefore, it requires more than just surface-level attention or casual analysis. We should feel a true responsibility to understand all aspects of life, including our environment.

The following point cannot be emphasised enough. One of my mentors, the late Jim Rohn, transformed millions of lives with an idea that can be paraphrased like this: The acquisition of common sense begins with a keen interest in two things—life and people. The most important way to understand others is to learn about their history and the factors that shaped them. This keen interest will motivate us to become active observers of life and human behaviour. The main lesson here is that we should expand our observation, not just focus on people within our community or country, but look beyond to understand a broader range of human experiences and perspectives. We should travel, enjoy ourselves, but make it an educational experience by taking some time to learn about other people's cultures and customs, and compare them to our own. In essence, engaging our minds in understanding different cultures and drawing comparisons with our own can be highly stimulating and expand our horizons.

Much of what is listed about the process of acquiring common sense is best achieved by becoming a consummate reader (or "borrowing" other people's brains). Reading books on history, autobiographies, biographies, nutrition, Nature, religion, business, social science, and the psychology of success—along with keen observation, listening to well-read and experienced individuals, and watching documentaries—will sharpen and heighten your insight, intuition, intuitiveness, and perceptiveness... all of which are synonyms of common sense. All of this will improve the accuracy with which you judge things, provided you do it with a firm intention and desire to grow, develop, succeed, and **understand life and people.**

Common sense can be a gift to the inquisitive

As previously suggested, common sense will not develop significantly just by casually observing life and people. By constantly seeking answers to the reasons behind people's behaviour, their circumstances, and the workings of life, wisdom will gradually be uncovered. So, become like a child and ask their favourite question, 'why', about every aspect of life. This curiosity is the driving force behind a child's growth, but many tend to lose it when they grow older. You will not gain much from something you do not have a keen interest in. The following important question that stimulates mental and emotional growth is, "How?"

He who asks a question is a fool for five minutes; he who does not ask a question remains a fool forever. – Chinese proverb

---

> **The more questions you ask, the more engaging your life becomes. Interesting individuals are those who have posed numerous thought-provoking questions and discovered many intriguing answers.**

Those who understand aspects of life that affect most or all of us have gained this knowledge through various forms of learning, guided by a consistent standard of reasoning. Because this understanding results from a reasoned process, the method for developing common sense is therefore teachable. Anyone who wishes to gain a deeper understanding of life and human behaviour can pursue this wisdom by engaging their full mental and emotional capacity. If such an attitude were widely adopted, common sense could indeed become common.

> **"I am bored!" "Of course you're bored, Rudy; you are a boring person!" – Vanessa Huxtable**

Common sense is highly esteemed

During disagreements, people are often accused of lacking common sense, of making 'no sense', or of having 'no sense' at all! Even crimes are described as 'senseless'. Our perception of someone's level of 'sense' affects how much respect and regard we have for them. Generally, we do not honour or respect those we see as idiots. The exceptions to this rule may be the people we love, such as friends and family.

It is evident that intelligence, or 'having sense', is essential to everyone. Many conflicts or disagreements stem from misunderstandings. These misunderstandings often come from an inability to reason and reach correct conclusions. Why do so many of us frequently arrive at wrong conclusions? The answer is a lack of helpful information for making sound judgements. After someone acquires a lot of know-how, they are described as having plenty of sense, or what should be 'common' sense.

> **The worst distance between two people is when they have a conflict caused by a lack of knowledge or inadequate knowledge.**

While it is true that most of our decisions are driven by emotions, it is our minds that shape those emotions. Therefore, it is the thought process responsible for shaping our feelings that needs to be educated. As top achievers suggest, being intelligent and educated does not equate to having common sense. Possessing such qualities and qualifications will not necessarily influence our emotions in a way that promotes feelings aligned with clarity and understanding about life and people.

Why is common sense considered such an uncommon attribute?

The straightforward answer is that we are not born with it, nor is it an essential requirement for us to 'get by' in life. Common sense is acquired by those who understand life and people and regularly apply this knowledge. Much of the knowledge and understanding that can help us get along with each other has not become common sense, and will remain uncommon sense, because of the following factors:

- Common sense partly comes from gathering knowledge driven by genuine curiosity about people and all aspects of life. However, many of us show little interest in anything beyond our immediate reality, which limits the depth and breadth of our understanding.

- There are no *widespread* formal systems for teaching people various constructive methods of thinking, such as simple logic or syllogistic reasoning.

- There is no widespread formal education system that encourages us to be attentive observers and to have a strong interest in human behaviour.

- Generally, it's everyone for themselves regarding who will or won't acquire the necessary knowledge of history, which essentially is knowledge of people, places, and things.

Not all the information and knowledge that humans have produced is important enough to help us develop what we call common sense. Some knowledge is trivial. For example, if you refer to a drink as 'almond milk' or 'soya milk', no one will criticise you or accuse you of lacking common sense, even though only mammals produce milk. It's a contradiction, but it's not significant enough to ruin your life. Much of the knowledge that helps people become more effective in the art of living has been efficiently passed down through books, our most longstanding and effective method of sharing information. The problem is that, throughout history, only a minority have been dedicated readers. Modern technology has allowed us to store information on tapes, CDs, DVDs, and MP3s. Despite this, only a small number of people have taken advantage of these tools to seek knowledge beyond the classroom.

We are in the information age, and at the forefront of this revolution is arguably the most excellent library ever built – the Internet. Most of us can access it, whether through our mobile phones or via a phone-to-computer connection in our homes. Yet, despite this unprecedented access to knowledge, ideas, and opportunities, people still say that common sense is not so common. All of the above sources of information offer fertile ground for developing common sense, as they provide both knowledge and mental stimulation. They nourish the mind with information while also giving it the exercise needed to think critically and practically.

Modern technologies have also given us unprecedented ease in practising the art of being a dedicated observer by providing documentaries and films of all kinds. Yet, many of us remain dissatisfied with people's powers of common sense. It cannot be said that there is a lack of knowledge. Therefore, if it is true that common sense is not common, it must be because most of us have not taken the time to learn. Most of us have not taken the time to absorb knowledge and impressions from available sources, nor to understand the lessons and habitually apply them. Why? It's called the power of choice, and it has everything to do with how strong our attitude is in shaping the person we have become.

So, even though we (the world) would all benefit if most of us had and used common sense, this has not happened. The problem is that once we become adults and set in our ways, no one can force us to change our attitude. Life is constantly evolving, so we must continually update our understanding of the world. For example, in the early 1980s, I knew an older person who had never grown up with television and was therefore unfamiliar with it. While watching a film, they asked, "How come the person was in one place and then appeared in another place in an instant?"

The concern often raised about a person's lack of common sense mainly relates to their actions in life and how they interact with us or others. As human beings, our free will leads to a wide range of attitudes. This diversity ensures that life remains complicated, as we are fundamentally complex ourselves.

At some point in history, after humans bonded together and acquired knowledge of how to survive the hardships of what would have been a strange planet, life became very complex. As some of us migrated into different environments, we were shaped into adopting various emotional and mental attitudes.

This complication has made common sense a rare trait. Here are some reasons why:

- Because we are complex, it requires an acquired understanding of human psychology and an analytical approach to decipher and understand people.

- Due to our diverse attitudes, not everyone has the desire or inclination to analyse themselves and others; therefore, not enough common sense is acquired.

- It requires caring and more than an average interest in life and people to gain even a basic understanding. Some of us lack the motivation to invest the time and effort needed to understand others beyond the surface. Others do care, but have never taken the steps to develop the knowledge and skills necessary to handle life's situations with sound judgment and common sense.

- Many of us have not fully embraced the philosophy of "Do unto others as you would have them do unto you." This philosophy serves as a valuable lesson in common sense. For example, if you sent someone a message asking for information and they didn't reply, would you like that? Would it improve your opinion of that person? Therefore, common sense suggests that if someone sends you a message, you should reply. The only exception is if you don't care.

- The power of choice is undoubtedly the main reason why people do not bring their best selves to the game of life.

- We begin life with our emotional self, but we are meant to gradually educate it so that intellectualised emotion guides at least most of our actions. This has not occurred.

- At each stage of our development, we may fall in love with or become comfortable with the person we are at that point – people embrace and get stuck at various levels of their growth. This is called arrested development and is a persistent reality. Let's say someone had the misfortune of moving with the wrong crowd, and in a moment of madness, they were goaded into swallowing a pint of gin in one go. If this reckless and dangerous act boosted their popularity, they could, conceivably, come to like and accept themselves as this 'new popular person', thus adopting this behaviour as their norm.

- Many people have been conditioned to admire ignorance, believing it's uncool to be intelligent or feeling intimidated by, or even averse to, using uncommon words.

- Most parents lack a ***systematic way*** *of* passing down valuable wisdom to their children.

- Although many of us recognise the key subjects for practical living, the full extent of what they are and the role they should play in our lives has never been formalised or ingrained in human consciousness. Most of us are socialised to view the knowledge gained from our academic subjects and obtaining qualifications for social advancement as the most critical intellectual pursuits. Consequently, after leaving school, most of us do not become avid readers, nor do we dedicate much time to deep reflection on a broad range of subjects and issues.

- As a result, many of us grow up unaware that there is essential knowledge, much of which is cited in this book, that must be actively sought to support our personal development. Consequently, only a few pursue this more profound understanding.

- While we do acquire a certain amount of common sense simply through living, our growth remains limited by the extent of our experiences. **Without deliberate learning**, even common sense is restricted by what life exposes us to.

- Our childhood curiosity often does not develop into adult inquisitiveness, a profound and continuous desire to understand life and people beyond appearances.

- In some cases, people know what they should do, but their emotions interfere and prevent them from taking the right action.

- Many of our societies impose so much emotional rubbish into people's minds that we now face a crisis of fearful and unhappy individuals. Survival and happiness are twin drives in human life, but a lack of happiness has led many to give up on survival through suicide. It is said that many people live lives of quiet desperation. In such a reality, how many would have the ability and the willingness to grow after being effectively programmed with mind-numbing information? Wouldn't this situation hinder the development of accurate knowledge, the foundation of common sense?

- Many have inadvertently tuned into mind-numbing entertainment that doesn't promote intellectual growth, resulting in the

emotional mind becoming far too dominant. This, in turn, reduces the role of the logical deductive mind. Furthermore, our complex emotions make it difficult for everyone to understand each other, but easy to cause conflicts. Many of these conflicts have become so entrenched that common sense cannot play a part in resolving them.

Common sense has two primary applications:

- Life and people – understanding human behaviour and activities.
- Life and our environment – understanding the Earth and the universe.

Common sense is highly regarded when it demonstrates a clear understanding of how things operate in practice, and when it is used to ensure things work effectively in real-world situations.

So, our drive to survive and be happy requires understanding and mastering the above applications of common sense. As a result of our desire to minimise conflict, get along with others, and live more harmoniously, the need for a shared understanding of life and human nature naturally arose. The more people who develop a clear understanding of life, of themselves, and of others, the easier it becomes for us to coexist peacefully and cooperatively. Similarly, our need to get the best out of Nature and the environment we have created, and to minimise and avoid dangers that are inherent in both, led to the development of a shared sense of Nature-based common sense. The following is a good analogy which captures the philosophies behind the birth of common sense, which you will read later in this book:

If ten people live in a house with potentially dangerous equipment, it benefits everyone if each person understands how to operate and maintain it safely. Otherwise, each occupant could pose a risk to the others. This analogy illustrates a simple truth: common sense is grounded in logic and science. Societies and the world as a whole function more effectively when people actively follow the principle of universal teamwork.

Our experiences have shown us that following these principles is more dependable than succumbing to our emotional whims and fancies. The desire for common sense also stems from the need to optimise or maximise our results in a way that does not threaten or violate anyone's fundamental rights. Additionally, common sense aims to optimise or maximise Nature's yield without causing it harm. Common sense clearly states, "If we harm Nature, we are harming ourselves!"

Other examples of straightforward common sense

- Climbing a coconut tree ten times in one outing to pick ten coconuts isn't common sense. Such an action fails the test of practicality and usefulness.

- Repeated climbing would not benefit the climber in terms of efficient use of time and would involve using excessive energy, as well as posing an unwelcome additional danger unless they were a reckless thrill-seeker. Practicality and efficiency dictate a single climb, allowing the coconuts to fall, if necessary, on a cushioned surface.

- The acts of dumping chemicals and toxic substances into the sea demonstrate a lack of common sense at the highest level, and in all honesty, we might as well call it stupidity. How can we logically justify dumping toxic waste into the sea? Why should it even need legislation to stop such a practice? Considering that so many of us rely on the oceans for food, isn't this effectively the same as pouring toxic chemicals into our cooking pots?

The harm we do to the environment is harm to ourselves because it's the house we live in, and this house sustains us.

Why are we so complex?

Free will ensures there is no fixed standard or uniformity of attitude and behaviour. Nothing compels us to grow and learn. The only aspect of our being that is driven to develop is our physical self. Our physical growth appears to be governed by an internal clock that triggers a relentless, unstoppable, stage-by-stage process of:

- Conception
- Birth
- Infancy

- Childhood
- Adulthood
- Maturity
- Old age, and
- Death

Nature also influences our mental growth. However, this is where it becomes complex. Nature does not offer a strict, unstoppable stage-by-stage process that compels us to reach our full mental potential. Instead, nature pushes us to a basic level that begins with emotional intelligence. Emotional intelligence starts in the *womb*. After birth, this emotional ability continues to develop, with a baby laughing when happy or crying when hungry, uncomfortable, or in need of reassurance and affection. Thus, a baby begins life by gathering information in a basic way: cold is bad, warmth is good, hunger is terrible, and food is wonderful. Most other mental developments during this period, and afterwards, are shaped by the environment and the input from those we interact with.

It was largely our interactions with Nature that helped the first humans develop their minds and intellects. This was because the knowledge exchanged between individuals then was not as extensive as it is now, due to the lack of accumulated knowledge. Through our interaction with Nature and the exchange of stimulating ideas, our mental and emotional capacities grew, enabling us to establish cultures, civilisations, and societies.

Our current reality serves as proof that we were never 'perfect' nor possessed great knowledge and intellect from the start. Nature demonstrates this simple lesson by showing that it takes time and processes for a tree to germinate, grow, mature, and bear fruit. This truth, relating to our development, can be illustrated with three points.

- In both recent history and our present reality, we continue to learn and make discoveries, with no end in sight. This indicates that knowledge could be infinite.
- Over many thousands of years, human progress rose and fell as civilisations and empires declined and knowledge was lost.
- There was a time when we were savages and less civilised.

What is the ultimate application of common sense?

We all agree that common sense is vital for our basic daily interactions with each other and our environment. You've seen that top achievers value it highly, but why is common sense so highly esteemed? Consider the dictionary definition: Does it suggest that common sense involves developing our best qualities and abilities? Look at the definition and the list of synonyms that follow. The definition presents common sense as a *trait* a person can possess, and the range of synonyms indicates that few qualities embody greater personal growth. It seems there may be little that surpasses common sense in terms of personal development.

A dictionary definition of common sense:

good sense and sound judgement in practical matters.

The Cambridge Dictionary defines Common Sense as, *"The basic level of practical knowledge and judgement we all need to help us live in a reasonable and safe way."* This definition indicates that *knowledge* and *judgement* function closely together: judgement allows us to understand life and people accurately, while knowledge provides the necessary foundation for living effectively and productively. A basic level of practical knowledge is essential in every aspect of life, and without it, we risk confronting anything from minor inconveniences to serious challenges.

Synonyms of common sense:

good sense, sense, sensibleness, native wit, native intelligence, mother wit, wit, judgement, sound judgement, level-headedness, prudence, discernment, acumen, sharpness, sharp-wittedness, canniness, astuteness, shrewdness, judiciousness, wisdom, insight, intuition, intuitiveness, perceptiveness, perspicacity, vision, understanding, intelligence, reason, powers of reasoning, practicality, capability, initiative, resourcefulness, enterprise...

Informal meanings – horse sense, gumption, nous, **savvy**, know-how, smarts; rare sapience

An examination of just a few of the synonyms listed above should reinforce the idea that common sense is our ultimate potential for personal growth. As mentioned earlier, insight is a synonym of common sense.

Are insight, wisdom, and common sense the same thing?

The following definitions are sourced from the Oxford Dictionary:

- **Insight**

  The capacity to gain an **accurate** and deep understanding of someone or something.

Insight is crucial for solving problems. For someone to have insight, they need some understanding of human behaviour. Once they are given the facts, they can often grasp the reasons behind a person's actions. This is because insight enables them to see the specific cause and effect, helping them to understand the reasons for a person's behaviour. Would you consider the above to be abilities of the highest order? How many of these abilities do we possess or are working to develop? Having insight represents a major development of our senses. It's almost like having the ability to see the future — to foresee future consequences based on current actions.

- **Wisdom**

The quality of having experience, knowledge, and good judgement; the quality of being wise.
    As you can see, the definition of wisdom is similar to that of common sense. And what makes us wise? Knowledge and experience. Through experience, we have learnt to build our houses to withstand hurricanes and winters. Wisdom gained from experience has taught us not to make our houses as if it's always summer.

Wisdom suggests that having a child is a bigger decision and responsibility than getting married. While successfully raising a child and maintaining a healthy marriage both demand skill and commitment, the failure of a marriage does not necessarily harm society. However, if a child results from that union and the parents lack the wisdom to nurture and raise the child properly, both the child and society will face the consequences. Yet, many still see the decision to marry as more important than the decision to raise a child.

> **Spending the majority of our income immediately after earning it, without saving or investing for the future, often results in hardship and poverty. This tendency is widespread even in developed societies.**

We all should aim to learn how to make sound decisions, and logical reasoning is crucial in that process. A key part of *wisdom* is good judgment, which involves **applying** knowledge appropriately to real-life situations. It's this practical knowledge that helps us avoid or solve problems. Simply gathering information, like a walking dictionary, doesn't make us effective. Knowledge is of little value if it remains unused or inactive.

True learning happens when we consistently act on what we know, and wisdom represents the highest part of this journey. We must learn how to act wisely. As the peak of common sense is so high and we are not born with it, it can be seen as climbing a ladder that we need to ascend to reach our full potential. Because life constantly requires us to solve problems and since common sense is deeply rooted in logic, it should be regarded as one of our most effective tools for problem-solving.

Humanity walking up the 'common sense ladder'

Should the understanding of how to survive, stay safe, stay healthy, succeed, gain recognition, achieve greatness, contribute to society, become fully conscious, and obtain wisdom be common knowledge? Why shouldn't they be, when some are essential and all of them are qualities that can elevate us from our almost 'blank-slate' beginning to reach our full potential? Of course, not everyone desires all of these qualities, but we should all understand how they are achieved. Then, we would be fully informed and better able to choose what we want to pursue and become. Are these realities due to mere luck, or are they primarily based on a process that can be studied, understood, and applied? They are.

COMMON SENSE LADDER

If you accept that the above thorough examination has clarified the true meaning of common sense, you are now better prepared to recognise when the term is being misused.

Two of the misuses of common sense are:

- Describing a situation as caused by a lack of common sense when it was not. People may perform actions that seem irrational, but in reality, they were acting maliciously; they know better but choose not to do better.

- Claiming that a statement is common sense when it is actually based on the person's misunderstanding.

In the art of communication, having a mutual definition and understanding of words and ideas is crucial. Over the years, I have had countless discussions, debates, and arguments that went on and on with no end in sight. Eventually, I realised an important fact: not all of us always have the same definition of things, and even words. This experience has taught me how to recognise when a lack of mutual understanding is the cause of disagreements. So, whenever I find myself in such a situation, I pause and ask the other person(s) to share their definition or understanding of what we are discussing. Once the difference in understanding becomes clear, it becomes much easier to resolve an argument or discussion, potentially avoiding a great deal of frustration. If you accept this as a sound, common-sense principle, you can apply it to prevent many misunderstandings before they escalate.

How did we develop what we call 'sense'? What factors contributed to our coming together to form societies, countries, and empires? In short, what caused us to evolve from our basic state of being to our current reality? How have these factors helped us develop 'sense'? How would analysing these factors deepen our understanding of what we call 'common sense'? As you probably already know, having common sense is much more than knowing not to record things you don't want anyone to find out about, such as making a song about your criminal activities and creating a video to go with it. It's also more than knowing not to insult someone before asking them for a favour. You should also know not to bet someone that they won't wake up tomorrow morning. Common sense goes beyond knowing not to tell your partner that they looked better when you first met, even if it's true.

CHAPTER TWO

The birth, history, and development of common sense

**When we got here, we got seed, we got soil, we got some
rain, we got some sunshine, we got some seasons, and
the miracle of life…How do we turn all this stuff that is
available into equity, promise, lifestyle, dreams, future, and
possibilities? – Jim Rohn**

---

*ompared to now, life was not nearly as complicated when it first
began in the wilderness, during the formative years of human
societies. Initially, life was mainly driven by the need for food,
shelter, and dealing with dangers from wild animals and natural forces. It
is reasonable to assume that almost all people accept this without needing
debate [paraphrasing part of the above definition of common sense]. Our
earliest lessons in common sense were learnt through our interactions with
Nature. The following discourses by Thomas Paine and Count Volney will
offer some sound reasoning for this conclusion.*

A theory of the birth and history of common sense

Common Sense was a pamphlet written by Thomas Paine in 1775-76… In
proportion to the population… at the time (2.5 million), it had the largest
sale and circulation of any book published in American history. As of 2006,
it remains the all-time best-selling American title…"–Wikipedia. It has been
described as the most influential political pamphlet of the 18th century,
affecting both the American and French Revolutions.

Common sense = sense – this makes sense!

In the pamphlet *Common Sense*, Thomas Paine proposed one of the earliest
ideas about the fundamental reasons we form societies. From his reasoning on
the origins of social organisation, we can identify the key factors that gave rise

to the understanding and sense needed for us to live effectively with each other and to shape our existence on Earth most efficiently. Thomas Paine wrote:

> Let us suppose a small number of persons settled in a remote part of the earth, unconnected with the rest; they will then represent the first peopling of any country or the world. In this state of natural liberty, society will be their first thought. A thousand motives will drive them to it; **the strength of one man is so unequal to his needs**, and his mind so **unfit for perpetual solitude**, that he is soon compelled to seek assistance and relief from another, who in turn requires the same. Four or five united could build a tolerable dwelling in the wilderness, but one man might work his entire life without accomplishing anything; when he had felled his timber, he could not remove or reassemble it afterwards. Hunger would push him to quit his work, and different needs would lead him in different directions. Disease, or even misfortune, could be fatal; for, although neither might be mortal, either would disable him from life and reduce him to a state where he might be said to perish rather than to die.

Being *unable to **endure perpetual solitude*** can be interpreted as an indication that we are, by nature, social beings. When you consider that we have desires and wants, and that ***"the strength of one man is so unequal to his needs"***, this forms the basis for our original understanding of the need to live together to benefit from mutual exchanges. This common sense arose from our earliest realisation that, as individuals, we were not fully equipped to deal with the forces of Nature on our own. Thomas Paine's pamphlet, **Common Sense**, inspired the thirteen American colonies to fight for independence from Great Britain. He did not use it in the same context as it's being used here. It was called *Common Sense* because he believed his arguments were logical and sound. Rationality and logic should be essential parts of what we define as common sense. Consider some of the points raised, which were so persuasive that George Washington, the Commander-in-Chief of the Continental Army during the American Revolutionary War, had them read to all his troops.

- It was absurd for an island to rule a continent.
- America was not a "British nation," but was made up of influences and peoples from all across Europe.
- Even if Britain were the "mother country" of America, that makes her actions all the more horrendous, for no mother would harm her children so brutally.

- Being part of Britain would have entangled America in pointless European wars and hindered its progress in global trade.

- The distance between the two nations made governing the colonies from England unwieldy. If a petition were to be presented to Parliament, it would take a year before the colonies received a response.

The principles of syllogistic reasoning are outlined above. Do you agree that these points make **sense**? Would America be even half as powerful as it is today if it had remained a colony of England? Where would we stand in terms of technological innovations? Who would now argue that America's independence was not a wise decision? At present, it's doubtful that even Great Britain would make such a claim.

Count de Volney (1757-1820) – theory of human development

In 1793, Count de Volney also wrote an interesting theory on the nature of the earliest human experiences and how these experiences shaped us. He wrote it in his book called *"The Ruins, or Meditation on the Revolutions of Empires and the Law of Nature"*. It was an expanded theory compared to Thomas Paine's on the factors that shaped the first human life and society. It provided insights into the answer to a fundamental question: how did human beings learned how to achieve our two main drives or objectives, survival, and the experience of happiness? You will see how the accumulated experiences he referred to likely formed the foundation of our earliest understanding of how to live, survive, and eventually thrive. These experiences, built over time, serve as the fundamental building blocks of what we now recognise as common sense.

Hopefully, you have now accepted that human life did not begin with a bunch of enlightened and sophisticated people. We have had too many examples in the relatively recent history of people developing from the most basic existence, or savagery, into sophistication and advancement, for us to entertain such an idea. It is instructive to note that Count de Volney was born and developed his theory during the Age of Enlightenment.

A world where there is no accumulation of scientific knowledge would have been very frightening for the first inhabitants.

Perhaps, after reading Count Volney's thoughts below on *"The primitive state of man,"* it will reveal to you the basis from which human beings initially developed 'sense' and why we might want much of this knowledge to become **common** sense. Do not be distracted by the language or whether his ideas fit the common belief about the exact details of the origin of humanity. He writes:

When the hidden power which animates the universe, formed the globe which man inhabits, he implanted in the beings composing it, essential properties which became the law of their **individual motion**…formed naked in body and mind, man at first found himself thrown, as it were by chance, on a rough and savage land: an orphan, abandoned by the unknown power which had produced him, **he saw not by his side beings descended from heaven to warn him of those wants which arise only from his senses, nor to instruct him in those duties which spring only from his wants**. Like other animals, without experience of the past, without foresight of the future, he wandered in the bosom of the forest, guided only and governed by the affections of his nature. **By the pain of hunger, he was led to seek food and provide for his subsistence; by the inclemency of the air, he was urged to cover his body, and he made himself clothes**; by the attraction of a powerful pleasure, he approached a being like himself, and he perpetuated his kind.

Thus **the impressions which he received from every object, awakening his faculties, developed by degrees his understanding, and began to instruct his profound ignorance: his wants excited industry**, dangers formed his courage; **he learned to distinguished useful from noxious plants**, to combat the elements, to seize his prey, **to defend his life**; and thus he alleviated its miseries.

Thus, self-love, aversion to pain, and the desire of happiness were the simple and powerful excitements which drew man from the savage and barbarous condition in which nature has placed him…Wandering in the woods and on the banks of rivers in pursuit of game and fish, the first men, beset with dangers, assailed by enemies, tormented by hunger, by reptiles, by ravenous beasts, felt their own individual weakness; and, **urged by a common need of safety**, and a reciprocal sentiment of like evils, they united their resources and their strength; and when one incurred a danger, many aided and succored him; when one wanted subsistence, another shared his food with him. Thus **men associated to secure their existence**, to augment their powers, to protect their enjoyments; and self-love therefore became the principle of society… **self-love, the principle of all reasoning, became the incitement to every art, and every enjoyment.**

When, therefore, men could pass long days in leisure, and communication of their thoughts, they began to contemplate the earth, the heavens, and their existence, as objects of curiosity and reflection; **they remarked the course of the seasons**, the action of the elements, **the properties of fruits and**

plants; and applied their thoughts to the multiplication of their enjoyments. And **in some countries, having observed that certain seeds contained a wholesome nourishment in a small volume, convenient for transportation and preservation, they imitated the process of nature**; they confided to the earth rice, barley, and corn, which multiplied to the full measure of their hope; and **having found the means of obtaining within a small compass and without removal, plentiful subsistence and durable stores, they established themselves in fixed habitations; they built houses, villages, and towns; formed societies and nations**; and **self-love produced all the developments of genius and power.**

Count de Volney's theory offers a concise explanation of how we evolved—from basic emotional intelligence, limited intellect, and rudimentary knowledge and abilities, to a more advanced emotional framework and higher levels of learning, rational intelligence, and capability. His ideas align closely with what we observe in real life: a baby is born helpless, and both children and adults must acquire knowledge through observation and training to become effective. In this way, his theory resonates with our lived experience and, as a result, makes a great deal of sense. What do you think?

How can we use Volney's theory to identify the original formation of common sense/know-how?

Most of Count Volney's theories are based on how our senses were developed to aid our survival. And part of the development of our 'sense' became common sense. Here is an analysis of the sections that are **in bold**. You will see that much of what Count de Volney has written can be substantiated in more ways than one:

> When the hidden power which animates the universe formed the globe which man inhabits, he implanted in the beings composing it, essential properties which became the law of their **individual motion.**

> **Question:** What are the laws that govern our (and other beings') **motion** or **behaviour?**

> **Answer:** the laws that govern us are thinking, imagination, emotions, and adaptability. The laws that govern other beings are mainly instinct and adaptability.

He saw not by his side beings descended from heaven to warn him of those wants which arise only from his senses, nor to instruct him in those duties which spring only from his wants…

This is simply stating a reality about part of what makes us unique. Unlike animals and other life forms, which have built-in programs for navigating their world, we are never born with an instruction manual on how to perform most tasks, such as planting crops, making clothes, constructing adequate shelters, or healing our bodies, to name a few. We had to choose to learn how to do most things and how to understand most things. And it is our desires that drive us to understand life and to make discoveries.

By the pain of hunger, he was led to seek food and provide for his subsistence…

The **sense** of how to seek food would have been born from this first human experience. Unlike many other life forms, we are not born with an instinctive understanding of how to find food or what we should or shouldn't eat. Instead, this knowledge must be learned and developed over time. This ongoing process of understanding forms the basis of what we now recognise as the study and practice of good nutritional habits.

By the inclemency of the air, he was urged to cover his body, and he made him clothes…

This was the start of basic knowledge on how to dress appropriately for cold and hot weather. This was not an end in itself regarding knowledge of how to dress. All knowledge is supposed to be improved on. Some additional knowledge that is supposed to become common sense about clothing has not. For example, **tight-fitting synthetic** materials do not facilitate good ventilation and blood circulation for the human skin and body and are therefore detrimental to health. This point extends to women's clothes that can harm their reproductive system.

The impressions which he received from every object, awakening his faculties, developed by degrees his understanding, and began to instruct his profound ignorance…

This is stating what should be common sense: much of what we have learnt, we gradually learnt from our observation and interaction with Nature. We have also learnt from studying ourselves in terms of our physical design. This knowledge then becomes common sense among those of us who have shaped our societies in terms of technology. For example, the drum/speaker was invented by imitating the eardrum. The camera was invented by imitating the eyes. Yet, despite all that we have learnt, we have merely scratched the surface of our profound ignorance.

His wants excited industry…" — This is a natural extension of the ideas previously discussed. Our senses, guided by our desires and needs, drive innovation and progress. If we had never felt the need to cross a river, we would not have developed the understanding or the means to do so. Likewise, if the desire to fly had never stirred in us, we would not have cultivated the knowledge required to build aeroplanes, hot air balloons, or gliders. The invention of the aeroplane, for example, emerged from close observation of how birds fly, demonstrating how human curiosity and necessity awaken both our senses and our ingenuity.

He learned to distinguish useful from noxious plants.

The know-how in this area is still evolving. While we share a universal common sense that knowledge of what we eat is critically important, mainly since Nature produces plants that can be poisonous to us, the ability to reliably distinguish between what is safe and what is harmful remains neither common knowledge nor common sense.

Thus, self-love, aversion to pain, and the desire of happiness, were the simple and powerful excitements which drew man from the savage and barbarous condition in which nature has placed him…"

Self-love and the pursuit of happiness are indeed fundamental aspects of human nature. Over time, our intelligence has elevated this pursuit into a more sophisticated awareness of how these desires might be fulfilled. In response, different cultures formed and structured societies in ways that reflected and accommodated their evolving desires and perceptions of happiness, since they had, as Volney observed,

> *"felt their own individual weakness; urged by a common need of safety, and a reciprocal sentiment of like evils, they united their resources and their strength…"*

Perhaps Count de Volney was inspired by Thomas Paine when he wrote "… felt their own individual weakness". Humanity cannot survive as individuals, and the ultimate opposite of this would be to have the seemingly impossible 'universal team effort' as a reality. **"... urged by a common need of safety,** and a reciprocal sentiment of like evils" are descriptions of what drove the first humans to recognise their commonality. The last bit of the quote, 'like evils,' is a quaint expression for having mutual enemies, and undoubtedly it was about Nature and dangerous animals.

"When, therefore, men could pass long days in leisure, and communication of their thoughts, they began to contemplate the earth, the heavens, and their own existence, as objects of curiosity and reflection; they remarked **the course of the seasons**, the actions of the elements, **the properties of fruits and plants**; and applied their thoughts to the multiplication of their enjoyments. And **in some countries, having observed that certain seeds contained a wholesome nourishment in a small volume, convenient for transportation and preservation, they imitated the process of nature**; they confided to the earth rice, barley, and corn, which multiplied to the full measure of their hope; and **having found the means of obtaining within a small compass and without removal, plentiful subsistence and durable stores, they established themselves in fixed habitations; they built houses, villages, and towns; formed societies and nations**; and **self-love produced all the developments of genius and power."**

This is another example of learning from Nature to thrive. This entire section refers to the development and implementation of agricultural science. Without the science of organised farming, we would not have societies and nations. It is this science that has significantly reduced the need for humans to have a nomadic lifestyle. This has drastically changed the way we live and enjoy life.

It took a high development of his senses for Count de Volney to write such an accurate description of what must have been the processes by which human beings first developed intelligence and know-how. And the very knowledge we acquired from observation and experience is the basis from which common sense would have been born. However, even after having a desire to have knowledge that is common to us, we never agreed or formalised the content of this knowledge. We have not had total success in amassing, teaching, and implementing the right way to do many things. Two such areas are nutrition and medicine. This is partly due to self-interest and group interest. We are paying a heavy price for this now.

In general, we now have a significant imbalance in people's knowledge and understanding. So, in effect, a lot of what should be common sense is not common-universal-knowledge/understanding, hence the frequency of someone saying to another in a dismayed or confrontational voice, "That's common sense!", or someone aiming an insult at another with the declaration, "You have no common sense!" Count de Volney's ideas have been used here in a context different from his original intent. The aim is to illustrate one of the first

major lessons that can truly revolutionise our thinking—a lesson that deserves to become part of our common sense: what matters most is not simply what a person says, but what their words provoke us to *think*. It is the ability to inspire reflection, inquiry, and deeper understanding that gives an idea its real power.

How different might the world be if common sense had advanced alongside technological innovation?

It is indisputable that we have benefited from accumulating or amassing knowledge. This is evident in the area of technology. Once we study and understand the basic science behind a discovery, we tend to build upon that knowledge. If it is preserved and passed consistently to the next generation, who continue to expand on it, technology can advance at an accelerating pace. Human behaviour and sophistication can be developed, maintained, and advanced in the same way. If there is a long break in transmitting sophisticated behaviour, we can revert to savagery or extremely gross emotional behaviour. There is evidence of this in history. Furthermore, apart from mental defect, do we not have many among us who behave like savages as a result of either being uneducated or poorly educated? Also, being complicated beings, this behaviour is often exhibited despite people being 'educated'.

As we bonded in the struggle to cope with Nature and dangerous animals and to sustain ourselves with food, our focus was concentrated on our basic needs. As previously stated, these basic needs were primarily about survival. It was through our struggle for survival that the first stage of what we now call common sense evolved. This first stage was basic emotional intelligence. This mindset dominated our early history, and for good reason. It was essential for survival against the many dangers inherent in Nature during our prehistoric past[1]. Daniel Goleman, in his international bestseller, **"*Emotional Intelligence*"**, described it in this way:

> **The emotional mind is far quicker than the rational mind, springing into action without pausing even a moment to consider what it is doing. Its quickness precludes the deliberate, analytic reflection that is the hallmark of the thinking mind. In evolution this quickness most likely revolved around that most basic decision, what to pay attention to, and, once vigilant while, say, confronting another animal, making split-second decisions like, 'Do I eat this, or does it eat me?' Those organisms that had to pause too long to**

---

[1]   Pre-history: the period before writing was invented to record human life and activities

reflect on these answers were unlikely to have many progeny to pass on their slower-acting genes.

Babies start with emotional intelligence, not intellectual intelligence, and so did early humans.

He further stated:

But with the coming of agriculture and even the most rudimentary human societies, the odds for survival began to change dramatically. In the last ten thousand years, when these advances took hold throughout the world, the ferocious pressures that had held the human population in check eased steadily.

What happened next?

So, what happened after we were no longer solely preoccupied with survival? Part of the answer is similar to what occurs after a crisis passes. During a crisis, most of our responses are instinctive and emotional. Those bonded together to defeat a common enemy do not have time to notice discomforts, and social graces are of little importance. But once we were no longer solely preoccupied with survival, the inevitable happened.

What is this inevitability? Count de Volney phrased the first part of the answer this way: **"When, therefore, men could pass long days in leisure and in communication of their thoughts…"** This suggests that spending time with our thoughts is how we begin to understand ourselves. It prompts us to ask deeper questions: Who am I? How did I arrive here? Why am I here? What am I capable of? One of the results of this inner dialogue is reflected in the ancient maxim: **"Man, know thyself, and thou shalt know the universe."**

During a time of remarkable intellectual growth, this principle manifested in tangible ways. As we expanded our self-awareness, scientific understanding grew, our imagination blossomed, and we began to conceive inventions, as well as delve into spirituality and religion. But what does *"Man, know thyself"* truly mean—and how did it relate to us at that time?

The phrase lacks a universally accepted meaning, and its origins remain somewhat unclear. However, one way to interpret it is through what I call the *blank slate* principle. The vast differences in human thinking, attitudes, cultures, and languages suggest that our minds are not preloaded with fixed knowledge or behaviour. Unlike other species, whose instincts create uniform

patterns of living, human beings are born with minds more like empty books, ready to be written on by experience, environment, and choice.

Because we are not strictly governed by instinct, we possess remarkable mental flexibility. We can think of anything, believe anything, and become nearly anything. Nature abhors a vacuum, and the human mind does not remain empty—it is filled with whatever we expose it to: wisdom or foolishness, knowledge or ignorance, kindness or cruelty, discipline or recklessness, gentleness or harshness, sensitivity or insensitivity. We learn language, develop accents, adopt values, and absorb emotional patterns. This variety of input generates the entire range of human behaviour—from empathy to violence, from artistic genius to delusion.

This reveals a powerful truth about human nature: **despite our advanced intelligence, we are the most programmable creatures on Earth.** Why? Because we have not only free will but also a wide emotional spectrum that makes us highly receptive to influence and capable of profound change. The adaptability of the human mind is evident in the wide range of human experiences, such as different sexual orientations, fetishes, belief systems, and even extreme forms of bodily modification.

Animals, by contrast, are far more limited in their capacity for change. Their lives are governed by instinct. That's why almost all lions behave the same way in the wild. Human beings, however, are not born with what we need for effective living—we must *acquire* it. And what we acquire is determined by what we expose ourselves to, what we reflect on, and what we choose to believe.

Can you crack this puzzle?

look closely at the numbers

The empathy 'puzzle'

If you struggled with the puzzle above, it's likely because you were viewing it from your perspective. But if you turned it upside down and saw the answer clearly, it stopped being a puzzle; the solution became obvious. You have solved it by employing empathy by looking at it from the driver's point of view. Empathy is a cornerstone of common sense.

Self-harm is an international pastime, and this demonstrates that the blank-slate principle is true more than anything else. In light of our built-in drive to survive, how do we rationally explain smoking and other drug intakes, which are broadly accepted as self-harm? What would make us go against our basic instinctive drive to survive, apart from the fact that we can be programmed to act against our self-interest? This screams the message that we need to be careful. The above consequences of the blank-slate principle show that with the wrong influence, we can become our own worst enemy. Our best defence is to employ the logical and common-sense part of our mind (***filled with accurate knowledge***), which becomes our instinctive guiding light.

My parents told me I would be world number one. I was brainwashed! – Venus Williams (legendary women's tennis player)

"Knowing ourselves" is understanding that all the attributes mentioned, such as wisdom, or foolishness, etc., that we can instil in ourselves, are choices, and choice is the characteristic of our fundamental nature; it is what separates us from other life forms. Knowing ourselves can also be related to understanding our potential in terms of creativity, and perhaps the purpose of our existence. Maybe it suggests that if we truly understood who and what we are, we would learn to live in harmony with the laws that govern our existence, chief among them being the law of cause and effect, which is both logical and foundational. This law applies to our bodies through nutrition and health, and to our minds through productivity and mental well-being. Recognising that many of our attributes are the result of choices opens the door to a more empowering understanding of life, one that ought to be considered common sense. The following experience of life can truly empower us:

Every character trait, personality trait, and attitude we choose to embrace carries consequences. After sowing the seed of a particular trait or attitude, we must be prepared to accept the resulting harvest, our personal "autumn", without complaint. Only then can we reflect and decide whether we want a different, perhaps better, outcome next time. If so, we must change the seeds we plant, especially our attitudes and choices. A word of caution: with some people, you may have only one opportunity to sow the right seed. The law of

cause and effect also applies to the positive aspects of life. If we desire a good life, we must first become aware of the price and be willing to pay it.

Understanding and embracing the whole dynamics of the universal law of cause and effect will give us a reservoir of common sense.

As humans evolved, the drama diversified.

Well, there we were, brand new human beings, almost like virgins experiencing many things for the very first time. Compared to now, we had limited knowledge of our capabilities or the full range of experiences available to us. As we began to fully engage our "thinking tool", the intellectual mind, it gradually expanded, along with our emotional mind, leading to more complex feelings. From this expansion of thoughts and emotions, filled with questions about ourselves and our existence, we eventually developed various philosophies on how to live. Over time, however, these evolving ideas led to significant shifts in how we interact with one another. Here are some of the central ideas and behaviours that came out of our earliest contemplations of life:

- We have conceived various spiritual concepts based on our perceptions of our relationship with the forces of nature and the universe.

- We started multiple religions based on various concepts and ideas.

- We formulated ideas of how to rule and control societies, such as monarchies and other forms of government.

- We developed economic, social, and political structures.

- We developed multiple and varied cultures based on our social philosophies.

- Out of the "blank slate" principle (of being programmable), we developed noble desires, such as the desire to be great by serving others. But we also developed ideas that were ignoble and evil, such as formulating and executing ideas to dominate and oppress others in an attempt to be regarded as great.

- Formal education was eventually 'segregated' in conjunction with the invention of the concept of class and royalty. This led to an inevitable gap in knowledge and understanding between the haves and the have-nots, reinforcing the belief that some people are inherently superior to others by birth. This reinforcement presents itself in living colour because education affects behaviour, and those denied adequate or higher education can be socialised into antisocial, uncultured, or everyday criminal lifestyles. This undermined or significantly reduced the possibility of any truly cooperative human effort ever becoming a reality.

- We developed personalities out of a desire to be different and became 'individuals'.

All of the above changes, and more, led to human division becoming the norm. This division, combined with a growing global population adapting to the mentioned structures and institutions, has naturally resulted in consequences such as:

- The emergence of different civilisations, races, classes, and cultures led to a deterioration in human relations, as our emotional minds shifted from embracing our commonalities to emphasising our differences.

- Many people have little or no concept of sharing a common interest with others.

- People gradually stopped believing that they needed each other as deeply as they once did. Over time, this led to subdivisions, even within the same cultures and religions, where specific individuals or groups would no longer marry or form close relationships with others.

- People developed various attitudes, biases, prejudices, and even hatred against those who don't share their point of view. This has become the basis for segregation, oppression, and elimination.

As a result of these differences, life and living undoubtedly became more complicated. Our accumulated 'survival common sense' knowledge and skills of the past became inadequate to deal with life's new complications. The need for 'new' common sense to deal with these new complications has grown to the point where we are now. Over thousands of years, many of our human capacities gradually unfolded, giving rise to various inventions and increasingly complex ways of living and earning a livelihood. However, despite our technological and material advances, and as the ferocious pressure of Nature eased, we have been gradually submerging into a different type of pressure, which is predominantly artificial.

Our need to develop social skills (a new common sense) has increased manifold. To be effective in dealing with the latest artificial societal type of pressures requires the rational mind to take centre stage. The logical mind, filled with knowledge and trained to make accurate deductions, will refine our thinking so that we can detect, process, and understand the nuances of human behaviour. While the emotional mind is essential as our radar for danger, it is less effective in situations that require reflective thought, as it tends to make snap judgements. These quick judgements can often be inaccurate, especially when dealing with complex human behaviour.

According to Daniel Goleman, **"In a very real sense, we have two minds, one that thinks and one that feels. The emotional mind has its own reasons and logic."** It's at the heart of why intelligent people can often be guilty of not using common sense because the emotional mind can take centre stage and push the rational mind aside. He agrees with this by stating, **"Our emotions have a mind of their own, one which can hold views quite independently of our rational mind."** Perhaps you have had experiences that demonstrated that this is a reality. Maybe, for example, you are having an intelligent and rational discussion with someone. The conversation then changes to a different and very emotional subject, and you are caught off-guard because, before you know it, the person has changed, and it's like you've met the fabled Dr Jekyll and Mr Hyde character. Without a strong common-sense philosophy, it is easy for us to become prisoners of our emotions.

We are still in the process of transitioning from a primary emotional response to life's events to a more intellectual/considered response, and it seems we are not close. Our emotional mind is still far too dominant. Relative to the size of the global population, it appears that only a small segment is truly well-read and well-informed, those who approach life and make decisions grounded in concrete information. This is partly due to the absence of a widespread reading culture. As a result, we are left with a world where too many people have emotional minds that far outweigh their rational ones. Billions are navigating life without the guiding light of self-awareness, emotional intelligence, or an understanding of others. They lack the skills necessary to achieve lasting success, happiness, and longevity, as well as the clarity that comes from historical knowledge and scientific understanding. If you add to the mix strong baseless beliefs, superstitions and the absence of general knowledge, you get many pockets of volatility that do not foster good human relationships.

The knowledge and ability to attain good human relationships are cornerstones of common sense. A dominant, uneducated, and emotional mind is like a repellent to enlightening activities such as reading and other sources of gathering knowledge. It often acts as a buffer against acquiring both the skill and understanding necessary for common sense to flourish. Without an extensive input of knowledge and ideas into human consciousness, many of the qualities which characterise common sense are challenging to attain.

The principle of what is common sense, and the role it is supposed to play in our lives, was never something that we *collectively and consciously* contemplated. At best, we had a few philosophers, such as Aristotle (384 BC – 322 BC), who had thoughts on it that are not in line with the way we think of it today. Aristotle proposed that it is the **"capability of the animal soul (Greek psukhē) which enables different individual senses to collectively perceive the characteristics of physical things, such as movement and size, which all physical things have in different combinations, allowing people and other animals to distinguish and identify physical things. This common sense is distinct from basic sensory perception and human rational thinking, but cooperates with both."**

Both the products of reasoning and the products of experience can produce accurate knowledge, or common sense. Practical reasoning is dependent on the accuracy of information and the ability to process it. The common sense that can flow from our experience is dependent on our ability to accurately interpret what either happened to us or what we observe.

Accurate knowledge imbued into syllogistic reasoning = good judgement = common sense

Thomas Paine's hypothesis on how we first addressed one of the fundamental problems common to all humanity is grounded in the principle of syllogistic, or deductive, reasoning, a method that can lead to conclusions so clear and logical that they become accepted as common sense. Here is a partial paraphrasing of Thomas Paine's syllogistic reasoning. It starts with a major and then a minor truth or proposition.

First proposition:
When he had felled his timber, he could not remove it, nor erect it after it was removed. Therefore, one man might labour throughout the common period of life without accomplishing much.

Common Sense Meaning:

An individual's physical strength is insufficient to advance human dwellings beyond the rudimentary unless he had some degree of technology.

From this basic reasoning, it would have become evident that **"four or five united would be more able to raise a tolerable dwelling in the midst of a wilderness"**. And this is common sense. The more accurate the first two propositions, the stronger and more reliable the conclusion. So, what if the principle of syllogistic reasoning became widespread, constantly advancing and improving, until it evolved into our instinctive way of thinking and acting when solving problems? Drawing from Thomas Paine's hypothesis, it becomes evident that syllogistic reasoning played a vital role in human evolution, development, and the very construction of the modern world.

While animals can rely on their physical abilities to meet the demands of instinct, humans must invent tools and technologies to fulfil their needs and desires. And the quality of the inventions will depend on the quality of the syllogistic reasoning that flows from our minds. Our physical strengths and abilities are not adequate to fulfil what necessity dictates. The stimuli that drive the development of our world are primarily due to our wants and our need to solve problems and survive. It is not because of an automatic processor imbued with unerringly accurate and 'wise' scientific principles that are already within us. If this were the case, none of the inventions we bring into being would be harmful to us, and this is not the case. The solutions that our minds provided were stimulated by the physical challenges we faced. And the quality of our inventions will depend on the quality of our attitude and knowledge. The need for group effort became self-evident after an individual contemplated building a 'substantial' habitat for multiple occupancy, and after humanity undertook the necessity of creating our world. From observation and knowledge, we learn that survival-related matters tend to force us to become resourceful in our thinking.

So, this problem-solving method of thinking would have been with us 'unconsciously' from the beginning when we contemplated something as rudimentary as building a house. Since this is the basic principle by which our mind solves problems, we would expect this aspect of our being to continue evolving and to handle increasingly complex challenges. It did. However, it is not known if this ever became a central force that drove all our actions, but we do know that we are now primarily driven by our emotions. We also know that if our intellect doesn't restrain our feelings, it can lead to disaster. History has taught us that our development has had peaks and troughs. And when we went through our worst periods of dysfunctional behaviour, our syllogistic reasoning ability was not the instinctive way of thinking that we employed to solve our major problems.

Understanding psychology is critical in solving problems relating to human interactions. This common sense must be widespread across human civilisations for there to be cohesion between different people. As populations and societies expanded and life became more complex, we would expect our understanding of human psychology and emotions to grow accordingly, sufficient to address the inevitable challenges that arise from our complex nature. However, the value of syllogistic reasoning and how to apply it effectively to the problems of coexistence never became a widespread or institutionalised part of education within civilisations.

Such syllogistic reasoning would naturally incorporate insights from human psychology and an understanding of the many factors that shape who we are and who we become. It would recognise that no two individuals share the same patterns of thought or emotional makeup. This diversity of inner worlds would be accepted not as a flaw, but as a natural premise, leading to the logical conclusion that conflict is inevitable. This should motivate us to seek better ways of solving complex problems. We have such knowledge in many of our current institutions, but it is not widespread. Conflict resolution is not common knowledge. If human awareness, particularly our understanding of ourselves, others, and how to effectively solve interpersonal problems, had evolved continuously since the dawn of civilisation and been passed consistently from person to person, we might now possess a level of social and emotional development equivalent to what we call advanced technology. This is not the case. We tend to gain understanding, and it remains within some groups. There is no universal team effort.

If we had, during our earliest civilisations, consciously embraced syllogistic common-sense reasoning as the best way to solve our interpersonal problems, and we were consciously aware of the danger of our emotions becoming the dominant force in solving such issues, it could have resulted in the widespread institutionalisation of such understanding. And if this understanding became a widespread, familiar, and instinctive way of resolving our grievances, and improved as life became more complicated, we would expect that after thousands of years had passed, the leaders and shapers of societies would be great problem solvers in respect to human discord. It would be reasonable to expect such individuals to be critical thinkers with a comprehensive understanding of human emotions and psychology. This depth of insight would enable them to navigate differences, foster empathy, and sustain human cooperation, an essential foundation for progress. Given that the study of human psychology has been ongoing for thousands of years, a syllogistically inclined mind would draw

upon this accumulated knowledge, applying it not only to analyse behaviour but to harmonise human relationships in the pursuit of shared goals.

However, that is not the case, as we will see after examining some horrific practices across Europe, America, and other parts of the world that supposedly aimed to curtail transgressions.

So, how long had we been on our journey of human self-actualisation? According to archaeologists, genetic and fossil remains indicate that modern humans (Homo Sapiens Sapiens) existed from about 200,000 years ago, although they date the first civilisations from between 5,500 and 8,000 years ago. We eventually became aware of the value of understanding our psychology, and it became a study, which dates back to the ancient civilisations of Egypt, Greece, China, and India. Therefore, by the time we reached the 12th to 18th centuries, one might expect our understanding of human behaviour and mental processes to have advanced enough for societies to implement policies that effectively addressed major social problems.

We know from the horrific capital punishments examined shortly, that there was not a linear growth in using syllogistic reasoning, steeped with a knowledge of psychology, to solve human discord and transgressions. Our emotional mind was far too dominant.

"Men have passed on the knowledge of how to mix cement, lay brick, splice a line, navigate a ship, make steel, and dozens of other crafts, yet in politics, statecraft, and social relationships we continue to repeat old mistakes." – Louis L'Amour

---

Before we use common sense to process the horrific and brutal capital punishment practices that took place in the centuries mentioned earlier, let's apply syllogistic reasoning and see how it could have revealed the common sense necessary to have deterred such behaviour. What if the thought processes used to address crime during the 12th to 18th centuries had been informed by an understanding of human psychology? What if the leaders took the common-sense view that our laws should not create more problems than they solve? By the time we get to those centuries, we should have accumulated sufficient knowledge about ourselves to know the most effective way to shape our behaviour. Recorded syllogistic reasoning was formulated during this period in Europe, which was called "The Age of Reasoning" or "Age of Enlightenment".

This suggests that there was never any continuous transmission of such ideas, despite their principles being accessible to the leaders and shapers of Europe at the time. So, if the syllogistic method of reasoning were the instinctive approach used in deciding whether to legalise gruesome punishments for certain crimes, it would start with the following propositions:

- Horrific forms of capital punishment will not make a person any more dead. Moreover, based on what we understand about human psychology and the social factors that contribute to criminal behaviour, such punishments are unlikely to serve as effective deterrents. The roots of crime often lie in deep systemic, psychological, and social issues, not simply in rational cost-benefit calculations. Furthermore, there will always be crimes of passion, committed in moments of intense emotion rather than calculated intent. No level of brutality in punishment can prevent such acts. Therefore, the use of extreme cruelty in the name of justice cannot be morally or pragmatically justified.

- As a result of it being done in public, it would have the awful side effect of retarding the growth of millions of people who would be socialised into accepting this as a form of spectacle or entertainment. This is because we humans are very programmable and impressionable; therefore, extreme and gruesome violence sanctioned by esteemed pillars of societies such as governments, monarchies, and religious institutions could serve to normalise such behaviour and foster a callous society. Furthermore, such practices could foster in the highly impressionable a macabre taste for brutality. (According to Catharine Arnold, it took six hundred years before the practice of public killings, which attracted thousands, was ended in London and moved behind closed doors, "as a concession to genteel sensibilities.").

- The majority of human beings do not relish killing another human being – the more gruesome the method, the deeper the repulsion will be. So, another awful side effect of public executions would be the traumatising of countless numbers of people who witness these acts, and perhaps hundreds of those who would be required to execute them.

- Based on the reasonable probability of the above statements being true, we should not adopt any gruesome form of capital punishment.

Many hangmen and axemen were traumatised. The traumatising of those who carried out executions is further attested to by the following quote, "You can't tell me I can take the life of people and go home and be normal. If I had known what I'd have to go through as an executioner, I wouldn't have done it. It took a lot out of me to do it." These are the words of Jerry Givens, former state executioner for the Virginia Department of Corrections, USA. Givens executed 62 people over 17 years between 1982 and 1999. This experience is related by a man who performed executions in our current, comparatively 'humane' way, so what would be the effect on those who performed gruesome executions?

We have never had, and still don't have, a formal system that educates us about the requirements for effective living. Effective living is the purpose of common sense. Yet, we have not, in the majority, progressed from habitually using our common sense solely for basic survival into habitually acquiring the additional common sense necessary to be effective in a culturally diverse and complicated world. From the outset, we relied on our basic common sense out of necessity. Or, to be more specific, we developed and used our emotional mind well. From the outset, our instinctive actions to avoid or overcome danger had, for the most part, to be the right ones; otherwise, we would not have survived. The drive to stay alive in the face of nature's threats and wild animals imposed a relentless pressure on early humans. Survival demanded attention, adaptation, and swift learning. Those who failed to observe and act wisely perished, while those who succeeded passed on the traits of awareness, memory, and responsive intelligence. In this way, nature itself became a rigorous teacher, shaping the foundation of human reasoning through the unforgiving tests of life and death.

As the human drama diversified, what happened next?

Ignorance brings chaos, knowledge brings enlightenment and order.

Intellectualism (devotion to the exercise of one's intellect or mental powers) grew over thousands of years and largely kept the emotional mind in check. However, like most things in nature, civilisations rise and fall; and, like the ebb and flow of the ocean, human sophistication has waxed and waned over time. During this process, the emotional mind's dominance has fluctuated between enlightened sophistication and the fostering of extreme, macabre, and ghoulish behaviour, to more tolerable but still irrational behaviour. Tolerable irrational behaviour relates to actions that cause harm to no one. Regarding the damage and deterioration of human society, caused by extreme behaviour in the punishment of crimes, the rational, enlightened, and sophisticated minds, loaded with common sense, would not have sanctioned the actions that were soon to be illuminated. The thought of such actions would have repelled such minds, and they would have realised that such would cause the society to deteriorate even further. However, the emotional mind, without the guidance of a balanced philosophy imbued with syllogistic reasoning, would, and did, tolerate extreme behaviour. Would syllogistic reasoning have allowed the following actions, taken from a book about life in 1700s London by Catharine Arnold – Underworld London: Crime and Punishment in the Capital City?

"The 1752 Murder Act allowed judges to make an example of murderers by ordering that their corpses should be displayed on a gibbet. Thus, in the 1770s, up to one hundred gibbets stood on Hounslow Heath, so that, according to the poet Robert Southey, 'from whatever quarter the wind blew, it brought with it a cadaverous and pestilential odour'. The Sunday after the highwayman Lewis Avershaw was gibbeted on Wimbledon Common in 1795, the city was deserted as Londoners flocked to view the corpse. For months after, this grisly spectacle was a popular outing.

> **Of the men, all will hang, but some will be cut down, still conscious, and forced to watch as they are disembowelled and their entrails burnt before their very eyes. A few will be hanged in chains or placed in a gibbet until the flesh rots from their bones. Alongside these unfortunates march the spectators, the family and friends of the dead, and those who consider public executions to be first-rate entertainment. For centuries, hangings were holidays, offering all the fun of the Tyburn fair. The crowd gorged on gingerbread, roast pork, and beer before shouting, 'Hats off!' and craning to see the condemned men kicking their way to death at the end of a short rope."**

An example of one type of gibbet

Did you read the government's gruesome methods of killing without cringing? That snapshot was not the worst of the barbaric practices! This kind of behaviour is unthinkable in today's world. Why? To begin with, we now generally accept a basic principle of common sense: human life is more valuable than property. As a result, people are no longer executed for theft. Historically, however, the brutal practice of gibbeting, publicly displaying the bodies of executed criminals, persisted as recently as 1921 in Afghanistan. Before that, it was also used in countries such as the United States, Canada, Australia, Germany, Iran, and Bermuda.

This is one of the extreme dips in the evolution of both our emotional and rational minds. Many of the characteristics of common sense, such as sound judgement, were at least not embraced by the ruling body then. Also, the common-sense synonym, discernment, which means taste, refinement, sophistication, enlightenment, sensitivity, and subtlety, was not embodied in the minds and hearts of most of those who governed at the time, as well as most of the governed. So, even though this was the period known as the Age of Enlightenment or Age of Reason—a 17th- and 18th-century movement in Western Europe that emphasised reason, analysis, and individualism over traditional authority—it's clear that this transformation was far from complete. This illustrates a simple truth: changing human culture can take a long time.

The practice of gibbeting, mentioned above, was part of what was referred to as being 'hanged, drawn and quartered', and was an extreme emotion-driven behaviour for at least two reasons:

- The behaviour was grossly macabre, repulsive, and horrific. If you do a little research on this, you will also wonder about the mental and emotional well-being of those who carried out and watched these acts.

- It was not a deterrent – tens of thousands are estimated to have met similar fates for many years afterwards. According to Catharine Arnold in *Underworld London*, while a man was being sentenced to death in court for stealing, thieves were working in the crowd!

A brief look at some of the other horrific punishments that were meted out for crimes without them being deterrents should make the following common sense/wisdom an irrefutable truth: ***The most reliable method of transforming human morals and behaviour is education and socialisation, specifically designed to elevate and refine human interactions.*** The philosophy behind some punishments defied all logic and good sense. Here, as reported by Catherine Arnold, are some other punishments that were supposed to deter crime but did not:

- A priest, Father Houghton (1535), had his genitals sliced off and roasted on a spit in front of him.

- As a punishment for attempting to poison his master, the Bishop of Rochester, Richard Rouse, was placed in a cauldron of cold water and boiled to death in 1531.

- Trial by water. An accused was thrown into deep water. If he floated, without swimming, he was guilty, but if he drowned, he was judged innocent.

- The arm of an accused was plunged into boiling water. The condition of the wound would determine their Innocence or guilt. Trials by ordeal ceased in 1215 after Pope Innocent III declared that ordeals were not a demonstration of God's judgement.

Aren't you grateful that societies have come to their senses and no longer practice such horrific, counterproductive, and uncivilised punishments? This examination of extreme 'problem-solving' behaviour is not just to highlight a past period of deterioration in our problem-solving practices, it is to show that the quality of global human interactions does not consistently grow and improve without a consistent, widespread and global improvement in education and training. Even the expansion of formal education among ordinary people will reduce the tolerance level for extreme behaviour. The law of the day had nothing to do with dispensing justice and existed merely to defend property, which was regarded as more valuable than human life. This attitude has changed in Europe as evidenced by our current reality. The Age of Enlightenment eventually transformed Europe's social, political, and economic structures.

But even though we no longer have institutional cruelty to the extent described above, we have pockets of extreme behaviour of 'problem-solving' such as honour killings, horrific mob justice, high murder rates, suicide bombings, bombings with weapons of mass destruction by governments, and in the Philippines, we have the state-sponsored killing of drug dealers without trial.

We can see from the above extreme and macabre behaviour that humanity has fluctuated from good to bad, to worse, to better. Contrary to common belief, the present is a lot better than many periods of the past. This is a lesson that knowledge of history can teach. Currently, the vast majority of us cannot relate to being entertained by such horrific cruelty, for we have evolved, based on education and environment. All of this demonstrates something about being human that is irrefutable: the human mind and emotions can be programmed into almost any kind of behaviour. If the emotional intelligence that arose from the need for human cooperation had been steadily nurtured alongside widespread intellectual development, perhaps we could have avoided the extreme declines in both emotional and intellectual intelligence that led to practices like gibbeting.

An intensive and widespread intellectualism would bring out the qualities that are synonymous with common sense, and therefore, common sense would be more common today without the years of rude interruptions. For the rational mind to be dominant, it must become strong enough to, when necessary, refine or veto our emotions. Ideally, we want to veto emotions that are irrational and serve no useful purpose. Emotional intelligence and common sense are intertwined.

What if the following Chinese proverb were our consistent guiding philosophy as we evolved: If you want one year of prosperity, grow grain. If you want ten years of prosperity, grow trees. If you want a hundred years of prosperity, grow people? Is it a sensible philosophy to adopt right now? What if we had, and have, a consistent global policy of 'growing' people, not just in academics but in all the knowledge and skills of common sense? Would we have a vastly different world than our current reality? I think so. What do you think? Here is an idea for you to consider. Could civilised nations return to their previous extreme, barbaric behaviour? Absolutely! History has already taught us, overwhelmingly, that given the appropriate circumstances, the human moral and emotional compass can regress.

> *Feelings are essential to thought, thought to feeling, but when passions surge, the balance tips: it is the emotional mind that captures the upper hand, swamping the rational mind.* – **Daniel Goleman, *Emotional Intelligence*.**

Our current mixed reality

Unfortunately, the declines in both emotional and intellectual intelligence did occur, and today, the emotional mind holds sway. Intuitive, reactive thinking (often called System 1) remains dominant, while the slower, rational, intellectual mind (System 2) has not evolved rapidly enough to keep pace with our industrial ambitions. Without widespread and refined emotional intelligence, the desires and needs of various groups and communities have eroded much of the cooperative value that once underpinned human progress. The erosion of this value is partly responsible for much human oppression. As you have already seen, this value originated as a result of Nature insisting that we exercise our 'sense' and recognise that cooperative effort was a necessity to carve out our survival and enjoyment on earth.

The fact that many of our new dangers, such as pollution, are not as clear-cut and easily recognisable as a dangerous animal, has resulted in a situation where it's "everyone for himself" in terms of who has the knowledge/sense to recognise what are clear and present dangers. This ability to identify 'new dangers' is not common, and so it's not common sense. Many of these 'new dangers' are related to 'food', lifestyle habits, and drugs, both pharmaceutical and illegal. Much of what we need common sense for currently does not press on us in the same way as it did at the start of human existence. All the dangerous situations during that time were easily identifiable as clear and present dangers, and they did not give any reprieve for those who acted with stupidity. There was no scope to rationalise the consequences of being caught by a dangerous animal. In today's world, we have a lot more dangers. However, many of them can only be identified as a clear and present danger *if we deliberately become the*

type of person who is a keen observer, reader, and listener. But most importantly, our emotional intelligence must grow so that we don't rationalise the consequences of taking dangerous drugs, or eating junk food, for example.

One of the dangers that is not easily identifiable is seen in this philosophy: ***Nature produces dozens of foods and herbs that are compatible with the science of the human body, but our factories produce thousands of 'food'. They're great for the economy but terrible for our health.*** We need an advanced common sense to deal with these seemingly complicated subjects. Much of the insight (common sense) we need in today's world is how to effectively navigate our complicated, social, religious, and economic world. **The world we now inhabit is filled with a vast diversity of people, each with distinct backgrounds, cultures, beliefs, and motivations, and we face a fundamental choice: either confront these differences in conflict or learn how to coexist with them.**

Our physical survival has shifted from primarily knowing how to find or grow food, build shelter, and avoid dangerous animals to a situation where we must learn how to earn money to buy food, acquire shelter, avoid dangerous people, and secure our future. The other half of the need for common sense involves developing an understanding of how to navigate and climb our social and economic ladders.

The difficulty of this varies from country to country and is influenced by social, ethnic, and racial factors. Our complex societies and diverse populations make it essential to understand not only basic human psychology but also its more complex dimensions. This new complicated world has socialised us to experience extraordinary pressure. And this pressure has proved too much for many, to a point where we have high levels of suicides, depression, and insanity.

The good news is that, once you improve your mind and emotions and observe the world through powerful philosophical eyes, you can thrive and find joy, even in this complicated world and while dealing with seemingly impossible situations. A strong, well-balanced personal philosophy is essential for navigating life effectively. **When your insight into life reaches a high level, you can confront life's challenges with clarity about what is truly required.** In other words, deep insight becomes the compass that guides effective, resilient responses to adversity.

In essence, once you understand life and feel competent enough to deal with it, you can relax. By this time, you would have learnt how to identify the things you cannot change and the things that you can change, and live accordingly. Common sense says we tend to be frustrated by, and are afraid of, what we don't quite understand.

Insight is rooted in emotional intelligence and self-awareness. It is a key trait of resilient individuals. It empowers us to recognise our emotional triggers, understand our internal patterns, and bounce back stronger from stress or burnout.

> **The first human beings on Earth began to uncover knowledge. Just as today, back then, individuals had varying capacities for understanding different things. Sharing knowledge—then as now—was the right thing to do. It makes sense that an 'each one, teach one' philosophy was how some knowledge would have spread and become common.**

This increasingly complex world demands not only greater common sense but also new forms of it, different from what was needed in earlier times. As we formed societies and faced the challenges of living together, we developed a desire for shared understanding, cultural norms and rules that would help us coexist with fewer conflicts and more effectively fulfil our fundamental drives: survival and happiness The desire for peaceful coexistence became the foundation for creating and enforcing laws designed to limit the unjust tendency to violate each other's rights. Unfortunately, this effort has met with only limited success.

Just have a look at the size of the world's prison populations. Survival and happiness are impossible without peaceful coexistence. Currently, coexistence is particularly problematic due to the complexity of our emotional and mental make-up. This complexity has driven many to act in a manner that is anti-diversity. Therefore, the very act of coexisting seems to be a threat to both our survival and happiness, based on the proliferation of injustices, oppressions, and wars. How to coexist harmoniously with diverse peoples is now a pressing question, one that demands the attention of our best thinkers and the application of both intellectual and emotional intelligence. Since common sense represents our highest form of practical awareness, it must play a central role if the solutions we develop are to be truly effective.

> **A significant portion of today's social problems arises from the diversity of people across race, class, culture, religion, and nationality. As the world population expanded, collective identity fragmented: we shifted from a shared human interest toward increasingly narrow group affiliations.**

One of the most dangerous aspects of our complex world is the growing presence of political and social propagandists—and professional liars—who are skilled at spreading false narratives, or "fake news." If we are not good at analysing what they say and deducing their intention, they will succeed in manipulating us to act against our self-interest.

Common sense and effective living

Common sense is all about effective living. We have not collectively studied, understood, and practised the fundamentals of effective living. We have been even less consistent in spreading the knowledge of effective living. The proof of this is the extent to which we have been consistent in terms of wars, of diseases caused by diet and lifestyle, of discontentment, and unhappiness. This state of affairs could only be regarded as practising effective living if it was/is intentional and beneficial to those who perpetrate actions that produce these outcomes in other people. Knowledge about the art of effective living has only taken off in our current world since Earl Nightingale's 1956 recording, "The Strangest Secret", which heralded the birth of what we call the personal development or self-help industry. This is the closest we have come to organised and widespread teaching of many philosophies and ideas that ought to be considered common sense, and it has inspired many to broaden their understanding. However, this work, the recording, and the text are still a minor part of the human societal landscape, partly because we are not socialised into viewing work like this with anywhere near the esteem with which we regard academics. The other factor is that reading, or listening to personal development recordings, is not a national pastime in any country.

As you have already read, analysing much of the early human experience was a strong basis for understanding the need for common sense. These basic principles can serve as a foundation for the deeper understanding needed to live effectively in today's world.

Animals are very effective in their environment because their senses are built-in. The sense (knowledge) that we desire[2] to become common refers to areas of knowledge that affect important aspects of our lives in today's world. If such knowledge were widely understood and adopted as common practice, it could elevate us to a point where many more of us function as effectively in

---

[2] Not all of us have a desire for knowledge (common sense) to become widespread. This is true both historically and presently.

our environment as animals do in theirs. If this sense (knowledge) becomes common, there would be more parity between people in terms of health, happiness, success, and survival.

Common sense is based on the accumulated knowledge and experience of our interaction with Nature and with each other. We are meant to accumulate knowledge as we go, enabling us to avoid repeating the same mistakes. We have had limited success with this, primarily because we have not formalised the widespread teaching of Aristotelian-like syllogistic reasoning as it applies to everyday life. Nor have we formalised a widespread teaching of an 'A-Z' of common know-how, common sense, or wisdom. Therefore, much of the knowledge that was supposed to become 'common sense' has not. This void has left the door open for many to become victims of common nonsense.

Common sense and common law

As societies developed and became more diverse, the spirit of voluntary cooperation began to decline, and laws became necessary. On the positive side, these laws were designed to protect us from the harms of selfish intent and injustice, while also providing a framework for the smooth functioning of increasingly complex societies.

These laws are supposed to be based on common sense. We are not perfect, so just as our judgements are not always sound, neither are our laws, which are supposed to be based on sound judgements. Judges are expected to give sound judgements, and common sense is said to be able to exercise sound judgement.

One aspect of common sense is based on accumulated, proven, practical, and workable remedies for solving problems. Common law is also known as 'precedent law', and this is based on the principle that previous, accumulated decisions of the courts are binding or persuasive on current decisions of courts faced with similar cases. The similarity of the description of common sense and common law, plus the fact that they are both supposed to govern our behaviour, suggests that this is why they share the word 'common'. Common sense preceded the making of laws. Therefore, common sense would be the basis of common law.

Are you convinced that our laws are supposed to have everything to do with common sense? If common sense serves as the foundation for our laws, that underscores its importance. If it doesn't, then there is something fundamentally wrong with the laws themselves. Based on the above description, it is highly likely that common sense is the basis of our laws, and therefore, we should formalise its teaching in schools. As already demonstrated, syllogistic reasoning produces common sense. Since this type of reasoning can be taught, we are left

with the duty of teaching how to acquire accurate knowledge to be used in the syllogistic formula.

Common sense has never ceased to be relevant. Apart from using it for physical survival, or the avoidance of danger, we would've learnt (through experience) things such as what plants are edible, and how to cope with adverse weather. The crossing of deserts taught us that a sighting of a bee is an indication that water is nearby because bees cannot live far from water. The absence of such survival common sense could easily lead to death.

Common sense can be time and place-specific

In the early days of American history, during the era known as the 'Wild West', when most men carried guns, a rule of survival (common sense) meant knowing not to call a man a liar or a coward unless you were prepared for a gunfight and confident you could win. If you did not possess this 'sense' and lacked gun-fighting ability, you would be dead, and the law or the public would not interfere. In today's world, such an insult, generally speaking, would not have such a drastic consequence. You could be sued, or end up in a fight, and if it went any further, the law could protect you. From this, we learn that some common sense is time and place-sensitive.

As previously mentioned, a modern-day survival common sense is our habit of teaching our children how to cross the street safely. Yet, despite this being widespread knowledge, both adults and children have often ignored it to their detriment. Perhaps living in societies where many people are employed to protect us, and where we are trained to follow rules, has made us less inclined to apply common sense.

As previously mentioned, a modern form of survival common sense is the habit of teaching our children how to cross the street safely. Yet, despite this being widely known, both adults and children often ignore it, sometimes with serious consequences.

Perhaps living in societies where many people are employed to protect us, and where we are trained to follow rules, has made us less inclined to apply our judgement. This is evident in how some people use pedestrian (or zebra) crossings. Because we are taught that vehicles should slow down when approaching a pedestrian crossing and stop when someone steps onto it, some individuals cross the road without checking whether the car is stopping.

Common sense tells us to make sure the driver sees us and is indeed slowing down. After all, we can't know the driver's state of mind or whether they've even noticed us. I make it a rule to establish eye contact with the driver closest to me, on my immediate danger side, before I begin crossing. Only then do I check the other side. On one occasion, the driver on my immediate danger side was approaching so fast that I stopped to ascertain what he was doing. He became agitated and waved at me to continue. I didn't care whether he was agitated or not because this was a decision I could not afford to get wrong. He had the protection of being in 'a suit of armour'. My suit is just flesh and blood. There would have been just one obvious winner if they had made contact. None of us is receptive to being injured, even if it's just a broken leg.

In the UK, Government figures have shown that nine people were killed on zebra (pedestrian) crossings in 2007, compared to only three in the previous year. There was also a sharp increase in the toll of those seriously injured, which reached 157, 20 more than in 2006. In the interest of safety and survival, apply common sense/sound judgement at zebra crossings. Some basic common sense that we need today can be attained through the understanding of:

- Basic and complicated human behaviour. Most of what we do is driven by our desire to be happy and to survive.

- Nature, natural law or natural science, the law of sowing and reaping as it applies to everyday living, sow nothing, receive nothing. We usually reap much more than we sow. If we practice bad relationships, in the main, we will have a poor return. From the basic workings of everyday, commonplace, man-made science, for example, we should learn that exposed electric wire is dangerous.

- The natural consequences of our thoughts and actions; for example, consistent negative thoughts foster negative life experiences – if you don't plan for your financial future, you will suffer when it arrives.

- The common phenomena of Nature, such as storms and earthquakes.

- Reasonable probabilities as they relate to explaining human actions – so, if told a story, you should be able to filter out improbabilities and lies.

For our minds to be effective at calming and civilising our emotions, our minds need accurate information. Accurate information is the nourishment for the logical mind.

Even as adults, most of our decisions are made emotionally. This is something we will not change. However, we will not be as effective as we can be if our emotions are not guided by accurate information. Not everyone may have a natural gift for science and technology, but everyone can attain wisdom. And it is only through a process of refining our emotions with accurate knowledge and information that wisdom will be obtained. It is only after a level of wisdom (common sense) is attained by the majority of ordinary people that sound judgement (common sense) will become the norm rather than the exception. Part of the process of developing sound judgment is learning to take 'second thoughts', deliberately pausing to override pure emotion with reflective reasoning.

This is about acquiring the habit of pausing to consider before making decisions and taking action. Accurate and sound thinking does not happen like magic. It requires the formulation of ideas based on **accurate knowledge.**

A flavour of common sense

Far too much of what we think and believe is absorbed through a process akin to osmosis. Many of the beliefs we accept and the habits we develop seep into our emotional and psychological makeup long before being vetted for logic, truth, or practicality. As a result, habitual patterns of thinking and feeling become the default method for many when reaching conclusions. In effect, a person's whole thought process can function on autopilot because they never question or test many of the assumptions they hold to be true. Therefore, for many, only *a few* aspects of life and living come under the glare of critical analysis sufficiently for them to thoroughly understand whatever they are focusing on. Many lack the skill for critical thinking. This skill does not exist in a vacuum. It takes extensive knowledge and understanding of human psychology. The starting point of this process is gaining an understanding of our basic needs and motivations, and then developing the ability to critically analyse human behaviour.

> **A large part of our attitude toward things is conditioned by opinions and emotions which we unconsciously absorb as children from our environment. In other words, it is tradition, besides inherited aptitudes and qualities, which makes us what we are. We rarely reflect how relatively small, compared with the powerful influence of tradition, is the impact of our conscious thought upon our conduct and convictions.** – Albert Einstein

Einstein is suggesting that we are often unaware of how deeply our conscious thoughts are shaped by conditioning. If you were asked which animal is the king of the jungle, would you say the lion? If you did, this is an example of picking up an idea and accepting it as truth without checking its accuracy. Lions do not live in jungles; they live on the savannahs. The incredible thing is that you have never seen a lion in a jungle, in person, or on television. You picked up this false idea like osmosis.

The fictional television detective, Columbo, primarily solved his cases by using syllogistic reasoning, which produced simple logical answers that fit the description of what we call common sense. The world was so enthralled by his methods that the series lasted eleven to twelve years. So, what was the 'tool' that he inserted into the syllogistic reasoning formula, and why was it so effective in solving his cases? His tool was an in-depth understanding of human psychology. He was effective because he was a master of applying this understanding to spot inconsistencies or aberrations in human behaviour. It usually takes one anomaly in the perpetrator's behaviour to trigger his suspicion. Once his suspicion is aroused, his mind would pick up on any other anomalies in the person's story or behaviour. Once these anomalies accumulate, the die is cast, and the proof of the perpetrator's guilt is inevitable.

In the episode *"Murder Under Glass"*, the victim was poisoned in his restaurant by a man he had dinner with. The murderer did it in such a way that the man seemed to have been poisoned after he left. After he solved the case, he told the man that he had suspected him two minutes after they met. The man declared that this was impossible. Columbo then explained to him that he became suspicious because he had not asked to be taken to the hospital, or have his stomach pumped, after being told that a man he had dinner with had been poisoned eating the same meal. Columbo was suspicious of him even though he knew the police had told him to come to the restaurant to help their investigation. This is because he understood that an innocent person would be so frightened by the thought that he could have poison in his system, he would insist that the police take him to the hospital first, or go on his own. How many of us would have had this process of thought?

How about the case where he found out that a man had opened his mail after coming home to find the dead body of his business partner on his lawn? Would you have spotted the anomaly in him opening his mail at such a time? In another case, *"A Trace of Murder"*, a woman conspired with her lover to frame her husband for murder. Her lover was a forensic expert who worked at the same station as Columbo. Not knowing that the two knew each other, Columbo invited the forensic expert to attend a meeting in a café with the woman and observed her for suspicious behaviour. This is an example of an expert in forensic science not having enough sense to realise the consequences of his actions. Or perhaps it was a case of acting without thinking. They ordered coffee. The man

took charge and placed a cup of coffee in front of everyone. Then he committed the act that alerted Columbo that they knew each other. In the middle of the table was a cup of regular sugar, and to the side, a cup of artificial sweetener. The man pushed aside the regular sugar and pushed the sweetener towards the woman. By this simple act, he transgressed a custom that an astute person would not miss. There are four ways that we usually drink regular coffee:

1.   Black (without milk, sugar, or cream)
2.   With sugar only
3.   White (with milk or cream only)
4.   With sugar and cream, or milk.

He never asked her how she liked her coffee; such a question is almost hardwired into coffee drinkers to ask. Furthermore, he compounded his error by giving her a specific type of sweetener. His lack of astuteness did not end there. He went to get the chauffeured car. He came back, got out of the back seat and waited by the door for the woman. When the woman approached the car, he didn't offer her the back seat. Instead, he moved and opened the front door for her, and Columbo observed this as further confirmation that they knew each other. He later confirmed his suspicion that the woman suffered from motion sickness and would, therefore, not sit in the back of a vehicle, which the man, by his action, knew.

We are fascinated by the application of syllogistic reasoning – common sense. We now have a television programme called Criminal Minds, which is in its twelfth season and is based on forensic profiling. The profilers assess the behavioural characteristics of the criminal (unsub, or unknown subject), gain an understanding of the reason for their actions, and then use this to identify the criminal. After identification, simple logic is often used to catch them. This is a specialist 'common' sense because most of us do not know the psychology of criminal behaviour. However, it has the same formula as everyday syllogistic reasoning (common sense) – accurate information, plus logic.

Astuteness = common sense

Human behaviour, like any other animal's behaviour, has patterns to it. Our patterns are mainly shaped by our thinking, our emotions, culture/ society, education, and the environment. Each of us is obliged to be adept at understanding at least those within our own culture. Once you are on this road of understanding, and the greater your awareness of the patterns of human behaviour, the more effective you will be in at least judging the reason(s) for people's actions. And if you are called on to determine the truth of a story, whether as a juror or in your everyday interactions, your perceptions will be wise and therefore invaluable.

Common sense on the value of history

One of the most significant determinants of the truth about almost any subject is knowledge of its history.

It is often challenging to awaken someone to an alternative understanding of life and reality if their reading habits are limited. The central missing link needed to piece the jigsaw puzzle of life together is a fairly comprehensive and accurate knowledge of history. This will provide direction to understand the factors that shaped the psychology of different people, such as knowledge of their origins, which reveals the environments that influenced them, their activities and their culture, which together help explain their worldview.

From this, we can understand what drives nations, races, cultures, and civilisations. We can now examine the significant events of the past, as well as those that are current, with an informed perspective. The value of history is difficult to overstate, as you can see from the following pointers:

- Having a solid understanding of a person's history enhances our ability to understand them.

- It's unwise to start a relationship with someone whom you don't know much about, including important information about events and influences in their past that have affected them.

- When someone says, "How can you say you love me and you don't know me?" they are referring to not knowing the experiences that have shaped them, and this is, in effect, not knowing their history.

- Likewise, we can improve our understanding of the world we live in by learning the history of its people.

- Understanding the events and beliefs which shape a country is necessary to understanding the people of that country.

- This principle of knowledge of its history applies to almost every subject.

- Knowledge of the history of economics, or religion, for example, will give a greater understanding of economics, or religion, likewise.

- The ultimate wisdom from the value of history is that today makes a lot more sense because we know and understand what happened yesterday. Knowing and understanding yesterday gives us the root cause of today, and this is the key to solving any problem or to providing a clear basis on how to proceed. So, we will know best where we are going when we know where we are coming from. History is relevant because it shapes today.

- If we suffer from amnesia, we cannot function to our full capacity.

Common sense on the sanctity of life

Is the sanctity or precious nature of life a universal truth? It may be, if that principle is limited to human life. However, even this is not straightforward; across cultures and throughout history, the value placed on human life has fluctuated. During the time of the American 'Wild West' and early modern Europe, a man could kill another in a face-to-face duel without any repercussions. During slavery, a slave's life was not sacred. The great Nature and Universe that govern our existence do not hold any life as sacred. Nature kills with indifference with what is often referred to as 'Acts of God'—storms, hurricanes, tornadoes, earthquakes, volcanoes, lightning, and so on.

So, in effect, the sanctity of life is a philosophy that came out of the inner world of our minds. The birth of the sanctity of life came out of our capacity to love. We love our life, and we love our family and friends, so we instinctively want to protect both and punish those who cause us to grieve. The sanctity of life is a very subjective philosophy, as it fluctuates depending on the point of view from which it's being considered and how we choose to relate to any particular life. In Hinduism, the cow is revered as a sacred symbol of life and divinity and therefore is not to be killed. Furthermore, the cow provides an abundance of essential products for Hindus, including milk, curd, and butter, which serve as an important source of nourishment. It is used in rituals, and its dung is used for fuel. However, on a wider scale, the cow is said to be the third most widely eaten animal in the world. Many of us treat dogs as pets, sometimes almost as family members, yet many Chinese people eat them. In the West, we mostly find this act abhorrent.

He is one of those people who would be enormously improved by death. – H. H. Munro (Saki) (1870-1916)

The fact that Nature, the great giver of life, is also indifferent to taking life is a demonstration of how unique we are. It demonstrates our unique ability to shape the world the way we want it to be. We are unique because, even though we are a product of Nature, we can decide which lives are sacred and precious, and we have decided, in the main, that human life is. This is why the vast majority of us will never commit murder and find such an act abhorrent. However, despite our morality, the twist in the tale is that we have made a distinction between murder, killing in wars, capital punishment, and in self-defence. We humans are rather strange. While we invented morality, and indeed morality often serves to nurture a healthy mind and spirit, our blank-slate nature has also enabled a history of profoundly horrifying oppression and genocide. This suggests an uncomfortable truth: our attitude toward the sanctity of life is not fixed. Rather, it fluctuates according to the state of our mental and emotional development. That we are a true enigma becomes evident when we reflect on these facts:

- We can be mercilessly oppressive.
- We have the capacity for unconditional love.
- We can show selfless compassion.
- We can harbour unshakable hatred.
- We can be mercilessly prejudicial.
- We can kill mercilessly.

Practical approach to problem-solving

Success psychologists teach that ambition and enthusiasm are not enough to pursue and achieve success; skill is also required.

They often speak to individuals who are dissatisfied with their current financial path and are determined to increase their income and secure their financial future. Yet, even among the motivated, personal development teachers like Jim Rohn have spoken about the uphill battle of encouraging people to change their reading habits or commit to skill development. Rohn, who lectured to millions over the years, frequently recommended the very books and principles that he credited with making him wealthy.

He estimated that only five per cent of those people went out and bought the books he recommended; the remaining ninety-five per cent "couldn't be bothered". They failed to internalise the transformational power of books and didn't grasp the fundamental truth that to achieve more, they had to change

and become more. It often came down to either a lack of awareness of two key pieces of wisdom or an unwillingness to fully embrace them.

The first bit of wisdom (known by only a few) is within the quote by Albert Einstein, which states that a problem cannot be solved at the same level of thinking that created it. A person's income reflects what they know, especially their level of financial literacy, and how effectively they apply that knowledge. To change their income, they must elevate their knowledge and skills. The second insight refines this: as Jim Rohn famously said, **"Success is not something you pursue; it is something you attract by the person you become."** In other words, we don't chase outcomes; we become the type of person who naturally draws success. First, we grow into that person; then we achieve and receive. This approach captures a deep level of practical wisdom, common sense in action.

The syllogistic reasoning formula, if imbued with the relevant and correct premise, is a powerful tool that can solve problems that seem unsolvable. Our manmade problems often feel intractable because they tend to be interpreted through emotionally charged lenses, rather than with our logical, rational minds. When decisions and policies are guided by emotion first, reasoning becomes reactive, biased, and fragmented, making durable solutions hard to achieve. Our logical, rational mind is the great enabler in solving problems.

The value of having accurate knowledge about childbirth and how to nurture children toward physical and emotional health cannot be overstated.

CHAPTER THREE

The first major life issue to which Aristotelian syllogistic reasoning applies: **Common sense on childbirth and the nurturing of children**

We now turn the spotlight of syllogistic reasoning on an aspect of life that affects all of us, childbirth. Since the quality of childbirth and care has everything to do with the perpetuation and quality of human life, we must apply the correct science and reasoning to it. If we have more problems giving birth than other lifeforms, this suggests that we are less well-suited than they are. If this is not the case, why do we generally have more problems giving birth than animals and other lifeforms?

Few, if any, topics are more vital than understanding how to facilitate the perpetuation of human life best, ensuring not only survival but thriving physical and emotional well-being across generations. Since this is such an important subject that doesn't require snap judgement, it is not suited to be dominated by emotions. Syllogistic reasoning had a transformational effect during the Age of Enlightenment because it is based on the principle that one should follow the logical argument wherever it leads, rather than be constrained by rigid dogma. If there is ever an aspect of life that requires the same approach, this is it. There are many philosophies on how to care for babies, with some focusing specifically on childbirth. The following are just a few basic approaches. Comparing different methods and evaluating their outcomes is a practical way to gain wisdom, which is, in many ways, just another name for common sense.

Does the following real-life drama demonstrate the dominance of our logical or our emotional mind?

Dr Sir Frederic Truby King (1 April 1858 – 10 February 1938) was a New Zealand health reformer who is best known as the founder of the Plunket Society, an organisation promoting infant welfare. According to Wikipedia, this society was formed to apply scientific principles to the nutrition of babies and is firmly rooted in eugenics and patriotism. Eugenics is a social philosophy that advocates for the improvement of human genetic traits through the promotion of higher reproduction of people with the desired genes. This philosophy can

also be described as advocating selective breeding, or rooting out 'weak genes', and is the same as Adolf Hitler's ideas about the 'Aryan race'. Knowing that Truby King supported the eugenics philosophy is an example of how knowledge of a person's history gives a better insight into the reason(s) for their philosophy and actions.

In 1932, Dr Truby King published a book, Feeding and Care of Baby, which contained his ideas about childcare. His ideas were also promoted through a network of specially trained nurses and a widely syndicated newspaper column. Perhaps you will agree that his interest in eugenics or 'selective reproduction' is related to his foundation philosophy of how to raise children: "Build character by avoiding cuddling and other attention". His methods are still practised today and were featured in a four-part British television documentary titled *"Bringing Up Baby"* (Channel 4, aired from 25 September to 16 October 2007). The series explored an experiment comparing three different approaches to baby care, aiming to determine which was the most effective. As you explore each method, consider whether the underlying philosophy and the claims made by each advocate align with what you would consider to be common sense, or even wisdom.

Apart from the Truby King Method, the other methods demonstrated were the Benjamin Spock Method and the Continuum Concept. Episode 2 of the documentary began with the statement: "Every new parent wants the best for their baby, but knowing what that is can be tough in a world where parenting tips change as fast as high street fashions. In the 1950s, discipline was in style, as mothers were encouraged to show their babies who was boss [Truby King Method]. In the 1960s, rules were out and baby love was in [Benjamin Spock Method]. And in the 1970s, it was all about going native [Continuum Concept]." The Continuum Concept is based on anthropological studies that will be explained as we examine this most important subject.

What is the best way of bringing up a baby? All three methods were 'road-tested' to see which one works best. The following are some of Truby King's methods of feeding and baby care that are still being practised, according to the documentary, "Bringing Up Baby". You may think it makes sense, or you may be aghast like an unknown person who wrote on a blog: "Sad. So sad to deprive a life of nourishment, but more so, love. The damage that can't be mended. The time that cannot be taken back."

Truby King's methods specifically emphasised regularity of feeding, sleeping and bowel movements, within a generally strict regimen that is supposed to build character by avoiding cuddling and other attention. Dr King's methods continued to be popular until the 1950s. An advocate of Truby King's method, Claire Verity, was one of the Channel 4 mentors and a childcare professional whose clients included Sting and Jerry Hall. According to the programme, she earns up to 1,000 pounds per day for her services.

Claire Verity – advocate and mentor of Truby King's 1913 routine-based method (has no children)

The following are some of the key philosophies and ideas of this Truby King advocate:

- She is against feeding babies in public.
- Four hourly feeds only.
- No visitors in the first week.
- **Claire Verity declared:** "At 7 PM, put the baby in its cot and its room and close the door. If it cries, it cries." So, the minute they come home from the hospital, they go into their cot in their room. **She suggested:**
- "I wouldn't advise any parent to have the baby in the room with them. A baby will listen to every single noise, and it won't sleep, and that's no good; it will blow the routine from day one."
- "Most times, when a baby cries, it's because it's tired or attention-seeking; in both cases, ignore them."

It shouldn't require syllogistic reasoning to demonstrate that which should be common or general knowledge: babies cry for other valid reasons, such as hunger, discomfort, illness, or the need for affection.

- The objective of her method is to get the baby to sleep from seven p.m. to seven a.m.
- No touching or kissing in between feeds. **Claire Verity stated:**
- "I don't understand why anybody needs to touch a baby or pick a baby up. A baby doesn't want to be cuddled all the time. All they want to do is to be left alone to grow.
- "I think people who pick up babies are stupid, absolutely stupid. There is no need to pick up a baby; leave it alone, don't touch it.
- "A baby thrives in a routine. It needs continuity and stability, and that's what the routine gives.
- "A routine is very beneficial for a baby because a baby likes continuity and security; they like to know that they are going to

get fed at a certain time, and they know they are going to bed at a certain time."

- Up to three hours outdoors on its own until feeding time, even from day one – lots of fresh air makes it sleep better at night and feeds much better.

- Initially, the mothers cried when they couldn't respond to their babies crying, or having to leave them outside and keep the door closed.

- To justify not responding to a baby's cry, she claims that babies can cry for no reason. **This is how she explained her objective:**

- "With my method/routine, I guarantee to put your life back in order within 24 hours after having the baby."

- She guaranteed that the baby would sleep through the night, feed every four hours, and be a happy, contented child.

- She claims formula food is just as good as breast milk.

- Baby should only be held while feeding, changing, and bathing. **This point was expanded on with this explanation:**

- "Ideally, no cuddling except when feeding, especially the first week or more; it's about getting them into the routine, bonding when feeding only."

- Feeding is about business, not bonding, it's about getting them into a routine.

- Limited contact, including eye contact while feeding, and she can have ten minutes of cuddling only. **Claire also stated:**

- "No eye contact while feeding; once he gets eye contact, he knows then he is in charge, and he is not. You're in charge, and you're feeding him. It's all about getting the milk down them."

- **In advising one mentee, she stated:** "When feeding with a bottle, keep the baby away from your body so that it doesn't get too comfortable and fall asleep. The point is for her to have a full bottle so that she sleeps for the next four hours. Look at the size of her, she is so tiny. How can you make something so small control your life? It's crazy. You are in charge, you tell her how you want it to be, and that's how the routine comes in."

- **She was asked by Benjamin Spock advocate, Dreena Hamilton:** "How much time are you going to spend adhering to the baby's needs if there is limited touching and talking?" **She responded:**

- "You don't have to physically hold a baby for it to feel secure. Security is being swaddled at night; being in its own cot, pram or buggy, or when the parents are around…What needs does it have? It doesn't need to go jogging around the park."

- The objective is for the babies to sleep through the night sooner and for the parents' lives to get back to normal quickly.

- Another tactic she uses to achieve her sleep objective is reducing the baby's daytime feeds so they are 'starving' by evening, encouraging them to take in more food at that time and, in turn, sleep longer at night. She also wakes them half an hour early from their afternoon nap to help ensure they are ready to sleep in the evening.

Does it make sense that a baby may be traumatised if it is allowed to feel undue hunger a few days or weeks after it was born, having never experienced hunger in its previous ten months of life?

Dreena Hamilton commented: "It would be really cruel to feed him loads and loads just because you want him to go through the night."

- In response to her mentee tearfully expressing that she felt she was being mean to her baby by not responding to its crying, **Claire Verity responded:** "You're not being mean, you have to just rise above it and understand that she is playing you up…she knows exactly what she is doing. She is looking for attention even at this age, all the time. Don't bow down to her, don't give in, you are in charge, keep going with the routine." This is about a baby who is a few days old!

- **Claire Varity:** "I think I am a complete bitch, 'course I am, what I do is quite mean but it works."

- **According to the narrator,** "Claire Verity believes babies are manipulative creatures who take over your life if you don't show them who is boss from day one."

- She was not satisfied with the baby sleeping from 11 p.m. to 7 a.m., so she adjusted the baby's diet by adding porridge to extend sleep from 7 p.m. to 7 a.m. **This goal was achieved, and the parents were able to act on the following suggestion:**

- "If you want to have a party, great, have a party; don't let it stop you, those babies won't wake up."

- The mentees followed this advice and had fifty party guests in their home without waking their twins.

- **Claire Varity's triumphant statement to the advocates of the other methods of baby care was:** "My babies are sleeping from seven to seven, are yours?"

- Her mentees eventually got lots of sleep after three days.

- Their social and sex life returned to normal quickly.

- This is success, right?

Tamsin Greig, the narrator of the programme, stated: "Scientific studies have shown that a newborn baby's cry produces hormonal changes in the mother". You will read where one of the mentees acknowledged that she felt ill from hearing her baby cry. **It was also stated on the programme:** "The 1950s approach was all about raising sturdy, disciplined children. Lots of love was seen as mollycoddling." The following quote from Truby King reveals a correlation with Claire Verity's philosophy: If you do let him master you completely, he won't learn to live properly, and your life won't be worth living.

Tamsin Greig also stated: "King's military approach to babies was particularly popular in post-war Britain when parents wanted disciplined and self-reliant children, it was the dominant approach to childcare for over 40 years. Truby King's career started not in childcare but in dairy farming, where he observed that a strict feeding timetable and lots of fresh air created healthy, contented little calves. When he applied this theory to babies, he found the same applied. So, all Truby King Babies were to sleep in well-ventilated rooms on their own and spend hours outdoors each day [on their own].

Since common sense suggests that the issue is about the emotional well-being of the baby, why would he draw inspiration from the well-being of calves? Some animals mourn the death of their offspring, but the cow is not one of them. Would you agree that it's a stretch to compare our emotional characteristics to those of cows, even though we are both mammals? Perhaps Truby King and those who advocate his method believe that plenty of fresh air can substitute for affection and the nurturing of emotional well-being. However, this approach gives little consideration to the emotional needs of newborns.

Dreena Hamilton – advocate and mentor of the Benjamin Spock method (has a large family)

Benjamin Spock wrote a book, ***The Common Sense Book of Baby and Child Care*** (1946). It is second on the 20th century's non-fiction bestsellers list, next to the Bible. According to Wikipedia, *"The book's message to mothers is that 'you know more than you think you do." Spock was the first paediatrician to study psychoanalysis to try to understand children's needs and family dynamics. His ideas about childcare influenced several generations of parents to be more flexible and affectionate with their children, and to treat them as individuals."* Its message was a contrast to the rigid and sterile philosophy of the Truby King method. It has been credited with helping to revolutionise childcare in the 1940s and 1950s in the West.

Its philosophy fitted into the 1960s when "rules were out and baby love was in". Because this method of baby care doesn't have rigid rules, there isn't a lot to describe in terms of the television documentary's demonstration. Nevertheless, there is sufficient information on crucial questions that we ought to apply common sense to. The question is, which method is best for the welfare of the baby and parents? **Here are some of the philosophies of Dreena Hamilton, a mentor of the Benjamin Spock method of baby care, and some incidents:**

- Mentor Dreena Hamilton is against breastfeeding in public.

- This method recommends that parents take quality time for themselves. During one such moment when her baby was crying in the next room, the mother said, ***"It's hard not to rush and jump to them every time they cry. I physically feel sick when I hear him cry."***

- The general rule is for parents to trust their instinct about what to do with their baby.

- This method is not in favour of visitors unless they can be of practical help in looking after the baby.

- Dreena, commenting on the Truby King's Method: **"I think it's cruel, hard, and awful to leave a very small baby to cry without contact and adhering to its needs. A baby needs to be loved, it needs to be touched, and it needs to be cuddled."**

- Critics said that Benjamin Spock's method produces spoiled and indulged children. Others say it inspires independence and freethinking.

- Dreena: ***"How does a new baby know what spoiling is? A three-year-old child knows what spoiling is. A three-day-old or a month-old baby, you can't spoil."***

- Infants raised according to Spock's approach typically slept in a separate crib or bassinet placed directly beside the parents' bed, enabling proximity without bed-sharing.

- The mother accepted that being tired and worn out, having been woken up several times per night, is part of the territory.

- Mentor's advice: **"If you can't breastfeed, don't feel guilty, do it your way."**

- Parents should work out their own feeding pattern and routine.

- Narrator: *"Childcare does not require rules. This advice was regarded as alarmingly modern by British standards. The advice was to rip up the rule book and do what you think was best. No right or wrong in bringing up a baby."* This is based on the 'mother knows best' philosophy.

- Narrator: *"You just can't love or cuddle a baby too much; there is no such thing".*

- Narrator: *"He (Benjamin Spock) claimed that if mothers were to follow his advice, they would produce more confident adults who will form healthy relationships in later life."*

- **Dreena:** *"Forced schedule is really, really bad. Don't expect a baby to come out of the womb, a primitive little creature, and suddenly say, 'Oh, it's ten o'clock, I'll have a feed; two o'clock, I'll have a feed. You have to have a balance of discipline and free reign, according to Dr Spock."*

- *"Let them tell you in the early weeks when they want to eat, when they want to sleep. People don't like it because it messes up their routine, but you shouldn't really have a routine."*

Claire Scott – advocate and mentor of the Continuum Concept (has two children)

The continuum concept is an idea coined by Jean Liedloff in her 1975 book *The Continuum Concept.* This idea states that human beings have an innate set of expectations (which Liedloff calls **The *continuum*)** that our evolution as a species has designed us to meet to achieve optimal physical, mental, and emotional development and adaptability.

In reality, she didn't originate the method; she coined its name. The baby-care approach she endorsed has been practised for centuries. Soon, you'll be able to assess its effectiveness and practicality using plain common sense. **This is how Claire Scott described it:**

"The continuum method is an approach to life and parenting. It involves constant contact with your baby for at least the first six months. It involves carrying the baby in a sling, sleeping with the baby in the same bed at night, and breastfeeding on cue (the baby feeds when it wants to, as it did in the womb). Babies are born and expect to be held, and if the baby is placed in a crib or cot, it feels a sense of loneliness… When the baby is held continuously and sleeps in the mother's bed, it develops a sense of rightness." **These are some of her other thoughts on baby care and other information:**

- It's very much about a holistic life; wearing a sling enables the mother to breastfeed without having to stop what she is doing.

- After birth, there should be almost immediate contact with the breast to ensure a successful breastfeeding relationship; not more than 20 minutes should elapse between birth and contact with the breast.

- Constant skin-to-skin contact and instant access to the breast.

- This method meets the baby's needs much faster, therefore, reducing the time the baby will cry.

- The continuum method is not difficult to implement because it's based on your instinct.

- If the baby is in a sling for the first six months, the baby must be included in what the mother is doing. It watches, listens, and learns, and then as the baby gets older, they start to join in themselves. Because they have had these experiences from birth, they are very adept at what they learn to do, and it just becomes a natural part of their lives. In contrast, the baby in the crib, the carrycot, or the playpen, for example, totally misses out on these experiences.

In response to Claire Verity's claim that babies cry for no reason, she stated:

- *"Babies cry because they have an unmet need…something is wrong or unfulfilled."*

- "The continuum concept is best for the baby bonding with its father."

- **"Breastmilk is the perfect food, and it's very easily digested and far more easily digested than formula milk. When a baby is in the uterus, it gets fed twenty-four hours a day. It comes out of the uterus, and it has a natural weaning stage. From birth, you**

feed it whenever the baby cues that it needs feeding. For the first six months, all the baby gets is breastmilk."

- "In the West, we are conditioned not to listen to our feelings, and we are conditioned not to listen to our babies."

- First night: peaceful for all…when the baby was hungry, food was on tap, so he never needed to cry.

- **"The long-term benefits of following the continuum concept are optimal well-being: mental, physical and emotional well-being."**

- "Central to this concept is that a baby should be brought up by a whole community, not just the nuclear family. Parents are encouraged to gather a tribe around them from birth. The 'tribe', such as parents, grandparents, siblings and friends, would gather, and the child is passed from person to person, and it fosters sociability and independence."

- Visitors are allowed and encouraged.

- **Mother, Alex:** *"I want to apply the continuum concept because I want the child to feel confident. It's a natural instinct within me to want to be with my child. I got pregnant for a reason because I wanted to have a child. So, the last thing I want to do is, as soon as I get that child, is to put it in another room as if it's some punishment for being alive."*

- Parents are encouraged to let children explore the world around them and feel confident that their inbuilt survival instinct will protect them.

- The continuum concept is based on an anthropological study.

- A key element is to have a support network of like-minded parents.

One of the surprising and insightful outcomes that were revealed to the mentees occurred when they met other like-minded parents:

- Children can work with knives from a very young age.

- **Narrator:** *The theory is: toddlers who have been held in a sling from birth, and in constant contact with adult activities, have learnt through watching their mums and dads the correct technique of how to handle a knife.*

The above point about using a knife was demonstrated when, after three weeks of following their respective programmes, the mentees met with older children who were raised by the continuum principles. The mentors of the Truby King and Benjamin Spock methods were alarmed to see babies as young as two and a half years using knives to cut up vegetables without cutting themselves. They cut cucumbers, carrots, diced mushrooms, and grated cheese. Isn't this profoundly insightful? Does this prove that this method accelerates the learning curve of the baby? It was stated, about babies using knives: ***"It is only suited for children who have been brought up on the continuum concept."***

The programme ultimately concluded that no single method could be crowned best for 'Bringing Up Baby', each approach has its advantages and drawbacks. Every participating parent believed they'd chosen the correct method, reinforcing the idea that what matters most is selecting the method best suited to the individual. So, that raises the questions: what are the pros and cons?

Significantly, the evaluations were based on the parents' experiences, not the babies', since infants can't communicate their perspective. And because the babies appeared to be healthy and thriving, any subtle or long-term adverse effects would have been difficult to detect."

For viewers who watch the programme, hoping to discover the best method for caring for a newborn, the programme's conclusions fall short. What it presented is insufficient unless the goal is simply assessing how each technique affects parents' lives. If you aim to optimise your baby's physical and emotional health, the programme's coverage is incomplete. Accordingly, additional information will be offered shortly for your consideration.

The Truby King method and the Continuum Concept are methods that are incredibly different in terms of human considerations and common sense. It was the Continuum Concept advocate, Claire Scott, who made a statement that captures the possibly unseen consequences of the Truby King method, and at the same time highlighted what the emphasis of raising a baby should be. Claire Scott's statement that "no one really knows" is provocative; it encourages us to reflect on the hidden, long-term impact of early childhood neglect. She highlights how something as seemingly simple as a baby's cry carries deep emotional significance: it is a call for connection, safety, and trust.

Her words invite us to consider the complexity of our emotional lives. As humans, we are profoundly shaped and often driven by our feelings. When emotional needs go unmet at a critical stage of development, particularly in infancy, the consequences can manifest years later in subtle yet profound ways: low self-esteem, difficulty trusting others, and emotional instability.

Now ask yourself: could the dysfunction we observe in individuals and society be rooted in these earliest experiences, some even before birth, in the womb? Could the seeds of adult emotional struggle be sown at a time when a baby is most sensitive and vulnerable? An essential benefit of emotional well-being is the capacity for empathy. This ability to understand and share the feelings of others is not inherited, it is cultivated through emotional nurturing, especially in the earliest stages of life. A baby's emotional development does not thrive in emotional deprivation. It begins not in adulthood, nor even in childhood, but from birth, immediately after leaving the "womb matrix" and entering the "earth matrix."

This emotional nourishment is as vital as physical nutrition, perhaps even more so for a newborn. Unlike adults, who can at least attempt to rationalise the absence of affection, a baby has no such capacity. But even for adults, rationalising the lack of love doesn't eliminate the need for it. The assumption that strength of character comes from emotional hardness is deeply flawed. True strength lies in emotional openness, in being responsive and attuned to the feelings of others.

The belief that affection, like cuddling or emotional attention, somehow weakens a child is misguided. Withholding such care may raise emotionally stunted adults, lacking the basic human ability to empathise. These individuals often struggle to identify and manage their own emotions, let alone respond appropriately to the feelings of others.

Without empathy, a person may misread or mishandle situations, perhaps in ways as glaring as offering "happy hour" tickets at a funeral, or as subtle as consistently ignoring another's pain. What's at stake is not just emotional intelligence or social grace, but something more profound: the moral compass that guides human connection. The absence of empathy doesn't just result in awkwardness; it can foster insidious, even harmful, behaviour.

According to science reporter Melissa Hogenboom, BBC News, ***"Scientific researchers have concluded that psychopaths have an empathy switch which is off by default."*** Do you think that it makes sense that the absence of empathy and sensitivity would characterise those guilty of the most heinous crimes in society? The article also stated: ***The ability to empathise with others, to put yourself in someone else's shoes, is crucial to social development in order to respond appropriately in everyday situations.*** – http://www.bbc.co.uk/news/science- environment-23431793

The absence of empathy and emotional sensitivity is starkly visible in some of society's most disturbed individuals, those who commit heinous acts without remorse. This raises a sobering question: how many of these people were raised according to rigid, emotionally neglectful approaches such as Truby King's method or its equivalents? Can we truly believe that dysfunction emerges randomly, without cause or history? Or must we acknowledge that early deprivation and misguided ideals of emotional restraint lay the groundwork for lifelong psychological harm?

One striking example of our collective detachment from emotional and biological intuition is the public backlash against breastfeeding. The Continuum Concept, a philosophy grounded in natural child rearing, faced significant societal resistance, particularly regarding the public breastfeeding of infants. So strong was this objection that, even as late as 2009, laws had to be passed to protect a mother's right to nourish her child in public—a right that common sense and biology already affirm.

Why such hostility? Because, in many Western societies, the act of breastfeeding has been mischaracterised as indecent exposure, grouped, astonishingly, with the display of genitalia. The female breast, primarily designed by Nature to feed offspring, has been culturally recast as a purely sexual object. This reveals how profoundly human beings can be conditioned, how societal programming can override instinct, biology, and basic empathy.

Not all cultures share this distorted view. In some societies, the female breast remains connected to its original, nurturing purpose. Yet in the West, a paradox persists: revealing cleavage for fashion or sex appeal is widely accepted, even celebrated. But the same breast, used to fulfil its evolutionary function, is seen as indecent when a baby seeks nourishment in public.

If infants had the power to speak for themselves, they would assert their right to nourishment wherever and whenever hunger strikes. They would demand freedom from stigma, and the dignity to be fed from the very organ designed by Nature for their survival.

The ultimate common-sense way for "Bringing Up Baby"

Should our culture regarding how to give birth, care for, nourish, and raise a baby be based on our perceptions or feelings of what is the right way, or should it be based on the science of Nature? Does it make sense that we should figure out what the natural or Nature's way is, and work with that program? Or should we continue as if we know more than Nature? The evidence that Nature has already won this argument, hands down, will be outlined shortly.

By now, you may recognise that common sense aims at our highest ideals. And truly, what could be more vital than ensuring the continuation of humanity through physically and emotionally healthy children? Common sense cannot be valuable if it cannot help us in basic, yet critical, areas of life. The following

may surprise you: the responsibility for being good parents begins before procreation and conception. Common sense suggests that couples would want to bring their best physical, mental, and emotional self to creating a baby. **Here are the rules:**

- Ideally, both prospective parents should maintain a healthy diet and lifestyle for at least one year before conception to optimise fertility, support healthy foetal development, and reduce the risk of complications.

- This healthy diet and lifestyle should continue during pregnancy and after. Here are the rules:

- If the mother drinks alcohol, the baby drinks alcohol. If the mother eats junk food, the baby eats junk food. Junk food is bad for our health.

- If the mother smokes, the baby smokes, and second-hand smoke has a similar effect. Here are the possible consequences: nicotine, carbon monoxide and tar cross the placenta and enter the baby's bloodstream. Carbon monoxide binds to haemoglobin more strongly than oxygen does, reducing the amount of oxygen the baby receives. Nicotine narrows the blood vessels, including those in the umbilical cord, which further limits oxygen and nutrient flow. Consequences could include: low birth rate, premature birth, stillbirth and miscarriage. It can also interfere with brain development, lung development, and heart development. They have a higher risk of sudden infant death syndrome, asthma and other respiratory issues, behavioural and learning problems in childhood.

- If the mother takes drugs, the baby takes drugs. This includes an anaesthetic or other pain-relieving medicines administered during epidurals. Effects can consist of: prolonging the second stage of labour, increasing the chance of needing assisted delivery, for example, forceps or vacuum suction.

- If the mother has prolonged stress, it can have negative impacts on the baby. This will be expanded on shortly.

Regarding alcohol consumption, the American Academy of Paediatrics has recommended that pregnant women shouldn't drink. And even though there are different opinions on this, there is a consensus among doctors that pregnant women should avoid drinking in their first trimester. Many have also stated that there is no way of knowing how much alcohol is safe, or when it is a safe time to drink alcohol during pregnancy. ***Because of this, the current recommendation of the government agencies of several countries is to drink no alcohol at all if one is pregnant or planning to become pregnant. Foetal (or Fetal) Alcohol Spectrum Disorders (FASD) is a continuum of various permanent birth defects caused by the mother's consumption of alcohol during pregnancy."***

Simple logic: If the consumption of small amounts of alcohol can impair the faculty of **some** adults, is it not likely also to cause harm to a delicate unborn baby? Regarding smoking and pregnancy, the American Cancer Society quoted this: *According to the 2014 Surgeon General's Report, there have been more than 20 million smoking-related deaths in the United States since 1964; 2.5 million of those.*

Deaths were among non-smokers who died from exposure to second-hand smoke. During that same time, 100,000 babies have died due to parental smoking (including smoking during pregnancy).

This is what Joseph Chilton Pearce, in his classic bestseller, Magical Child, had to say about the effect of stress on the unborn baby:

If the mother's body is producing massive amounts of adrenal steroids during pregnancy, as a result of chronic anxiety, maltreatment, or fear, the infant in the womb automatically shares in these stress hormones; they pass right through the placenta. That infant is locked into a free-floating anxiety, a kind of permanent body stress…locked into this tension, the infant in utero cannot develop intellectually or establish the bonding with the mother in preparation for birth. However, nature cannot program for this variable and wait for the damaging effects of chronic stress to be removed. Growth (at least physical growth) goes right ahead while intellectual growth struggles along as best it can in its crippled state, slipping further and further behind. If the infant does not spontaneously abort, it will be born deficient in intelligence, if not in body, highly prone to early infantile autism or childhood schizophrenia, or dysfunctional in a wide variety of ways.

Other effects of stress on mother and child

When you're stressed, your brain activates the sympathetic nervous system, signalling the adrenal glands to release a chemical cocktail, including epinephrine (adrenaline) and cortisol. Cortisol suppresses the immune system. A suppressed immune system makes you more susceptible to illnesses. An unwell mother will

affect the health of the baby during and after pregnancy. Persistently high levels of these chemicals may impair memory and learning, and increase your odds of depression. All of the above should be widely understood by now, and as such, it's reasonable to consider it common sense.

The following, which is a vital part of the childcare equation, was not dealt with in the Channel 4 documentary about "Bringing up Baby".

Common sense on women giving birth

> **How were children born before there were doctors?**
> **Whatever it was, it worked!**

A pregnant woman or one giving birth is not supposed to be 'a patient'. Pregnancy is not a sickness. Giving birth is supposed to be a healthy event. The earliest records we have of the existence of doctors date back over four thousand years. If we subtract this from the length of time archaeologists say we have been on this planet, perhaps we survived healthily without doctors for over 195,000 years.

In *Magical Child*, Joseph Chilton Pearce also stated that 'matrix' is the Latin word for womb. In describing the child in the womb, he said, "The mind-brain develops bonds (forms of communication and rapport) with both its present matrix and the new matrix into which the child must eventually shift as genetic maturation unfolds. While in utero, the infant prepares for their eventual separation from the womb by establishing bonds of communication with the mother. (These bonds are probably partly hormonal, as well as psychological and below ordinary consciousness.). This bonding process provides a bridge between matrices so that the unknown of the new matrix (outside the womb) will have sufficient points of similarity with the known of the old matrix. Then, the mind-brain can accommodate, learn about and adapt to the new. Nature would never (of her own choice) propel the child into a new matrix without sufficient preparation because s/he would be unable to adapt or survive in the new environment. And remember that nature programs entirely for success."

Common sense tells us that the correct way Nature has programmed women to give birth to babies is in a squatting position. They were not designed to give birth while lying on their backs. This is physically challenging and an impediment to the smooth birthing of a baby, and a major contributor to excessive birth pain. It is on a similar principle why we go to the toilet in a squatting position and would find it difficult to do it lying down. A baby is a lot larger to expel than answering the call of nature. Common sense compels us to ask: if humans are truly the superior life form on earth, why is childbirth so awkward, complicated and risky that it requires expert assistance, unlike other animals?

It has to be a delicate balance for the baby to move from the safe and secure place of the womb to an unknown environment. Common sense suggests that a stressful birth would traumatise the infant since it is super sensitive at this point. The baby is giving up a very intimate and comfortable place to be introduced to the earth matrix and would prefer to do it trauma-free, with no drugs. Coming into the earth matrix requires immediate continuity, not 'cold turkey' separation; it requires gradual weaning after undergoing its physical separation from its mother. The continuum method is based on this instinct (sense). This is why one mentee following the Benjamin Spock method said she physically felt sick when her baby was crying in the next room.

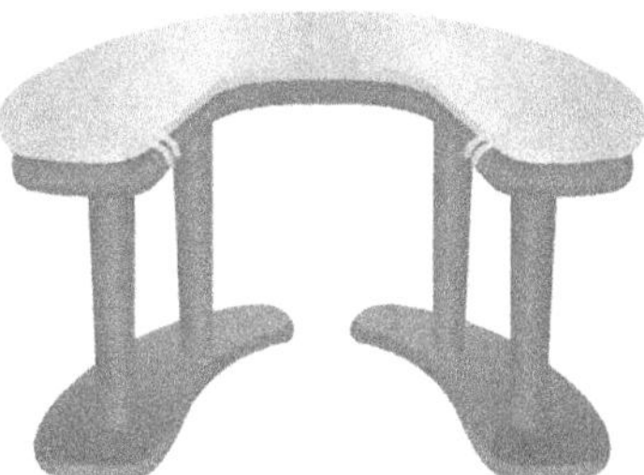

A Birthing stool - figure 1

The culture we have today was formed out of a mindset of survival against Nature, or man against Nature. This mindset has not evolved to one of working *with* Nature. And so we see in the case of childbirth, we go against the natural order of things. As a consequence of this mindset, we construct infrastructures and machines to assist the birthing process. Joseph Chilton Pearce suggested that we have made the assumption that we have a superior brain so that we might outwit Nature, and we believe we must outwit Nature to survive her. As a consequence, he suggested that the cooperative flow of energy with the life system is then quite lost to view. Within the currently organised childbirth system, some of the common characteristics are as follows:

• Most babies are born in hospitals and delivered by strangers wearing masks and gloves.

- Babies are often separated from their mothers after birth. Does common sense suggest that this would traumatise the baby, considering that it was physically attached to the mother for up to ten months, and experienced no other reality? Perhaps this might evoke unnamed feelings of being abandoned in the infant's emotional bank account? A study titled ***Early Contact Versus Separation: Effects on Mother-Infant Interaction One Year Later***, authored by K. Bystrova, Associate Professor in the Department of Hospital Paediatrics at the St. Petersburg Paediatric Academy, aimed to evaluate and compare the potential long-term effects of delivery and maternity ward practices, particularly those involving mother-infant closeness versus separation, on the quality of mother-infant interaction one year after birth.

- The conclusion was: ***Skin-to-skin contact, for 25 to 120 minutes after birth, early suckling, or both, positively influenced mother-infant interaction one year later when compared with routines involving separation of mother and infant.***

- Very bright *artificial* lights are prominent in delivery wards. Since the baby lived in a dark womb for all its existence up to this point, does common sense suggest that this might be problematic, and perhaps cause harm? Well, according to the American Academy of Ophthalmology, ***"At birth, babies are very sensitive to bright light, so their pupils remain constricted to limit the light coming into the eyes"***.

- The mother lies in the most common position known as the lithotomy position. She is on her back with her feet raised.

- If a mother experiences excessive, unbearable pain during labour, she is likely to be offered an epidural or a spinal. This is a local anaesthetic injected either into the space around the spinal cord or directly into the spinal fluid to provide pain relief.

- It works by numbing the nerves carrying pain messages from the lower part of the body to the brain.

- This injection of drugs might have the effect of slowing down labour and increasing the chance of needing assisted delivery, such as the use of forceps, or ventouse (vacuum suction cup) delivery.

Surgical forceps are a scissors-like tool used to clamp the baby's head and pull them out.

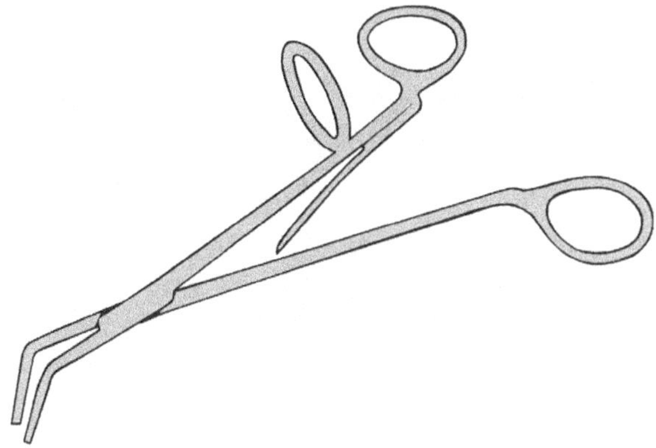

Surgical Forceps – Figure 2

Consequences of using forceps for delivery include bruises or cuts, and bleeding in the skull.

Consequences of vacuum extraction include minor scalp injuries and severe bleeding within the skull, as shown in figures 3 and 3.1 to follow. As illustrated in the photo, a ventouse delivery involves using a vacuum device with a suction cup to assist in guiding the baby's head out during birth.

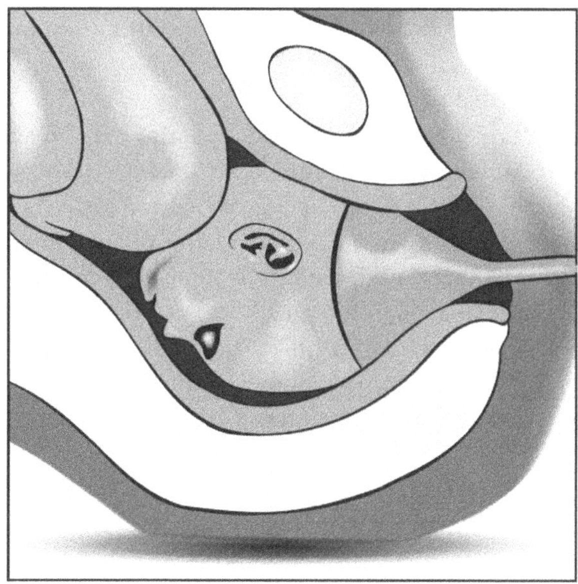

Vacuum extraction – figure 3

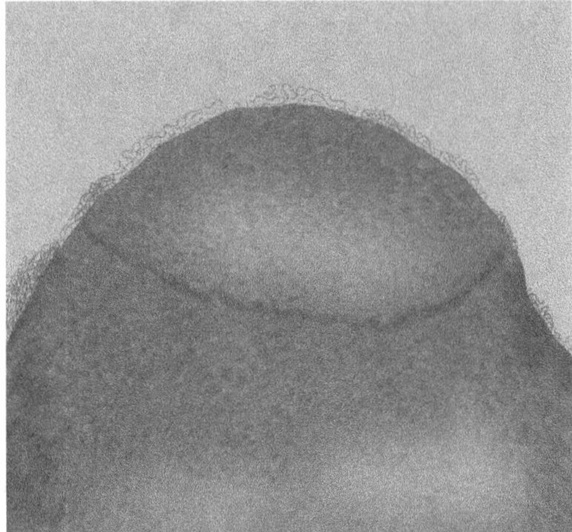

Figure 3.1

Should the consequences of vacuum extraction come as a surprise to anyone? Are we not aware that a newborn's skull is not fully formed, and that the centre remains soft and vulnerable? Even if that weren't the case, shouldn't it be obvious that such an artificial method of delivery would be traumatic for an unborn infant? This illustrates how one flawed principle can lead us to adopt an even worse one. We've become experts at performing procedures that ideally should never be necessary, yet we are praised for our innovation and so-called life-saving advancements.

Joseph Chilton Pearce, *in Magical Child*, explained it this way: The infant is exposed to an intelligence determined to outwit nature, an intelligence distrustful of anything natural, an intelligence with a vast array of tools at its disposal with which to outwit and, in fact, supplant nature entirely. And in that outwitting and supplanting, damage is done that is incalculable. Future historians will shudder in loathing and horror at the hospital treatment of newborns and mothers in this very dark age of the medicine man and the surgeon. What is the common phenomenon of this system as it relates to babies? **Joseph Chilton Pearce continues:**

> European and American researchers have long observed that infants do not smile until some two and a half months after birth (on average). Nor does the early infant display sensorimotor learning or general adaptations during this time. Because such a prolonged period of incapacity, with no signs of intelligence being manifested, is quite

unique in this world, many learned papers have been written about the smiling syndrome and post-birth lack of intellectual response in infants. Freud, in early neurological studies of infants, wrote about this strange vegetative condition, and theories have grown out of this theory in a typical academic style. Our body of knowledge finally included as a matter of fact that babies do not (indeed should not) smile during this ten to twelve week period after birth because intelligence is non-existent during this time.

He further wrote:

The question arose: Why is intelligence so slow in forming? No other species has anything comparable to this long delay in at least some form of intelligent adaptation. In answer, theories arose, of course, giving rise to other theories, concerning this period of stupor, total helplessness, semi-consciousness, massive sleeping, excessive crying, and a general precarious hold on life…naturally, an acceptable answer emerge: The human infant is born prematurely…and naturally, another question arose: Why is the human born prematurely? Again, an answer dutifully emerged, one in keeping with the whole fallacy. We are born prematurely because of our big brains. Notice that the head of the youngster at birth is much larger than the body. Problems arose when humankind got up on its hind legs and started walking upright because this posture closed in the pelvic area and narrowed the birth canal considerably. With this huge head, full of all those brains, if the infant were to grow to full term in utero, his head would be too large to pass through the now-narrowed canal, so the human infant must be born prematurely to get out at all.

He stated that this idea was postulated by Jerome Bruner, whom he described as a brilliant researcher at the **Harvard *Centre for Cognitive Studies***. Did you read the above in a state of incredulity? Did your common sense agree with Pearce that this is a fallacy? Well, let's look at the post-birth experiences of practising the common-sense method of squatting and no hospital delivery.

Pearce wrote:

In 1956, Marcelle Gerber, under a grant from the United Nations Children's Fund, travelled to Africa to study the effects of malnutrition on infant and child intelligence. She concentrated on Kenya and Uganda and made a momentous discovery. She found the most precocious, brilliant, and advanced infants and children ever observed anywhere. These infants had smiled continuously and rapturously from, at the latest, their fourth day of life. Blood analysis showed that all the adrenal steroids connected with birth stress were totally absent by the fourth day of life. Sensorimotor learning and general development were phenomenal, indeed miraculous. These Ugandan infants were months ahead of American or European children. A superior intellectual development is held for the first four years of life. Just in case you are thinking that race is relevant, consider the following, also written by Pearce in Magical Child:

New European-type hospitals were being erected in Uganda at the time of Gerber's studies. Only the upper-class Ugandan families could afford such luxury, and the women of this class naturally followed the fashion of having their children in hospitals. These hospital-delivered infants, it turned out, followed the same civilised schedule as American and European infants. Gerber found that they did not smile until some two and a half months after birth. Nor were they precocious in any sense. They showed no signs of sensorimotor learning, displayed no uncanny intelligence for some two and a half months, at which point some signs of intelligence were apparent. Blood analysis showed that high levels of adrenal steroids connected with birth stress were still prevalent at two and a half months. These infants slept massively, cried when awake, were irritable and colicky, frail and helpless. So the issue was not in some racial predisposition toward early intellectual growth. The issue lay solely with what happens to the newborn infant in hospitals. He also wrote the following story:

"Frederick LeBoyer was a conventional French obstetrician who delivered 9,000 babies by standard methods. He noticed that France, a nation of 50 million people, had over one million dysfunctional children. He began to question general birth practices and realised that hospital deliveries were damaging the infants. He quit his practice, retired to India for three years, where he carefully studied native procedures for child delivery in very remote, so-called primitive areas. He combined what he saw with his own scientific background and developed a synthesis. He returned to France and began a new form of delivering infants into the world. And the babies he delivered smiled, beautifully, continuously, rapturously, from some twelve hours after birth. I personally know of several infants, delivered in the home by their own parents, who have smiled continuously from the first hour of life. And why not? They have been met with love, care, concern, and above all, gentleness and quiet."

What are the other characteristics and benefits of these natural births, which are non-hospitalised and unassisted by drugs, machines, or other tools?

- The child was never separated from the mother, who massaged, caressed, sang to, and fondled her infant continually.

- The mother carried her non-swaddled infant in a sling, next to her bare breast, continually.

- She slept with her infant. The infant fed continuously according to its schedule.

- They virtually never cried.

- Their mother was bonded to them and sensed their every need before it had to be expressed by crying.

- The mother responded to the infant's every gesture by assisting the child in any and every move that was undertaken, so that every move initiated by the child ended in immediate success.

- At two days of age (forty-eight hours), these infants sat bolt upright, held only by their forearms, with a beautifully straight back and perfect head balance. Their finely focused eyes stared sentiently and intelligently at their mother's eyes. And they smiled and smiled.

Does common sense suggest that the infant would benefit from this continuation of staying connected and bonded to its mother, in the immediate moments after birth? Would it not be beneficial even if the birthing stress was natural, and even more so if the stress was traumatic? When adults are traumatised, we benefit from counselling and support, and it is not usually easy to fix. Would comfort from its mother, the source of its ten months of bonding, be paramount to a traumatised newborn infant? This familiar, reliable, and trusted source of comfort is the only ideal source of comfort to at least reduce the trauma experienced during moving from its comfortable matrix of the womb to the outside matrix that has unknown elements. If the trauma an adult suffered can last a lifetime, even though they have words to name and rationalise what happened, could the trauma suffered by a newborn infant, whose only sense and language are emotions, also last a lifetime? Perhaps the following points raised by Daniel Goleman, in his book *Emotional Intelligence*, are relevant to the question:

"The interactions of life's earliest years lay down a set of emotional lessons based on the attunement and upsets in the contacts between infant and caretakers. These emotional lessons are so potent and yet so difficult to understand from the vantage point of adult life because, believes LeDoux, they are stored in the amygdala as rough, wordless blueprints for emotional life. Since these earliest emotional memories are established at a time before infants have words for their experience, when these emotional memories are triggered in later life, there is no matching set of articulated thoughts about the response that takes us over. One reason we can be baffled by our emotional outbursts, then, is that they often date from a time early in our lives when things were bewildering and we did not yet have words for comprehending events. We may have the chaotic feelings, but not the memories that formed them."

Does your perception accept that, at a minimum, this is very likely to be true? Here is another vital childbirth practice—one that is critical, yet unfortunately, was not adopted sooner. How many lives have been affected because of this delay? We will probably never know. According to tommy.org:

Delayed cord clamping (DCC)
"Cutting the cord immediately after the birth has been routine practice for 50-60 years, but more recently, research is showing that it is not good for the baby, as it means the baby misses out on a large amount of blood (214g). This has led to recent changes in guidelines and practices regarding delayed cord clamping. Waiting until the cord has stopped pulsating and becomes white is becoming increasingly normal practice in births where there is no medical reason to speed things up."

Babies who have immediate cord clamping (particularly boys) have also been shown to be more likely to:

- be anaemic at four months of age
- have decreased fine motor skills (coordinating small muscles, such as hands and fingers) at the age of four years
- have decreased social skills at the age of four years

When DCC may not be practised:

- If the mother is bleeding heavily
- There is an issue with the placenta, such as placental abruption, placenta praevia, vasa praevia or the cord is bleeding, so the blood is not getting to the baby.

According to americanpregnancy.org:

- More mothers than ever before are inquiring about delayed cord clamping. [Good news]
- The iron in the blood increases the newborn's iron storage, which is vital for healthy brain development.

Hopefully, the above will now become routine and common practice. For the general public, this should become common knowledge/common sense. They should enquire if those delivering the baby are versed in the science of delayed cord clamping (DCC.)

A child's life is like a piece of paper on which every person leaves a mark. – Chinese Proverb

---

Without structure, discipline, and love, children will often not become well-adjusted, successful and happy adults.

Basic common sense for raising a child

It is obvious that the fact that we were all once children does not qualify us to be good parents. Why is this? Each year of our childhood had its compartment of emotions, and the full scope of what these emotions were is not available to us as adults. This is why we find it necessary to study child psychology. The comedian Bill Cosby stated the following truth, as a joke, "You would've thought that since we were all once children, we would know how to raise children, but it doesn't really work this way." He is right; it does not work like this. Being good parents does not depend on relying on remembering all the emotions children express at various stages of their development, because we can't. It's not about remembering that they need affection. We instinctively comfort those we love. Therefore, we will give them affection unless we are dysfunctional. It's not about remembering the way we thought as children; it's about having the sense to understand that children are like a blank slate that has to be written on for it to be of any value, or like a computer that requires effective software for it to function. The basic software for a child is love, discipline, structure, knowledge, and rules. Some of the other basic things they have to be taught are:

- Acceptable and unacceptable behaviour.

- Encouragement to tell the truth. Claire Huxtable tells Rudy in *The Cosby Show*, "…No matter what it is, you can always tell me the truth… because I will still love you." If you don't teach them to tell the truth, they can grow up to be lying adults.

- Etiquette.

- Toilet training.

- How to relate to adults in terms of respect.

- How to relate to adults in terms of being safe.

- How to relate to family members in terms of respect and being safe.

- How to eat and live healthily. You are in charge of your child's health, so you must learn how to teach them these skills. The dietary habits you instil in the child will become the basis for their future healthy or unhealthy practices.

- Mental and emotional discipline. A child's cognitive and emotional growth requires thoughtful guidance and support. This foundational shaping influences their future potential, attitudes, and lifelong behaviour.

It should be common knowledge that we must deliberately teach our children all of this, and more. It is unwise to leave it to chance that they will stumble upon the information and the disciplines they will need for practical living. Our current complicated world has increased the demand on our rational, logical minds. The dangers threatening our survival and happiness have increased tenfold. Yet, unlike in early human history, when threats were likely universally recognised, there is now far less consensus about what those dangers are. There was a time when instinct alone guided us through life's challenges, but those days are behind us. To survive and be effective in our diverse, complicated, and competitive world requires us to employ the full scope of our ability to think.

How to survive and be healthy is now a significant issue. So, at some point, after we are born, we have the responsibility of learning how to survive. We have to learn how to acquire knowledge about health and nutrition and apply syllogistic reasoning to this knowledge. It doesn't get more important than this.

CHAPTER FOUR

The second major life issue to which Aristotelian syllogistic reasoning can be applied: **Common sense lessons for health and nutrition**

The healthiest life is one that's lived thoughtfully, with the goal of making your body and mind feel as nourished and as alive as they possibly can. – Oprah Winfrey

---

An addiction to unhealthy foods can be more problematic than an addiction to drugs. This is because, according to the US Surgeon General, two out of three people die because of what they eat. Additionally, there is little stigma surrounding unhealthy foods, and many people remain unclear about what constitutes an unhealthy diet. Given this, and considering that food is a profoundly emotional subject, it becomes a matter of survival for the logical mind to step in and take control. Life and health should be the top priorities when applying common sense. This is because, if we leave life prematurely, the other applications are of limited value to us. Surely, the application of common sense regarding health and nutrition has to be regarded as a basic fundamental use of it.

The most significant omission of common sense is not recognising that, as human beings, we have a responsibility to study nutrition to understand how to maintain the health of both mind and body. This is no different from understanding that apart from putting petrol/gas into our cars, they also need servicing and care. In the natural world, animals are never overweight; they do not have cancer, heart disease, diabetes, multiple sclerosis, and many of our life-ending and life-impairing diseases. There are two ways we can interpret this. It is either that they are better designed than we are, or they benefit from not having an option to adopt a diet that is contrary to their body's needs. There is a third way to interpret this: the human body does not require a specific 'food science', and we suffer from multiple diseases because of a random 'throw of the dice' that infects us with other 'things'.

Man surprised me most about humanity. Because he sacrifices his health in order to make money. Then he sacrifices money to recuperate his health. And then he is so anxious about the future that he does not enjoy the present; the result being that he does not live in the present or the future; he lives as if he is never going to die, and then dies having never really lived. – Dalai Lama

---

Syllogistic reasoning

- The science that governs a car's function and health determines how it should be treated and maintained, not the opinion of the driver. If that science is ignored, the vehicle will break down—or even blow up.

- Likewise, the science that governs the function and health of the human body determines how it should be treated and cared for, not the opinion of its occupant.

- Therefore, if the science of the body is not complied with, it will break down or die as a consequence.

- All living things are hardwired with a drive to survive.

- Animals have a program that they are hardwired to follow, called 'instinct'. This includes a program of what to eat to survive to the fullest extent.

- Human beings are also hardwired with a drive to survive. This does not include a program of what to eat to survive to the fullest extent.

- Therefore, human beings are required to figure out what diet will enable us to survive to our maximum capability.

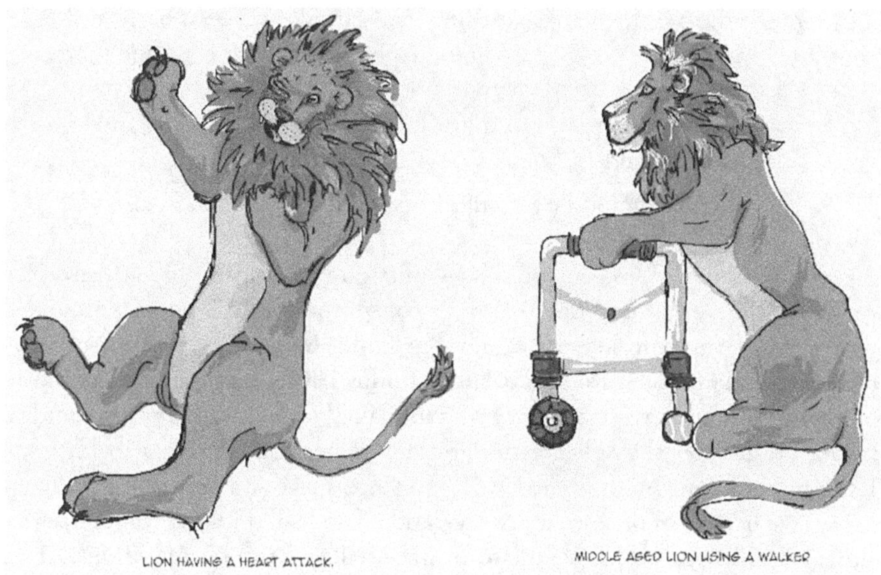

The above scenario does not occur in the natural world for lions or other animals. You will never see a lion using a walker unless it had an accident.

Daniel Goleman stated, "The most ancient root of our emotional life is the sense of smell, or, more precisely, in the olfactory lobe, the cells that take in and analyse smell. One layer of cells took in what was smelled and sorted it out into relevant categories: edible or toxic…"

We currently lack a well-developed sense of smell that could help us identify what is truly edible. For years, I noticed some attractive berries growing near my workplace, but I never ate them, simply because I couldn't be sure they were safe.

I finally ate them after I saw someone doing so, and he assured me that they were fine. Another example is this: on the 29th September 2015, Kate Connolly of The Guardian newspaper reported that record numbers of people during the European migrant crisis became ill, with one fatality, after foraging and eating poisonous mushrooms in Germany. They mistook those they found as being the same as edible varieties found in their homelands. It's tough being human. We are left to figure everything out, often through trial and error.

Over time, through long and convoluted processes, our dietary and lifestyle habits have evolved, often without clear intention or understanding. As society grew more complex, so did our habits. Many of the nutritional norms we follow today were created arbitrarily, shaped more by taste preferences than by nutritional compatibility.

Some of the most delicious-smelling foods are also the least healthy. It takes emotional intelligence not to be dominated by smell when choosing foods.

- To eat is a necessity, but to eat intelligently is an art. – François de la Rochefoucauld
- Nutrition should be a compulsory subject in schools at all levels.

A common-sense approach would have nutritional compatibility at the centre of all decisions regarding food or drink consumption. This point is validated by what the Surgeon General said about 'food' being the cause of so many deaths. Our emotional mind has latched onto habits that are detrimental to our survival, and these habits are invariably highly addictive, therefore hard to break. We are now the only creatures on this planet that eat primarily for taste, rather than for nutrition or survival. And since survival is one of our primary drives, we need a lot of common sense(rational, logical thinking) to reverse this situation. We have to learn how to bring intelligence to our emotions, or, as Jim Rohn puts it, "our emotions need to be educated as much as our intellect."

If you had a horse that is worth a million dollars, would you let it stay up half the night, drink coffee and booze, smoke cigarettes and eat junk food? How about a ten-dollar dog? Would you treat him that way? Five-dollar cat? What about a billion-dollar body? – Zig Ziglar

---

The mind never ages; an ageless mind within a body that is in good condition is worth the discipline.

There are two essential aspects of life and living that we need to understand—knowledge that should become common sense and guide the way we live.. These aspects of life start with two questions: what is the correct human lifespan, or how long are we capable of living? And what physical and mental conditions should we be in during most of our lifespan? The answer to the first question is one hundred years or more, and the knowledge of how to achieve this should become common sense.

The answer to the second question is "Good condition", and the knowledge of how to accomplish this should also become common sense. Here is a quote from *Demystifying Cancer*: "The body has an internal 'clock' that genetically determines how long we can live." It is not astonishing that we can live comfortably and healthily to age one hundred and beyond. Most animals can't live this long because their 'clock' will not permit it.

A mayfly will live for only one day! Nowadays, however, despite clear indicators that we can live comfortably beyond one hundred years, it is pretty standard for the majority of us not to get near this age. The strange thing is, this does not alarm us. Yet, if we observed the same thing happening in the rest of the animal kingdom, there would be an international panic. There is no panic when this happens in our world because of a word that has become our great enemy in the crusade for health: normal. Poor physical health, regardless of a person's age, is often viewed as a 'natural' or 'inevitable' aspect of life. Yet in the natural world, animals tend to show greater consistency in both their physical condition and lifespan. This is because they eat what they are designed to eat. In other words, what they eat is in harmony with the science of their body.

The desire for good health is universal, so the knowledge of how to achieve it should be as well. If this knowledge does not become common sense, then experiences like that of Annette Larkins will remain rare exceptions rather than the norm.

Here is a person who is a living demonstration of perhaps the most potent dietary practice there is. This is the incredible story of Annette Larkins, who is aptly described as an ageless beauty.

Annette Larkins

There is an ancient maxim that will be repeated twice in chapter five: "Let your food be your medicine and your medicine be your food." Annette Larkins is living proof that when we allow food to be our medicine, it can not only be healing but also serve as a fountain of youth and longevity. It was her age, youthful appearance, and unique lifestyle that prompted WPTV News to send reporter Tania Rogers to interview her at seventy. It was revealed that she switched to a raw vegan diet to improve her health and increase her energy, but she experienced even greater benefits than anticipated.

She described the food in her garden as her fountain of youth. Her husband, who is only nine years her senior, said: "People would ask what I was doing with a young girl, or '…you brought your granddaughter with you.'" Just in case you're thinking that this is a case of her having 'good genes', these were his comments:

"If I had to depend on my genes, I would be dead. My mother died at age forty-seven of breast cancer. Her mother died at age thirty-six of breast cancer, and she had sisters who also died of breast cancer. Diabetes is common in my family." She declared that she has lots of energy and is very vibrant, and

her faculties are as sharp, or sharper, than when she was young. And as a rule, she wakes up no later than 5.30 am. Her husband takes daily medications for high blood pressure, diabetes, and other conditions, but she doesn't even take aspirin. At the end of an interview, she said, "I do not just want to survive; everybody is doing that, I want to thrive." It should become common sense that we are supposed to thrive, not just survive. It is a common declaration among people that they are "surviving".

Our free will, the ability to do whatever we choose, is a significant reason why we struggle with consistency in maintaining good health and longevity. Given the information above and the example of Annette Larkins, does it not suggest that we have significantly drifted off course? One example is not adequate as a research sample. However, you can research and find others, and apply syllogistic reasoning to the principles of the facts and information being presented here. The absence of a widespread common sense (proper knowledge) regarding our correct diet has had the knock-on effect of distorting our perception of what old age is. For most of us, a 70-year-old is an older person. In reality, based on our 'internal life clock, ' this should represent middle age. If our genetic capability is about 120 years, we have a distorted view and expectation of how a 70-year-old person should look and their ***physical condition***. Many have suggested that she could pass for a person in her late thirties to early forties.

It is difficult for most of us to pursue the knowledge/sense of good health and adopt the dietary practice that would enable us to live the way Nature intended. This is because food is a very emotional thing. And most of us have emotions towards food that are akin to an unguided missile. To reap the benefits of Annette Larkins, would you forgo your usual pleasures and learn new pleasures? Did you know you can recalibrate your mind and emotions to make this possible? Would it be worth experiencing an additional twenty or more years of not just being alive but being vibrantly alive? Would this be worth a disciplined effort? Are you aware of any definitive instructional manual on what to eat, or not eat, that came with us at the outset of life? Free will is part of what makes us human, and our logical brain should produce the common sense that can be the 'tool' that is supposed to guide us to good health, longevity, and happiness. Common sense is meant to be our guidance system, just as instinct is for animals. Yet our poor outcomes in many areas of life suggest that we often fail to use free will to our most significant advantage.

Since our bodies function according to scientific principles, shouldn't our understanding of how to keep them healthy also be scientific, rather than driven by our acquired tastes? Should this become common sense? Since our bodies are based on scientific principles, should it be compulsory for all of us to learn human biology, health and nutrition? Does this make sense? What if we include the fact that the Surgeon General has declared that two out of three people die in America because of what they ate? Is this a case of, 'case closed?' The basic knowledge of how our body works and the science of nutrition should become common sense. Nature produces dozens of foods that are compatible with the science of the human body, but our factories produce thousands of so-called 'foods'. It's great for the economy but terrible for our health.

Inefficient design?

As you've already read, our free will puts us at a disadvantage compared to other creatures. If we had a built-in instinct (knowledge) of the correct food to eat and were **compelled** to follow this diet, we would enjoy a similar health experience as wild animals. Wild animals do not experience innumerable diseases and widespread premature death caused by illnesses. They generally live to the age of their genetic capability. This is not the case with us. Many of us resist being compared to animals, and this attitude stems from a lack of appreciation and understanding of just how deeply connected we are to Nature. For many of us, our relationship with Nature is merely a cursory acknowledgement that we are connected to the plants and trees. The question we need to ask is this: Do our widespread diseases and premature deaths mean that humans are biologically less efficient than wild animals? Or are these problems the result of choices we make through the exercise of free will?"

Wisdom = common sense. Common sense = knowledge that most, or all of us, should have.

I once told someone that I juice fruits and vegetables every day, and he expressed doubt about him doing it because of the time it takes. In reality, it doesn't take much time, but this is irrelevant because of a simple truth: I have nothing better to do. Your body is the only place you live, currently, and everywhere you go, you have to take it with you. A good analogy for this is that you have a choice of either showing up in a battered Sedan or a well-tuned Ferrari. Is it wise that you should take the best care of the only place that you have to live in? Should this be common sense, or should we take better care of our dogs and cars than ourselves? So, repeat this as a common-sense mantra, "I have nothing better to do than take the time to look after my number one asset, my health." *If you recognise the need to change your diet for better health, then it is best to do so because you're inspired, instead of waiting until you're desperate.* When should you be concerned about your health and take care of yourself? Should it be when you're sick, or when you're healthy?

When do you suppose most people become concerned? Common sense says it's easier to maintain good health than to repair the body when it's sick. Which option *should be* common sense and common practice? What about your car? Do you service it after it breaks down, or before it breaks down? Which option is common sense? Should it be common sense of how to achieve good health and longevity, or should it be down to the consequence of the law of averages, where occasionally a few of us achieve this despite a lack of understanding?

What should be common sense as to the correct human diet?

If I had a say in how the human body is designed, I would make it compatible with spicy, salty, fried foods (foods I love but don't eat), and most foods – in effect, no scientific or nutritional principles would apply. However, our body comes with its unique science, and like any other science, its rules have to be obeyed or we pay the consequences. When the time comes to pay, most of us are usually unwilling to pay.

What if the Surgeon General is correct about the role diet plays in premature death? Is determining what we should consume a worthy subject to spend extensive time on? Should there be a common sense about food – what to eat and what not to eat? Should it be the case that, 'If there is no immediate negative reaction after eating something, it can be eaten?' Should we have a better understanding than this? Do you ever plant a seed and get an immediate tree? Even when we play the lottery, don't we have to wait for a little while before getting a result?

The thought, whether conscious or unconscious, that says, "I have hardly eaten any fruits or vegetables for the past many years, but I feel fine," is based on an inadequate understanding of life and health. Because of the above thought, the passing of time is taken for granted. The lack of knowledge about health and nutrition has a direct impact on your feelings/attitude towards food. While you may have been born with sufficient good health to resist illness, it should be common sense that health disasters are often the result of the cumulative effect of neglect. We are incapable of knowing when we will have health problems. Many have died from a heart attack without warning. Therefore, the best option is to find out what eating habits are necessary for good health and adopt them. Your knowledge and feelings should come together in such a way that you govern your life in your self-interest, for survival, health, and happiness. Many know the right thing, but cannot break the grip of their addiction to unhealthy eating and lifestyle habits. The unique combination of knowledge and feelings that we can acquire to guide us to our self-interest is the ultimate ingredient for the syllogistic formula that produces the common sense/wisdom necessary for practical living. This is because good health is our number one currency, for it affects every aspect of our lives.

When it comes to eating, humans are, without question, the dumbest animals on the planet. – *Mike Anderson, The RAVE Diet Documentary*.

Here is a statement that may surprise you. **On the question of what the correct human diet is, there is almost universal agreement. The problem is, this agreement is mostly unconscious. Nearly everyone seems to agree that fruits and vegetables are essential.** There is even a saying, "An apple a day keeps the doctor away." If common sense is applied to this saying, it would be clear that it doesn't mean we should eat only one apple.

For the most part, we apply common sense and avoid cooking our fruits, except in cases like apple pie and other traditional recipes that sacrifice the fruits' benefits for the sake of variety and custom. The proverbial "apple a day" is not practised by vast numbers of people, and the eating of vegetables is regarded by many as merely 'dressing' to the main course. So, even though many of us have the common sense that we should eat raw vegetables, as we eat raw fruits, this activity is often a mere dash of 'mixed salad'. Worse, most of us cook our vegetables and seldom eat any that are still alive. Because food is deeply tied to our emotions, simply knowing that we need to eat fruits and

vegetables for good health and longevity isn't enough to make it a common practice. The actual practice would require a shift in, or the development of, our emotional intelligence.

How do we rationalise what meat is edible? Some people eat or don't eat dog, snake, snail, rat, cow, goat, grasshopper, lion, flies, alligator, crocodile, and almost anything that moves. Is this rationale based on the science of the human body, or is it based on custom/culture?

There is no universal agreement on what our correct diet should be because of the often vexed question of whether we should eat meat.

Food with a dash of salad

Food with a dash of wisdom

The popularly accepted definition of our dietary type is that we are omnivores. An omnivore is defined as an animal that can naturally feed on both animal and vegetable substances. Why do most people accept that we are omnivores? This is accepted because we are social beings, and this is the current dietary practice of most human beings. In effect, this is the only reality most of us are aware of. As a result, vegetarianism is often dismissed as a fad, an oddity, or extremism, and those who adopt it are sometimes labelled, ironically, as 'health freaks.' The fact that people would regard a person as a health freak because they appear to be overly concerned about their health tells its own story. It reveals a situation where people are so programmed to eat for entertainment, taste, or pleasure that the idea that we are to eat primarily to sustain our lives in a state of good health is now an oddity at best, or freakish at worst. This is because we are disconnected from the science that governs our lives. Our very unique nature as human beings has resulted in a situation that makes it extremely difficult, perhaps impossible, for our diet to be guided by a universal common sense. Here are some ideas to consider:

- Humans appear to be the only species on Earth that prioritise taste over health when it comes to eating. This is a reality because we have the power of choice.

- All other life-forms are programmed to eat for survival.

- Contrary to the claim that we are herbivores, dietary science suggests that we are mainly frugivores. What's the evidence to support this? Fruits contain more potent and essential minerals than vegetables, require no cooking to consume, and, unlike some vegetables, do not contain digestion inhibitors. These traits suggest that humans are naturally more frugivorous than herbivorous.

- The fact that we eat both meat and vegetables is no more proof that we are meant to be omnivores than the fact that we smoke proves that we are *supposed to* ingest smoke. Those who take the view that we have evolved to eat meat should realise that being able to eat meat does not demonstrate that we are suited to do so. The fact that the lungs can adapt to accept a regular diet of smoke, even though it contains no benefits, and is harmful, indicates that the body is very adaptable.

- Eating meat, drinking alcohol, or smoking merely demonstrates that we can force our bodies to accept any substance that does not have a level of toxicity that would cause immediate death. The body will accept poisons in small doses over time. It will also accept unhealthy 'foods' for varying periods.

The food for all living things, including ourselves, was pre-made by Nature. We did not have to wait until we learnt how to cook to survive. Animals are not premade food since we can't eat them raw. To eat them, we had to learn how to catch and cook them, and we couldn't at the onset of our life on earth.

The science that suggests we should only eat plant foods is varied. However, here are the primary ones. Many of them have been listed because of the importance of the subject, and because extremely emotional subjects are always strongly resisted:

- We are not unique to the point where we are not similar or connected to other lifeforms.

- We are designed like other frugivorous and vegetarian animals. We have very long intestines.

- Omnivorous animals have much shorter intestines.

- We can look at the chimpanzee, for example; it is classified as an omnivore, as it eats both plant and animal materials. If you compare it with an orangutan (also a member of the ape family) which primarily eats fruits (but only eats lower quality foods, such as bark, leaves, and termites in times of scarcity) you will see that its intestines are more than twice the length of the chimpanzee's, even though it is a smaller animal.

- Carnivores have greatly enlarged stomachs, which encompass between 60 and 70 per cent of their entire digestive tracts. Frugivores and herbivores have smaller stomachs because they process smaller, more frequent amounts of food.

- The kidneys of carnivores and omnivores create extremely concentrated urine, again differing from the kidneys of frugivores and herbivores, which produce weakly concentrated urine.

- We chew our food just like fruitarians and vegetarian animals, in a sort of circular motion, repeatedly, and roll it into a 'ball' before we swallow it. This is the first part of our digestive process.

- Natural meat-eaters do not chew their food. They 'cut and swallow'. They chomp up and down, with a minimal sideways motion. Some of us appear to try to imitate these animals, and what did our parents tell us? Take your time and chew your food!

- Frugivores, herbivores, and omnivores have enzymes in their saliva to aid in the breakdown of *plant matter.* However, omnivores do not practice repetitive chewing, as do frugivores and herbivores. In the case of carnivorous animals, they do not have such enzymes.

- Our digestion starts in our mouth with our saliva. Saliva contains a digestive enzyme that is alkaline and used for the digestion of carbohydrates and natural sugars. These sugars are derived from plant materials.

- The fact that humans chew their food repetitively, even when eating meat, proves that we are not natural meat-eaters. This is because repetitive chewing stimulates the release of the enzyme ptyalin (salivary amylase), which is designed to break down carbohydrates and natural sugars, not meat proteins.

- Repetitive chewing and having a carbohydrate-digesting enzyme within their saliva *indicate that carbohydrate digestio*n is intended to start in the mouth, demonstrating that the animal is a herbivore.

- Any animal that does not practice repetitive chewing is designed to eat meat alone because the stomach is where enzymes exist to digest meat. An enzyme that breaks down protein would damage the inside of the animal's mouth because it is very acidic. This is why carnivores don't chew but swallow their food (meat) in whole chunks with only simple crushing.

- Natural meat-eaters (carnivores and omnivores) are well adapted to eat raw meat. They are also capable of digesting the hair from the animal. We cannot eat raw meat extensively without developing illnesses. We are also not capable of digesting hair.

- A carnivore's teeth are long, sharp, and pointed. Some omnivores have teeth similar to those of carnivores. Humans, like other herbivores, have teeth that are not sharp, but flat-edged.

- These are useful tools for biting, crushing and grinding grains and nuts. Do not misinterpret the significance of the fact that humans have canines. They are very inadequate for tearing raw meat; therefore, they are not comparable to those of certain omnivorous or carnivorous animals.

- A carnivore's stomach secretes powerful digestive enzymes that have about ten times more hydrochloric acid than that of a human or another herbivore. This powerful acid enables it to destroy things such as E. coli bacteria, Salmonella, trichina worms (parasites), or

other pathogens found in meat. These things will not survive in the stomach of a lion or tiger, etc.

- That we are not designed to be carnivorous is evident by the fact that many carnivores can secrete digestive acids powerful enough to dissolve and digest bone. We are incapable of this feat. The pH balance in the stomach of a carnivore can be one or less than 1 (very acidic) with food in the stomach. The acidity of our stomach, with food in it, can only range from 4 to 5.

- The evidence is overwhelming that meat and dairy products are the primary dietary sources of LDL cholesterol, commonly known as "bad" cholesterol. Elevated LDL levels are a significant contributing factor to heart disease, which remains the leading cause of death worldwide. Given that consuming animal products significantly raises LDL cholesterol. This is a key driver in plaque build-up, and it features heavily in heart disease and strokes. This proves that we are not natural meat-eaters.

- Cholesterol does not cause illness in true carnivores or omnivores, even though they consume raw meat, and carnivores consume large amounts. For instance, animals like lions and tigers, natural meat-eaters, do not develop heart disease as humans do. This highlights a key physiological difference: humans are not biologically suited to eat meat.

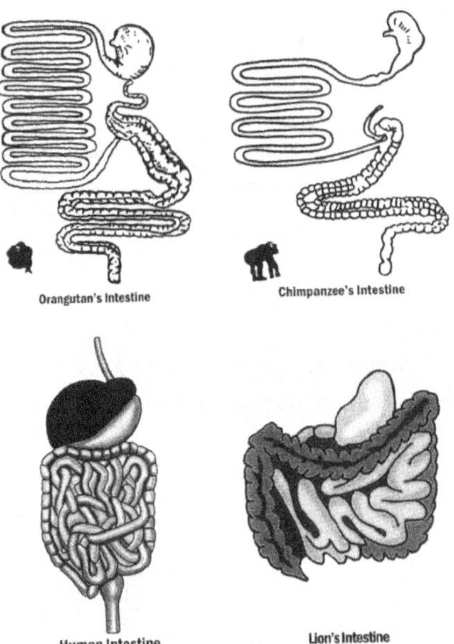

- As can be seen by the diagrams, our intestines are comparatively longer than an animal that periodically eats meat, such as the chimpanzee. It is also twice as long as that of a carnivore, such as a lion. These animals' intestines are 3 to 6 times the length of their trunk. A frugivore and herbivore's small intestine is 10 to 12 times the length of its torso and winds extensively in various directions. This structure allows food to remain in the intestine long enough to absorb essential nutrients and minerals before passing into the large intestine."

- Our intestines are more in line with the orangutan, whose primary diet is fruit. The benefit for the meat-eating animal of having a short intestine is that it allows waste to be expelled quickly. This is important because meat, by its nature, contains toxins, such as adrenaline, which the animal releases upon being killed. Our intestines are long, which means they do not facilitate the rapid elimination of meat. As a result, meat can remain in the digestive tract for extended periods, sometimes up to 72 hours. By this time, the body starts to absorb the gases and toxins produced by the meat. Also, the relatively short intestine of a carnivore or omnivore enables it to easily eliminate fatty wastes that are high in cholesterol before they start to putrefy.

If you are on a dietary path that is averse to good health, and you desire to change, it makes sense to change gradually, not suddenly. The exception to this rule is if you are in a state of urgent desperation. Food is addictive, and like any addiction, going 'cold turkey'[3] is difficult to sustain.

The human body maintains good health with a slightly alkaline pH balance. The vast majority of fruits and vegetables are alkaline-forming foods. The same cannot be said for virtually all animal-based foods. They are all acid-forming foods and carry the unhealthy baggage of cholesterol. Within these realities lies the truth as to what the correct human diet is supposed to be: herbal, fruit, nuts, vegetables, and plant-based foods.

---

[3] 'Cold turkey': the sudden withdrawal from addictive drugs and substances, and/or the unpleasant feelings experience from this withdrawal.

Here is some additional information that ought to be common sense. If you still think you have to eat animals, the least part of an animal you should want to eat is its liver. Why? The liver is the most toxic part of the animal. However, like most things in life, there are different points of view, and this is where the power of reasoning is useful. In your research, you may have read or heard that animals' livers are rich in iron, copper and pre-formed vitamin A (vitamin A obtained from animal and animal products), and this is true. But in light of the arguments already presented about meat and dairy products, it's up to you to decide the relevance of this information, especially if you are aware that there are many non-animal sources of these nutrients. You may have also come across information that seems to dispel the idea that the liver is toxic, such as, 'One of the functions of the liver is that it renders toxins inert and shuttles them out to be expelled'. This is also true, but since the liver is constantly doing this, what if the animal was killed when it had a special load of toxins it had not yet 'rendered inert'?

If it wasn't bad enough that we shouldn't eat meat, those who do eat it also have the following information to insert into the syllogistic reasoning formula that produces common sense. In 1960, a US Food and Drug Administration (FDA) employee named Charles Durbin told a gathering of poultry producers, "Chemicals and drugs have revolutionised agriculture in the past 15 years. In animal husbandry, growth-promoting chemicals permit the production of more meat with less feed; drugs…eliminate or control serious diseases.… Pesticides help the farmer control insects that would otherwise seriously affect his livestock... Over 50% of the drugs used by veterinarians and feed mills were unavailable to them in the early 1940s. Truly, agriculture has entered the chemical age."— Modern Meat: Synthetic Hormones, Livestock, and Consumers in the Post-WWII Era - Nancy Langston, UW-Madison.

Appearance versus the reality of health

"I know someone who exercised, ate healthily, but still got sick and died!"

Simple logic says this is supposed to be a scientific conversation. How do they know they were eating healthily if they had not studied nutrition and health? There have been times when this has been said by someone who is not in tune with the simple concept of cause and effect. They have also been deceived by their misunderstanding of how the body works. Some would make the general, fatalistic, non-scientific statement that "if it's your time, it's your time!" This erroneous philosophy has led many to treat this subject with indifference and remain very casual with their eating habits. Out of this come many opinionated concepts of a 'balanced diet' – meaning a little bit of everything. There is also a very subjective concept of eating everything in moderation. It is never clear how moderation is measured. The question is whether moderation is a relevant issue. Is it okay to eat a moderate amount of poison every day? How about a 'moderate' amount of junk food? What about the cumulative effect? Do you know what the body needs to maintain good health? Should this knowledge be common sense? You have to make up your mind as to how the health reality works. Is it based on science, or is it random and temperamental? It cannot be both. Here is the first scientific health lesson that ought to be common sense:

- Barring being given a strong dose of poison or extreme shock, the body cannot move from a state of **perfect health** to a state of ill health and death in an instant. It usually takes years of abuse.

- Any pronouncement about a healthy diet has to be based on natural or body science.

- The more acidic the blood is, the less oxygen it contains, and the faster a person ages and degenerates. On a practical level, this means we should do everything to keep the pH on the high side of the range, as close as possible to 7.45, by eating as many alkaline foods as possible. That would be, you guessed it – live, raw foods, especially green foods. – Dr Tim O'Shea

Common sense in matters of health is meant to place us on equal footing with other life forms, allowing for as smooth a journey as possible from birth to death, one where we are capable of caring for both mind and body in alignment with Nature's design. However, achieving this level of competence requires recognising that being human and having free will present us with complex choices. Cultural perspectives often shape how people select and prepare food, and because cultures vary widely, they promote different philosophies about what and how we should eat.

When animals heard I stopped eating meat, they all celebrated and declared, one less to worry about!

Common sense for food combining.

Protein and carbohydrates should not be consumed in the same meal. For example, combining meat (protein) with potatoes, rice, or bread (carbohydrates)

should be avoided. This also applies to other combinations, such as cheese (protein) with bread (carbohydrate). The question of why is related to the body's science, and the body's science is in charge of anything that it is called on to digest. It is not our opinion that should decide this. Here is the body's science as it relates to this matter:

- Carbohydrate digestion starts in the mouth when the digestive enzyme, amylase, which is in the saliva, begins to interact with the food you chew. Saliva is alkaline.

- Protein, on the other hand, is not digested at all in the mouth. It needs the acidic environment of the stomach, where a protein-digesting enzyme, pepsin, is activated.

- Here we have two substances that require opposing chemical environments for digestion, one alkaline, the other acidic; foods that are incompatible within the digestive system.

- Having properly chewed your food, the saliva that is mixed with the potato or rice (carbohydrates) requires time to break them down. The Meat and potatoes enter the stomach along with alkaline saliva, which begins the digestion of the potatoes. However, once the protein-digesting enzyme pepsin is activated to digest the meat, the alkaline enzyme cannot continue its task in an environment that has become acidic.

- Acidic and alkaline enzymes tend to neutralise each other, forcing the stomach to produce additional enzymes to aid digestion, an inefficient process that drains the body's energy.

- This is why such combinations induce drowsiness. If you've been eating this way, did you not find it strange that you felt tired after eating?

- The truth is demonstrable, so it is easy to put this to the test. Eat meat with vegetables, and carbohydrates with vegetables. If this doesn't produce your accustomed energy-sapping effect, this new experience should become common sense. What if you are told that a lifetime of this energy-sapping way of eating is not only unhealthy but also speeds up your ageing process? Does this make sense to you? What if you apply the basic understanding that energy is everything, and the ultimate loss of energy is death?

Common sense on eating fruits

If you eat a meal and then consume a fruit, the fruit is ready to pass through the stomach into the intestines, but it will be prevented from doing so because of the meal eaten beforehand. In the acidic environment of the stomach, the meal and digestive juices combine with the fruit, causing it to decay and ferment, and become acidic. The decay produces gas and causes bloating.

So, this is the body's digestive science, which logically suggests eating fruits on an empty stomach or before meals. In effect, breaking this rule can have the negative consequence of not eating, or rarely eating, fruits.

Common sense as it relates to health and spirituality

> **If your spirituality does not have a physical manifestation, something is not working.**

How is it that the principles that relate to nutrition are not considered as being part of what is often referred to as spirituality? Since the well-being of the invisible part of us, mind and spirit, is dependent on the well-being of our physical self, can we separate them? Can we declare that we are very spiritual, but dishonour the science and principles that govern the body? Are we not just one organism, mind, body, and spirit, or physical and mental? Since we can safely assume that we are designed to live to our genetic capability, in a state of good health, how can anyone claim to live a 'spiritual' life, but consistently break the laws upon which longevity depends? Our physical existence is essential to our spiritual nature because the spirit requires a body to manifest as a person. Spirit means mind and life energy. Interestingly, the body can remain physically alive even when the mind no longer functions properly, as seen in cases of coma or severe mental impairment. However, the mind cannot function without the energy of life. This highlights a profound truth: while the mind and life energy coexist, they are fundamentally distinct.

Ultimately, when the body breaks down, we die. We are holistic beings—mind, body, and spirit."

Syllogistic reasoning on the drinking of milk

The widespread acceptance of something does not always equate to it being common sense; it has to be based on truth. Mike Anderson had this to say on his DVD, Eating - the RAVE diet:

"Calcium brainwashing is even worse than protein brainwashing… you will consume adequate amounts of calcium on any natural diet. In fact, calcium deficiency of a dietary origin is not only unknown in the United States, but there has not been a single recorded instance of calcium deficiency of a dietary origin in the entire history of the human race.

…the dairy industry claims that Americans somehow have a calcium deficiency and therefore must consume more dairy products. But why would Americans be so special and have this calcium deficiency when populations around the world do not? And those populations consume a fraction of the calcium Americans do, yet they do not have osteoporosis problems, and they get their calcium from plant foods, not dairy products. The reason Americans are so special is because dairy lobbies have paid off politicians and set US calcium requirements sky-high to sell their products. The same people selling calcium are setting our calcium requirements, and dieticians, doctors, and the public have bought into this because the government promotes dairy products. To think that the mere act of consuming more calcium, like taking a magic pill, will somehow make bones strong is pure and simple advertising. The primary cause of osteoporosis is a lack of weight-bearing activity due to a sedentary work and lifestyle.

Mammals produce milk to feed and nourish their offspring. No mammal drinks their mother's milk after it becomes an adult, and this includes humans – at least, I hope not. So, Nature is demonstrating in plain view that milk is baby food, and this ought to be common sense. Here are the basic facts against adults drinking milk:

- Cow's milk is food if you are a calf. So, cow's milk is for cow's babies, and human milk is for human babies. No mammal will continue to drink milk after it has been weaned, except humans. Nature has decided that milk is baby food, not for adults. Milk is only produced in sync with the birthing process.

- We are the only mammals who drink another mammal's milk, and this is because we have free will.

- *Lactose* is a sugar found in milk and, to a lesser extent, in dairy products.

- Lactose intolerance is the inability of adults to digest lactose, and it ranges from 5% to 90% among humans.

- Lactase is an enzyme necessary to digest milk. Most mammals usually cease to produce the digestive enzyme lactase, becoming lactose intolerant after weaning.

- While some human populations have developed lactase persistence, in which lactase production continues into adulthood, milk is 'liquid-meat', and therefore carries similar baggage as animal flesh. So, the same rules apply as to whether we should eat meat.

Common sense about water

http://www.huffingtonpost.com/dr-susanne-bennett/drinking-water_b_1680027.html

Water makes up approximately 60 per cent of the human body. Your blood is 93 per cent water, and your muscles are about 75 per cent water. Optimal water intake is essential for human survival." – Dr Susanne Bennett.

Eating fruits is the best way to optimise your water intake, because optimal hydration includes consuming minerals, especially during periods of fluid loss. So, it's better to 'eat' your water, and fruits contain essential electrolytes and minerals for good health.

Tap (pipe) water

You are not supposed to drink or cook with tap water. Here is why:

- Chlorine, a toxic gas in its pure form, is commonly added to tap water as a disinfectant.
- Chlorine is highly toxic. It's not meant for consumption.
- Boiling tap water removes only volatile compounds such as dissolved chlorine, hydrogen chloride, fluorine gas, and hydrogen fluoride. However, it does not eliminate non-volatile substances, such as calcium chloride and calcium fluoride. In other words, traces of chemicals will always remain in the water.

If you use tap water for cooking and drinking purposes, it's best to consider investing in a sound filtration system. If this is something that most of us should understand, it should become common sense.

Common sense on losing weight

- If you're carrying excess weight, it's not always necessary to follow a strict diet; simply focusing on eating healthy, whole foods can naturally lead to weight loss.

- It's difficult to get fat while eating healthy foods unless you are a glutton and do not exercise. Regarding healthy foods, remember that the evidence already presented demonstrated that meat is not a healthy food.

- Calories are the measure of the energy provided by our foods. Excess calories will be stored as body fat. Counting calories is not based on common sense if you are counting unhealthy calories that are extracted from bleached white flour. This flour has been stripped of fibre and nutrients, making it unhealthy. Additionally, during the bleaching process, it may retain chemical residues such as benzoyl peroxide and chlorine gas."

- Do not measure your health based on weight loss. Being slim does not always equate to being healthy.

- Be patient, lose weight gradually. It took time for the body to gain weight. A sudden loss of weight can cause the body to compensate by increasing cravings. This is due to a chemical rebound effect: the body becomes accustomed to carrying excess weight, and when that weight is suddenly lost, its memory remains wired into the body's systems.

- Junk food, processed food, and denatured food cause your appetite control mechanism to malfunction. The same principle applies to quench your thirst. Drinking sodas and other empty calories tends to increase the craving for such products instead of quenching your thirst. Mineral water quenches thirst, but fruits are superior, as previously explained.

- People eat a lot of food because the vitamins, minerals, fibre, and moisture have been removed from the food. When you eat such foods, the body will not get sufficient energy, hence the urge to eat more. When you eat whole foods, your body will be satisfied on a fraction of the calories it takes with junk food. Live, uncooked foods are very good for sating the appetite.

- It makes no sense to diet on (or eat less of) the same food that caused you to become overweight. It makes no sense to eat less of the food that is low in nutrients.

- Exercise alone is inadequate for effective weight loss. You are not exercising common sense if you try to get rid of a big stomach by just exercising. This is because excess weight is mainly due to poor dietary and lifestyle habits. If you're eating junk food and exercising, you're speeding up the destruction of your body. This is because exercise places more demands on your body by breaking down body tissue, which the body will automatically try to repair. If the material used for repair is of poor quality, it places additional strain on the body by forcing it to expend energy extracting limited nutrients from inadequate resources.

- Digesting food requires energy, and junk food often demands more energy to process than whole, healthy foods. As a result, the body may expend more energy than it gains. Additionally, it must work harder to counteract the harmful additives and non-nutritive substances found in junk food. If the body can't digest it, it will store it or try to eliminate it. This attempt can manifest as acne, other skin rashes, vomiting, and even diarrhoea. Junk food is usually acidic, has preservatives and other unhealthy chemicals. An overly acidic diet is often the cause of cancer.

- Diet pills only help flush out water weight, not fat weight. Diet pills often contain similar ingredients to those used in speed tablets. They have side effects such as heart palpitations, angina, and seizures; hence, they are not to be used.

- Fruits, vegetables, and whole grains are ideal for weight loss.

- For those not engaged in a nutritional programme, it is essential to understand that depletion of the body's nutrient stores is a more likely cause of hunger. This has been proved by those who eat uncooked, highly nutritious foods. In such situations, hunger is very infrequent.

- Common sense says we must study the science of nutrition because no instruction manual or instinct came with us at birth as to what we should or shouldn't eat.

- Animals in the wild are never overweight because they always eat what they are supposed to eat.

- Domesticated animals can be overweight because we often feed them what they are not supposed to eat.

- Human beings are often overweight because we eat foods we are not supposed to eat, eat when we are not supposed to, and combine foods we are not supposed to combine. In short, we have unhealthy eating habits.

- We should all learn that the body has a cycle for eating, repairing, and eliminating. We are not nocturnal creatures, so we should not eat late at night. Between seven and eight o'clock should be the latest. The earlier the better. Late eating interferes with our sleep cycle and is, therefore, an unhealthy practice.

Non-foods

Did you know that junk foods are also referred to as *starvation foods?* Consuming these types of foods can lead to being overfed but undernourished, as they deprive the body of essential nutrients and oxygen. Oxygen is the substance that the body can do without the least amount of time, and since junk foods starve the body of it and nutrients, they are, therefore, anti-life. Good health requires our body to be slightly alkaline. If the body becomes too acidic, your health and life are at risk. Consequently, it makes sense to eat foods that are alkaline-forming in the body. A measurement of the body's acidity or alkalinity is a measure of its pH, and therefore, a measurement of its well-being. Since foods affect the body's pH balance, knowledge of these foods and their pH effect ought to become common sense.

Foods that have a moderate to strong alkaline-forming effect

These foods are rich in oxygen, enzymes, and vitamins, hence they're good for health:

Watermelon
Lemons
Cantaloupe
Celery
Limes
Mango
Honeydew
[melon] Papaya
Parsley
Seaweed
Grapes

Watercress; Asparagus; Kiwi; Pears; Pineapple; Vegetable juices; Apples; Apricots; Alfalfa; Sprouts; Avocado; Bananas; Garlic; Ginger; Peaches; Nectarines; Grapefruit; Oranges; Most herbs; Peas; Lettuce; Broccoli; cauliflower

Foods and substances that have a moderate to strong acid-forming effect

Alcohol; Soft drinks (pop) Tobacco; Coffee; White sugar; Refined Salt; Artificial sweeteners Antibiotics (and most drugs); White flour products (including pasta); Seafood; White vinegar; Barley; Most boxed cereals; Cheese; Most beans; Meats; Most types of bread

Please note that these lists are not comprehensive.

Syllogistic reasoning regarding our skin and health

- Because our skin is porous, substances like gases, alcohol, and chemicals applied to it can be absorbed into the bloodstream and circulate throughout the body.

- Anything that enters our bloodstream will affect our health.

- Therefore, we should ensure that what we put on our skin is suitable for our body. Logic suggests it's best to apply colognes or perfumes to our clothes rather than directly to our skin.

- Regular detoxification is a significant part of the body's defence against ill health.

- Sweating is part of the body's cooling and detoxification process.

- **Antiperspirants** are anti-health if they prevent or restrict the body's elimination of toxins.

- If this restriction is prolonged and toxins remain in the body longer than they should, it can contribute to poor health.

All of this should be common knowledge – common sense, which is sound judgement rooted in accurate knowledge applied logically.

Common sense on health, fitness, and lifting weights

Health and fitness are not the same. Here is why:

- You can be fit and not be healthy. This is because health is about the correct workings of your organs and the pH balance of your body's biochemistry.

- Fitness can be achieved primarily by working out physically (in the gym and on the track), yet tolerating a lousy diet at the same time.

- You cannot have a lousy diet and be healthy. Therefore, fitness primarily relates to the conditioning of your muscles and lungs. Yet you will see a definition of fitness that says: *The condition of being fit and healthy.* This perception is common but misleading.

It is not uncommon for individuals who have become addicted to the feel-good factor of the gym and weightlifting to have extensive discussions on how to increase strength, improve their physique (being 'cut'), and build muscle mass. What is uncommon, or perhaps never happens, is for this discussion to include ideas for health and well-being. Should the following be common knowledge to aid the above points about health and fitness?

- Many athletes have health problems.

- There have been football/soccer players who were plagued with injuries, then improved their diet, and subsequently reduced the frequency of injuries.

- Football/soccer players have collapsed on the playing field and had to discontinue their careers, while others have collapsed and died.

- Dr Ruth Heidrich, for example, who received her PhD in Health Management in 1993, was a marathon runner at the time she developed cancer—according to Dr Heidrich, her doctor, Dr John McDougall, told her that it was her diet that caused her breast cancer. She refused chemotherapy and radiation treatment and switched to a one hundred per cent plant-based diet. Over thirty years later, she is cancer-free and credits her new diet for saving her life.

- An athlete puts significantly more stress and strain on their body than most people. A diet that is rich in foods and substances that suck moisture from the body's tissue, such as white flour, white rice, table salt, and sugar, will shorten their lifespan and cause them health problems. This also applies to foods high in cholesterol, such as meat and dairy products.

Our muscles shouldn't be bigger or more agile than our brain. Our brain should drive all our activities.

Common sense about oxygen and sleep

We all know the fundamental value of oxygen in sustaining life. However, did you know that it can help you relax and, therefore, sleep? Regular deep breaths are good for health. If you sit in a chair or the bath and take rapid, deep breaths for at least ten minutes, you will feel a pleasant sensation of electricity running through your body, becoming relaxed and more receptive to sleep. This remedy is free and has no side effects, compared to alcohol and sleeping pills. Should this knowledge become common sense?

Common sense on smoking

- We have repeatedly misaligned ourselves with Nature and used our bodies for what it is not intended, with acts such as smoking. We should all have the sense to understand that even if a natural substance like marijuana has medicinal value, the body is not structured to process and extract such medicine from the smoke.

- Since it is a certainty that many who smoke accept that it causes cancer and death, how is it possible for them to acknowledge this reality, yet persist in smoking? We can reasonably assume that these persons are not trying to kill themselves because there are many quicker ways to do it. So, how do they cope with what the psychologists call cognitive dissonance? This refers to the mental stress or discomfort experienced by an individual who holds two or more contradictory beliefs, ideas, or values simultaneously. Common sense says they must have, at a minimum, pushed this possible consequence of their action into a vague, distant possibility. There is no way that they could cope if this possibility were a pressing, imminent reality. Could a person act indifferently to a gun pointed at their head, for example? So, how do smokers who know that smoking kills cope with this information? Firstly, we humans are masters of self-deception, and one way of coping is to alter our beliefs about the dangers of our actions – in this case, smoking. They, therefore, ignore the overwhelming evidence of the millions who have died from tobacco and instead cling to the rare exception—the individual who smoked their whole life and lived to old age. Sure enough, they may know or have heard of someone who has smoked heavily for forty years and seems to be still healthy. They will then communicate this to themselves or tell those who try

to discourage them from smoking. This cognitive dissonance also applies to eating harmful foods.

- The introductory psychology discussed above, concerning the complexity of the human mind and emotions, should be common sense. It would then serve as a springboard to find solutions for those who find themselves in such situations.

What if I were to tell you that smoking is good for asthma, hay fever, foul breath, throat diseases, head colds, and bronchial irritations, would you believe me? What unfavourable words would you call me? Would you say I lack common sense or that I am just a plain idiot? As you can see below, these claims were made in the 19th century and up to the late 1950s and early 1960s.

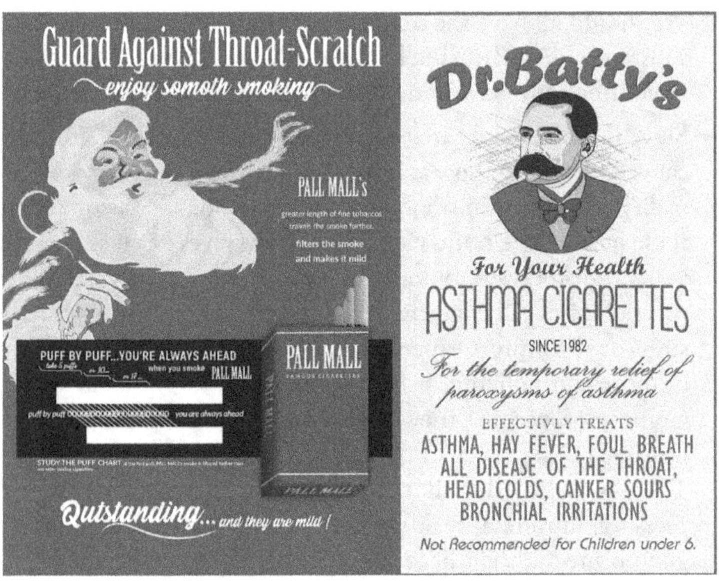

According to the Asthma Foundation Victoria of Australia, "These cigarettes did not contain tobacco, but they contained herbs that were considered to help reduce asthma symptoms. Whilst now the idea of smoking to help asthma may seem obscene, cigarettes for the majority of the 19th and 20th Centuries (and earlier) were considered to be beneficial for health." So, this idea that medicine can be extracted from a substance through smoking has been around for some time. These cigarettes were discontinued. However, was it because of an eureka-common-sense-awakening? It doesn't seem that this was the reason. They were taken off the market because "The herbs contained substances that had hallucinogenic effects and caused heart palpitations. And because more medications came about with fewer side effects."

Common sense versus common understanding

The tomato was feared in Europe for more than 200 years

The story you will read shortly demonstrates that common understanding is not necessarily common sense. It also shows that for knowledge to become common sense, it must be grounded in truth, because common sense is meant to serve us positively.

It must be a navigation tool that, if used by the majority of us, would help advance society. This story demonstrates that an idea or belief can be widely perceived, understood, and accepted without debate, and still be incorrect.

In this case, the fear of the tomato was not based on common sense, but on 'common nonsense'.

So, even though using our ability to perceive, understand, and judge things produces common sense, our perception must be based on accurate knowledge. It is only if our judgement is based on correct knowledge that there would be no need for debate, even if the 'understanding' is common to nearly all people. The description of the basic 'sense'/knowledge we need for practical living evolved from Aristotle's syllogistic reasoning, and its principle was influential during the Age of Enlightenment (or Age of Reason), when there was a shift from dogma and tradition being the sole, dominant guiding force. This type of reasoning is also at the heart of scientific advancement, insisting that we follow wherever the logical argument leads us.

According to K. Annabelle Smith (Smithsonian.com), "In the late 1700s, a large percentage of Europeans feared the tomato."

"A nickname for the fruit was the 'poison apple' because it was thought that aristocrats got sick and died after eating them, but the truth of the matter was that wealthy Europeans used pewter plates, which were high in lead content. Because tomatoes are so high in acidity, when placed on this particular tableware, the fruit would leach lead from the plate, resulting in many deaths from lead poisoning. No one made this connection between plate and poison at the time; the tomato was picked as the culprit...

"But what ultimately ruined the tomato's reputation was John Gerard's publication of *Herball* in 1597, which drew heavily from the agricultural works of [Rembert] Dodoens and [Charles] l'Ecluse (1553)... Gerard's opinion of the tomato, though based on a fallacy, prevailed in Britain and the British North American colonies for over 200 years."

Many Europeans falsely perceived that tomatoes were poisonous during the late 1700s. This conclusion was based on their apparent ability to judge things, and it was widely accepted without question. Therefore, this belief would have been considered to be common sense. In reality, it was a common misunderstanding. In the main, having a common understanding was not intended to be based on an idea or philosophy that we invented, but which has no practical application. It was designed that the sense/knowledge that is to be made common would be based on an accurate understanding of how life, Nature, and our environment work. And since life, Nature and the environment affect all of us, the knowledge/science that governs them should be familiar to all of us. This common sense, then, would be a combination of a basic and an advanced understanding of life that we would use to guide us in our interaction with each other, and with Nature and our environment. The acquisition of such basic and advanced knowledge would enable us to reach our full potential.

> **Society is supposed to be a team effort, and the more proficient the team members are, the more advanced and effective the team will be. This is the concept behind the idea of the need to have common sense or common knowledge.**

The true knowledge about lead poisoning from lead plates was not common knowledge or common sense then. Is it common sense now? How about aluminium pots? According to Maggie New, writing her article in http://www. livestrong.com/article/143570-poisons-from-aluminum-cookware/

… In the 1960s, safety concerns began to be raised over possible leaching of aluminium into food. The popularity of aluminium pots and pans is mainly based on two things: They are cheap, and they conduct heat very effectively. However, many suitable alternatives soon emerged, including stainless steel, porcelain, glass, and iron. The only poison that can leach into food by cooking with aluminium is the aluminium itself. The reason this became a concern is that large amounts of the material have been found in the brains of Alzheimer's patients, which proves that aluminium crosses the blood/brain barrier. This does not establish a causal link, which would be needed to say definitively that aluminium in the brain causes Alzheimer's disease.

Do you think the finding of large amounts of aluminium in a person's brain is sufficient information to warrant it becoming common sense that it is dangerous to use aluminium pots? Should this common sense become part of our health and safety guidance system? Should this be the case even if it is said that aluminium found in the brain has not been established as a definite cause of Alzheimer's disease? What do you think? The article further stated:

The body derives no benefits from aluminium, and in large quantities, it is harmful. The question then is one of quantity. If the food is not highly acidic or alkaline on the pH scale, less leaching occurs. "Leaching is most likely when the foods being cooked or stored are highly alkaline, like baking soda, or highly acidic, like tomato sauce, lemon juice, oranges or vinegar," according to the Tree Hugger website. In the case of tomato sauce, 3 to 6 milligrams of aluminium have been found per 100g serving after being cooked in an aluminium pan. This is approximately 10 per cent of the average person's daily aluminium consumption.

Are you now convinced that, at a minimum, it should be common sense that aluminium pots pose a health risk? Did you know that pots can be made from glass, and that this type of cookware is considered one of the healthiest options? Should this be common knowledge? I bought plastic water bottles and noticed that they were listed as BPA-free. I didn't know what BPA was, but figured it must be something bad; therefore, the product was better without it. My attitude was similar to buying food items that are labelled as free of additives. However, I eventually looked up BPA and found an article written by Jenna Bilbrey on the scientificamerican.com website:

In 2012, the U.S. Food and Drug Administration banned the sale of baby bottles that contain bisphenol A (BPA), a compound frequently found in plastics. The ban came after manufacturers responded to consumer concerns about BPA's safety after several studies found the chemical mimics estrogen and could harm the brain and reproductive development in fetuses, infants, and children. Since then, store shelves have been lined with BPA-free bottles for babies and adults alike. Yet, recent research reveals that a common BPA replacement, bisphenol S (BPS), may be just as harmful.

BPA is the starting material for making polycarbonate plastics. Any leftover BPA that is not consumed in the reaction used to create a plastic container can leach into its contents. From there, it can enter the body. BPS was a favoured replacement because it was thought to be more resistant to leaching. If people consumed less of the chemical, the idea went, it would not cause any or only minimal harm. Yet BPS is getting out. Nearly 81 per cent of Americans have detectable levels of BPS in their urine. And once it enters the body, it can affect cells in ways that parallel BPA."

Since plastic containers are one of the most widely used food vessels, should the above be common knowledge? Once again, glass seems to be our safest bet, even if it is just for storage, so now I've spent some money on glass containers. What better usage is there for money?

It is questionable whether most people should reasonably be expected to accept this next point, because it has been almost globally misrepresented. Most of us will not accept contradictions to what the overwhelming majority believe. Fortunately, world-renowned life coach and researcher Anthony Robbins has shared this information, so here it is, along with some explanation.

Common Sense on the Germ Theory

The germ theory states that certain diseases, such as the flu, are caused by specific microorganisms known as pathogens. Since common sense is based on truth and is, in the main, demonstrable, is the germ theory true, and has it ever been demonstrated? Can this theory stand up to the indispensable aspects of common sense, simple logic, and facts? It appears that this matter was settled by Nobel laureate Robert Koch (11 December 1843 – 27 May 1910). You will undoubtedly encounter contradictions in his ideas and those of other authors in this book, particularly in the subject matter discussed. It's up to you to decide. His ideas are known as Koch's postulates and were introduced to me in Tony Robbins' *Living Health* audio series. Koch's postulates are criteria for determining whether a disease is infectious and caused by a *particular* microbe. He postulated:

1. ***The germ must be found in every case of the disease.*** It is a well-known fact that so-called infectious diseases may arise in the absence of the so-called pathogenic germs that are supposed to cause them, proving that germs do not cause disease. A germ cannot be a cause if it does not accompany the condition it is supposed to cause. A causeless effect is not possible.

2. ***The germ should never be found apart from the disease.*** However, they are. The germs of diphtheria, pneumonia, tuberculosis, etc., are often found in perfectly healthy people who do not have, have never had, and do not subsequently develop the disease. A germ cannot be a cause if, when present in the body, the condition it is supposed to cause never develops. An "effectless" cause is not possible.

3. **The germ must be capable of culturing outside the body.** Never has a culture been made with normal, healthy living tissue. **Medical theory suggests that germs "attack and destroy" healthy tissue within the body; however, no germ has ever been observed to multiply in normal tissues or normal secretions in a laboratory setting. Germs are often seen in association with**

disease, as they feed on the decay. Until it can be demonstrated that germs have an affinity for normal, healthy tissue, the germ theory remains unsupportable. The germ must be capable of producing by injection the same disease as that undergone by the body from which they were taken. However, they are not. In a series of experiments conducted in 1921 with 62 volunteer Navy personnel, researchers attempted to induce flu infection using various methods, for example, injecting blood from active influenza cases, spraying 'infectious' germs into the volunteers' throats, and contaminating their food. The results were: no appreciable reactions. If specific germs cause specific diseases, then they should cause those diseases, and only those diseases, every time they are injected into the body. A cause must be constant and specific in its influence, or it is not a cause.

Koch's postulates are based on facts and simple logical syllogistic reasoning.

When you get a cut and your body begins to heal it, you may sometimes notice a small amount of pus near the scab. This pus does not indicate disease; instead, it's a by-product of your defence system using white blood cells to fight off invading germs. The pus is evidence that your body is winning the battle. Similarly, the mucus we cough up when we have a cold is the end product of our defence system getting rid of accumulated toxins and germs. So, logically, the only appropriate help you should give to the body in this situation is not some drugs, but detoxification.

Simple syllogistic logic on food health

Fatty foods can clog up our blood and, consequently, cause our system to malfunction. Therefore, excessively fatty foods increase the probability of our bodies malfunctioning. Excessive use of alcohol can weaken our bodies and cause them to malfunction. This is one of the factors of a hangover. Therefore, excessive consumption of both fatty foods and alcohol can over-stress our bodies and cause us to be ill.

If you ever wonder why many people tend to get sick after returning from a holiday, it is often because most people tend to eat a lot more than they usually do, and load up on many things they don't normally eat. Let's walk this through with simple logic using what we know of human behaviour. We tend to eat and drink more at a party than at home. Similarly, we tend to eat and drink more

while on holiday because we're relaxed and enjoying ourselves, especially when visiting a foreign country with a variety of appealing food and drinks.

If the diet is the typical animal-based type, there is more cholesterol for the body to process. Also, if alcohol or other toxins were consumed, it should not be a wonder that the body would require a detox at the end of the holiday. For example, the flu is the body's way of getting rid of toxins. A change of weather is not to be blamed. Many people have experienced a change of weather without ever, so-called, 'catching' a cold. A compelling truth is this: cold countries and tropical countries are known to have identical flu seasons. How do the above correspond with the common belief and promotion of the 'fact' that we 'catch' flu from an infected person? And how about the belief that we can 'catch a cold' because rain fell on us? The experiments mentioned earlier, conducted in 1921 with 62 volunteer Navy personnel, should at the very least raise serious doubts about this belief. Perhaps being mindful of this experiment will eventually relegate the 'catch a cold' belief to the realm of common misconception.

Smallpox is considered one of the most virulent of contagious diseases, and it is generally believed that persons exposed are almost invariably attacked unless protected by vaccination. This is one of the most stupendous exaggerations to be found in medical literature. My experience has been that very few people take it when exposed to it. – John Tilden, MD (1851-1940)

"External, material objects are never causes of disease, merely agents waiting to cause specific symptoms in susceptible hosts. Rather than warring on disease agents with the hope of eliminating them, we ought to worry more about strengthening resistance to them and learning to live in balance with them more of the time." – Andrew Weil, M.D.

Germs or viruses require a partner for them to become a problem to humans. The 'partner' is the body's environment – the environment is a combination of the biochemical state of the body and the health of the body's lymphatic or defence system. Suppose the body's biochemistry has a healthy alkaline pH balance and a healthy lymphatic system? If this were the case, it would be sufficient to deal with a few natural viruses or germs that may be introduced into the body. A healthy body would have to be overloaded and then overwhelmed with germs for death to occur, and this would not happen in everyday living. Otherwise, a healthy lymphatic or defence system can deal with such germs. The lymphatic system referred to is not restricted to the blood antigens that attack germs. This system is also a term that loosely refers to the actions of the pancreas, liver, kidneys, bacteria, and various cells. So, in effect, such a virus or germ would have to turn off a very complex and robust system for a person to die. The liver is the largest glandular organ in the body. It is highly robust and performs multiple critical functions, including detoxifying harmful substances such as alcohol and drugs.

The liver also functions as an organ of the immune system through the activity of the Kupffer cells, which line the sinusoids. Kupffer cells play a crucial role in capturing and digesting bacteria, fungi, parasites, worn-out blood cells, and cellular debris. The large volume of blood passing through the hepatic portal system and the liver allows Kupffer cells to clean large volumes of blood very quickly. No natural virus or germ is going to suppress a healthy body's defence system and cause it to die. A good analogy is that a germ cannot live on a clean surface or in a sterilised environment.

Only snake venom, various poisons, and artificial chemicals can kill a **healthy body** with *just minute quantities*. And in many instances, the liver is powerful enough to process and eliminate diluted snake venom. It can also remove small amounts of arsenic. I've been bitten by scorpions (not the most venomous ones) a few times without needing any medication. My tongue got a little heavy, but eventually, my body's defence system dealt with it. Are we supposed to accept that viruses can kill the body, which is powerful enough to eliminate small amounts of arsenic, other toxins and venoms? Especially when we consider that trillions of bacteria live in the human body and play a critical role in our health and well-being. These microbes play a crucial role in digestion, regulate immune responses, protect against harmful invaders, and even consume decaying matter, facilitating decomposition both within the body and in nature. In that context, none of this makes sense.

> **As our world becomes increasingly complex, so does the knowledge required for survival and happiness. Free will has often led to neglecting our minds and bodies through poor diet and lifestyle choices. In response, the commercial world has offered solutions, some helpful, others harmful, through the pharmaceutical and medical industries. This has added yet another layer of difficulty: the challenge of discerning what constitutes good, bad, or better medicine. Doing so requires syllogistic reasoning grounded in accurate knowledge. In such a world, ignorance is not bliss.**

CHAPTER FIVE

The third major life issue to which Aristotelian syllogistic reasoning applies: **Common sense regarding pharmaceutical medicines and the medical system**

Considering all we know about the inherent dangers on this planet, there has never been a time in history when ignorance was bliss. What people didn't know then, killed many, and what people don't know today, is also the cause of many deaths!

Suppose the primary goal of political leaders is truly to ensure the health and well-being of the people, rather than to protect the profitability of the pharmaceutical industry. In that case, they must re-examine the current healthcare system. A serious effort must be made to incorporate a comprehensive naturopathic approach to wellness as a legitimate option within public healthcare. This requires changing existing laws to give natural medicine equal legal and institutional standing.

At present, naturopathic doctors are prohibited from publicly claiming to cure major diseases such as cancer, despite relying on natural, non-processed or minimally processed herbs and nutrition. Natural medicine is often more affordable than pharmaceutical drugs and emphasises prevention, particularly through dietary and lifestyle changes. A quote from chapter ten speaks directly to this issue:

"By the late-17th century…the effectiveness of herbal remedies and natural medicines became increasingly accepted." So, what changed?

There is a reality called profit over morality. To think that it doesn't apply to medicine, perhaps the most lucrative industry, is being selective in our distrust of what some people will do for big money. "The medicine is good; they just overcharge us for it." Really? Is there vastly more profit in a treatment medicine than in a curing medicine? After over one hundred years of research, there is still no cure for the major diseases that kill or permanently impair us.

Considering what is at stake, is it worthwhile to look into this further? The evidence presented here should make the case to take such a look.

The pharmaceutical industry isn't like somebody started a company that just grew...oligarchs made a plan to overtake the medical sector, to take over the medical schools...up to the late 1800's and early 1900's, the primary treatment for any ailment was herbs...they decided to synthesise treatments, and that's where the patenting came in...they can then put their name on it...you cannot then get it unless you get it from them... synthesised herbs do not have the identical molecules[4]. Synthesising adds toxicity[5] to the end product. – Paraphrasing Dr Amun and Dr Amsu (Natural medicine practitioners)

Why is patenting problematic for humans? A medicine is patentable based on the extent to which it has a unique synthetic combination of chemicals. If a new drug has even trace elements of an old drug, it is not patentable. Drug companies tend to ignore treatments that cannot provide a framework to protect their expensive investment, that is, drugs that are not patentable, especially if the disease creates high demand. This eliminates natural substances, as they cannot be patented. So, drug companies are locked into only producing patentable drugs, since they are driven by profit. The criteria for patentable drugs are so strict that, in an article entitled **"How Patent Law Can Block Even Lifesaving Drugs**, written in the New York Times by Austin Frakt, **A patent for a hypertension drug was invalidated because it was deemed to have been created by a well-known process."** However, what if synthesising is the problem? It is. The toxicity it generates and the side effects are the clues.

> **"FDA approved Novartis's new $475,000 cancer drug among the most expensive ever. Swiss pharmaceuticals group Novartis has said it will charge $475,000 a patient for its new cancer therapy, putting it among the most expensive drugs of all time." Swissinfo. ch [David Crow (New York) August 2017]**

This hyper-expensive drug is described, like all other such drugs, as a treatment, not a cure. According to the Financial Times, "The treatment, known as chimeric antigen receptor therapy or CAR-T, has shown great promise in clinical trials, with the ability to send tumours into remission in blood cancer patients with just weeks to live. But the therapy is complex and expensive, with a process

---

[4]   This is the reason for side-effects that are prevalent in using pharmaceutical drugs.
[5]   It goes without saying that this is harmful. This is why toxicologists are involved in every stage of drugs development.

that involves extracting a patient's blood cells in a hospital, transporting the plasma – normally by air – to a laboratory, and re-engineering them before they are returned."

Remission: "A temporary diminution of the severity of disease or pain." "Cancer remission is when the signs and symptoms of cancer have **lessened or are undetectable**. In blood-related cancers like leukaemia, this **means** you'll have a decrease in the number of cancer cells. For solid tumours, that **means** that the tumour size has decreased."

Simple logic

A disease can only be cured if the root cause is eliminated
Cancer cells and tumours are symptoms of cancer, not the root cause
Therefore, getting rid of cancer cells and tumours cannot cure cancer
If this were untrue, remission would always terminate cancer

Patients are often optimistic after being told they are in remission. Would they be if they understood that it means, at best, cancer cells, the **symptom of the disease**, are no longer visible? What if they understood that the root cause was there before the cancer cells were visible? This new drug, Car-T, which is said to send tumours of blood cancer patients into remission, is so highly regarded, and the cost is astronomical, as stated above, but it is not a cure. Remission is not an indication that the person is cured. Remission is quite common with other types of treatments, yet millions of people die after having the 'benefit' of remission. Since it doesn't cure cancer, why is it so expensive? Novartis are the only one who can explain why their treatment drug and method are so costly. It should be absurd that a drug that doesn't cure is so expensive. Should the value of a drug be based on a person living a little longer, and other costs? There is evidence that cancer can be reversed permanently with dietary and natural remedies. Governments owe it to their people to investigate this.

Can food cure disease? Yes, scurvy, a disease that killed many, was cured by lemons or their component, vitamin C (ascorbic acid). The following should be common knowledge/common sense: according to Wikipedia, "Scurvy was a limiting factor in long-distance sea travel, often killing large numbers of people. During the Age of Sail (1571–1862), it was assumed that 50 per cent of the sailors would die of scurvy on a given trip. A Scottish surgeon in the Royal Navy, James Lind, is generally credited with proving that scurvy can be successfully treated with citrus fruit in 1753. Nonetheless, it would be 1795 before health reformers such as Gilbert Blane persuaded the British Royal Navy to give lemon juice to its sailors routinely." From this evidence and the story of Annett Larkins, common sense suggests that when Hippocrates said, **"Let your food be your medicine and your medicine be your food", he was talking about nature's live, uncooked foods.**

"Treating diabetes, heart disease, cancer, etc., is a 1.5 trillion-dollar industry." – 'What the Health' documentary

---

"Economics and politics simply intertwine in shaping conventional medicine's approach to cancer. Very simply put, treating disease is enormously profitable, preventing disease is not." – British Cancer Control Society.

Considering the role of patenting and corporate interests in treating illness and disease, it is reasonable to expect that governments should allow equal testing and evaluation of both natural remedies and pharmaceutical drugs. The choice of medicine should be guided solely by the goal of achieving genuine wellness. Since medical outcomes are measurable, the natural consequence will be that people tend to prefer whichever form of medicine consistently provides the best results.

Simple logic that ought to be common sense

Even a cursory knowledge of human biology suggests that an ever-increasing number of patented drugs, a unique combination of synthetic chemicals, cannot be in harmony with the natural science of the human body. Side effects and deaths are proof of this.

Deaths by drug medicine and doctors' error (iatrogenic deaths)

According to a report published in The Lancet (Vol. 351, Issue 9110, p1183, April 18, 1998): **"Adverse drug reactions (ADRs) are a leading cause of death in the USA, say Canadian researchers. Bruce Pomeranz and colleagues at the University of Toronto estimate that ADRs could account for more than 100 000 deaths in the USA each year, making them the fourth commonest cause of death after heart disease (nearly 750000 deaths), cancer (530000), and stroke (150000) (*JAMA* 1998; 279: 1200–05)."**

> **Five years later, this iatrogenic death rate had not reduced.**

The Nutrition Institute of America funded an independent review of "government-approved" medicine that was published in 2003. Professors Gary Null and Dorothy Smith, along with doctors Carolyn Dean, Martin Feldman, and Debora Rasio, titled the report 'Death by Medicine.'

The researchers found that the leading cause of death in America was not heart disease (at 699,697 per annum in 2001), or cancer at 553,251 annually) It was conventional medicine. They found that the iatrogenic death rate (death caused by doctors and/or medical treatments) in the US was 783,936 a year. They concluded that, "It is evident that the American medical system is the leading cause of death and injury in the United States."

The report compilers predicted that over ten years, iatrogenic deaths would total about **7.8 million**, "…more than all the casualties from wars that America has fought in its entire history." "This is a death rate that is equivalent to six jumbo jets falling out of the sky every day." Among the breakdown in this 7.8 million is 1.06 million for 'Adverse Drug Reaction', and 371,360 for 'Unnecessary Procedures'.

Furthermore, the report authors believed the numbers were much higher because most iatrogenic deaths aren't reported as such: **only 5 to 20% of iatrogenic deaths are reported for fear of lawsuits, and to preserve reputations,** as well as because **codes for reporting them are often absent.** The number of deaths due to conventional medicine may, therefore, be 20 times higher than the numbers given.

These statistics are controversial, as they are often contested for being too high. However, because doctors and hospitals generally do not readily acknowledge errors or adverse drug reactions (ADRs) and rarely publish such data systematically, they leave the door open to public distrust and ongoing controversy. Even if the actual figures were only half of those reported, the issue would still be deeply concerning.

This qualifies as an issue that will affect most of us; therefore, this situation should become common knowledge and common sense.

The ancient Greek physician, Hippocrates, is credited with being the father of Western medicine and is quoted as saying, "Let your food be your medicine, and your medicine be your food."

Based on the statistics above, how can we explain that natural treatments, such as dietary adjustments, herbs, and other holistic methods—are now considered 'alternative' or inferior forms of medicine instead of being recognised as part of mainstream healthcare? At the very least, this should lead us to question how pharmaceutical medicine became dominant, despite primarily focusing on managing symptoms rather than providing actual cures. How can we reconcile this with the philosophy of the father of Western medicine, which emphasised addressing the root cause of illness? If reason guides us, we naturally seek a cure. However, if the programmable emotional mind prevails, it can be conditioned to accept living with disease while endlessly treating symptoms. This illogical approach does not fit within the syllogistic framework that underpins common sense. Could the dominance of pharmaceutical medicine be linked to the enormous financial gains and the potential for higher profits? According to the World Health Organisation (WHO), 2016, the industry is valued at US$300 billion annually and is projected to grow to US$400 billion in three years.

How the medical system works should be common knowledge/common sense

What is your attitude towards medicine? Have you been minding your own business while letting the doctors and physicians mind theirs? The problem with having such an attitude is that both of you should be focusing on the same matter when it comes to your health. And you should care more about this matter than the doctor, because it is your health and life that are at stake. The medical system affects all of us. Therefore, an understanding of how it works should be common sense. Here are some basic facts that we should all research and become familiar with about the medical system, which most of us use.

- The medicine mainly practised today is called **allopathic medicine**, which relies mostly on **drugs** and surgery. It is primarily a medicine that treats or suppresses the symptoms of the disease, but does not generally treat or eliminate the cause. A simple example of symptom treatment is taking a painkiller for a headache. It numbs the nerves so that the pain doesn't register, but it doesn't deal with the root cause of the pain. Allopathy does not have a cure for any of the major diseases, such as cancer, diabetes, heart disease, or even the common cold.

- Does it make sense that we should be content with a type of medicine that overwhelmingly treats the symptoms of a disease, and not get rid of the root cause? Does this not mean you still have the disease? Why would any reasonable person be content with this unless they have been led to accept that this is the best option available?

- The doctor is not necessarily an expert on the drugs he prescribes – this is the prerogative of the drug company that developed and tested them. He prescribes medicines that have been approved and waits for new developments from those involved in research.

- The job description of doctors, such as general practitioners, does not include looking for cures. They are expected only to *practise* what they were taught.

- The focus is on treating diseases, not on promoting wellness.

- Drugs do not improve strength and energy; nutrition does. Did you know that most medical doctors are not knowledgeable about nutrition? This is true because medical schools typically offer little to no education on nutrition, vitamins, or minerals.

- Dr Ray Strand, the author of *Death by Prescription*, confirms: "In medical school, I had not received any significant instruction on the subject. I was not alone. Approximately 6 per cent of the graduating physicians in the United States have received any training in nutrition. Medical students may take elective courses on the topic. Still, few do… the education of most physicians is disease-oriented with a heavy emphasis on pharmaceuticals — we learn about drugs and why and when to use them."

- The allopathic business model fosters insidious self-interest, which was confirmed in an article written 18.06.2015 by F. William Engdahl in the NEO journal:

"Dr Richard Horton, the editor of the world's most respected medical journal, The Lancet, published the following: 'Much of the scientific literature, perhaps half, may simply be untrue. Afflicted by studies with small sample sizes, tiny effects, invalid exploratory analyses, and flagrant conflicts of interest, together with an obsession for pursuing fashionable trends of dubious importance, science has taken a turn towards darkness.'

"… Horton states bluntly that major pharmaceutical companies falsify or manipulate tests on the health, safety, and effectiveness of their various drugs by taking samples too small to be statistically meaningful or hiring test labs or scientists where the lab or scientist has blatant conflicts of interest, such as pleasing the drug company to get further grants. At least half of all such tests are worthless or worse, he claims." He also stated: "As the drugs have a major effect on the health of millions of consumers, the manipulation amounts to criminal dereliction and malfeasance."

Mr Engdahl also quotes other voices: "Dr Marcia Angell is a physician and was long-time Editor-in-Chief of the New England Medical Journal (NEMJ), considered to be another one of the most prestigious peer-reviewed medical journals in the world. Angell stated, 'It is simply no longer possible to believe much of the clinical research that is published, or to rely on the judgement of trusted physicians or authoritative medical guidelines. I take no pleasure in this conclusion, which I reached slowly and reluctantly over my two decades as an editor of the New England Journal of Medicine.'

"Harvey Marcovitch, who has studied and written about the corruption of medical tests and publication in medical journals, writes, "Studies showing positive outcomes for a drug or device under consideration are more likely to be published than 'negative' studies; editors are partly to blame for this but so are commercial sponsors, whose methodologically well-conducted studies with unfavorable results tended not to see the light of day."

F. William Engdahl also stated: "Corruption of the medical industry worldwide is a huge issue, perhaps more dangerous than the threat of all wars combined. Do we have such hypnosis and blind faith in our doctors simply because of their white coats that we believe they are infallible? And, in turn, do they have such blind faith in the medical journals recommending a given new wonder medicine or vaccine that they rush to give the drugs or vaccines without considering these deeper issues?"

Physicians play an essential role in supporting the health of society. However, maintaining our health is ultimately our responsibility. It is up to each of us to live and eat in a way that promotes wellness, helps prevent disease, and reduces the need for symptom-focused medications wherever possible. Consider the perspectives of two physicians on the use of such drugs:

Twenty-five years during which I used prescribed drugs, and 33 years in which I have not used any, should give my belief that drugs are

unnecessary and, in most cases, harmful, some credibility to those who seek the truth. – John H. Tilden, M.D.(1851-1940)

What hope is there for medical science to ever become a true science when the entire structure of medical knowledge is built around the idea that there is an entity called disease which can be expelled when the right drug is found? – John H. Tilden, M.D.

I have argued for years that we do not have a health care system in America. We have a disease-management system - one that depends on ruinously expensive drugs and surgeries that treat health conditions after they manifest rather than giving our citizens simple diet, lifestyle and therapeutic tools to keep them healthy. – Andrew Weil, M.D.

Angelina Jolie – a casualty of a system bereft of common sense?

In this section, we will look at the interesting case of Angelina Jolie's decision to remove her breasts as a preemptive action against cancer. But let us consider first some information available and some of the motivations that could affect the decisions we could make when dealing with cancer:

- Conventional medicine says there is no cure for cancer.

- The logical mind wants a cure.

- Therefore, the logical mind **will not** drive us to steadfastly hold on to a no-cure approach and shut out every other possibility. However, the emotional mind will, and so do those who gain financially.

- Blood reaches every part of our body. Therefore, simple logical syllogistic reasoning suggests that it is unlikely that organ removal, chemotherapy, or radiation treatment will eliminate or kill all mutated or cancer cells. This is because once a person develops cancer or mutated cells, they enter the blood, and once in the blood, they are distributed throughout the body.

For our brain-computer to efficiently generate common sense or sound judgement, it needs accurate knowledge. Because health and disease are highly emotive subjects, these emotions often overshadow logical reasoning. This is especially true regarding cancer. Therefore, it is essential to provide scientific information that is not widely known. This information should at least help reduce the resistance to using simple logic or common sense to make sound judgments when dealing with cancer. Here is some information that is highly relevant and valuable for the logical brain-computer on the subject of cancer.

How essential is oxygen to living cells?

Dr Otto Heinrich Warburg (8 October 1883 – 1 August 1970) was a German physiologist and medical doctor, recognised as one of the leading biochemists of the 20th century. In 1931, he was awarded the Nobel Prize in Physiology or Medicine for his research into cellular respiration (cellular breathing). In 1924, Dr Warburg hypothesised that cancer, malignant growths, and tumours are caused mainly by tumour cells generating energy through the non-oxidative breakdown of glucose. He dedicated considerable time to studying cell life, specialising in cellular respiration.

He believed that since life and death occur at the cellular level, oxygen is the most vital element for life. Consequently, he asked: if something cuts off their oxygen supply, would it cause some cells to die and others to mutate? Mutated cells are considered cancer cells. These cells have been damaged and typically exhibit a reduced capacity to utilise oxygen effectively. To explore whether oxygen deprivation causes cells to die or mutate, he isolated cells from rats and placed them in glass jars. One jar was fully oxygenated, mimicking conditions inside a rat's body. The other jar had oxygen reduced by about 80%. In this jar, all the cells died. A similar outcome occurred at a 75% oxygen reduction. At a 60% reduction, all cells appeared weakened; some died, but most mutated. Does this suggest a link between insufficient oxygen and cancer?

- Insufficient oxygen to the brain causes strokes.

- When tissues and organs are overloaded with acidity, the transport of oxygen is impaired. This suffocation means the cells cannot breathe properly. Every cell in our body needs to breathe in new oxygen and to clear acidic carbon dioxide to function correctly. – Marcus Julian Felicetti (a naturopath and yoga therapist), September 24th, 2012.

- Dr Harry Goldblatt also published a study on the relationship between oxygen and malignant cells in the Journal of Experimental Medicine (1953). He did the same experiment as Dr Warburg and obtained the same result. However, he decided to take it a little bit further. He took fully oxygenated cells and placed them in rats. And he took cells that had mutated because of insufficient oxygen and injected them into other rats. The rats that had been injected with the fully oxygenated cells did not develop cancer. Every one of

the rats that were injected with the oxygen-starved, mutated cells developed cancer.

- Why is it that people very rarely die of cancer of the heart? Have you ever heard of this happening? I certainly haven't. People very seldom get cancer of the heart because that's where the most highly oxygenated blood is, and as the evidence shows, cancer doesn't like oxygen. Cancer likes an anaerobic environment. The more anaerobic the environment, the more favourable it is to cancer growth. The fact that the heart is constantly pumping blood and oxygen seems to have made it almost immune to cancer. According to the Mayo Clinic:

- "Heart cancer is extremely rare. For example, one study reviewed more than 12,000 autopsies and found only seven cases of primary cardiac tumours. At the Mayo Clinic, an average of only one case of heart cancer is seen each year. Although still rare, most cancers found in the heart have come from elsewhere in the body."

- These include lymphomas (cancers of the lymphatic or white blood cells), melanomas (skin cancers), and sarcomas (cancers of the soft connective tissue).

- Dr Warburg reported that cancer cells maintained a lower pH balance, as low as 6.0 (they were more acidic), due to lactic acid production and an increase in carbon dioxide (CO_2). This suggests that cancer thrives in an acidic environment.

- Dr Wendell Hendricks of the Hendricks Research Foundation wrote, "Cancer is a condition within the body where the oxidation has become so depleted that the body cells have degenerated beyond control. The body is so overloaded with toxins that it sets up a tumour mass to harbour these poisons and remove them from general activity within the body."

Are Dr Otto Warburg's findings outdated? Is the suggestion that cancer doesn't like oxygen just an opinion? Is it just a coincidence that heart cancer is so rare that even when it is found there, it did not originate there?

Cancer Research UK: their research that indicated the cure for cancer

The Sunday Express newspaper published a 'landmark' article written by Jo Willey, their Health Correspondent, entitled **"Oxygen kills cancer"** on Sunday,

August 2nd, 2009. She cited the source and basis of the information as, *"The research, published today in the journal Cancer Research, was carried out by scientists from the Cancer Research UK–MRC Gray Institute for Radiation Oncology & Biology at the University of Oxford. They treated mice with certain drugs that improved the stability of blood vessels in the tumours."*

The article declared, "A NEW way of destroying cancer, radically increasing the effectiveness of radiotherapy, was last night heralded as a 'very exciting' breakthrough by scientists.

Previously, experts have tried to cut off the blood supply, fuelling tumour growth to starve and kill it. However, the new method enhances the blood vessels within the tumour, increasing the oxygen concentration... If the oxygen supply within a tumour is increased, cancerous cells become far more sensitive to treatment.

"Instead of boosting a tumour's growth potential, it [oxygen] has the opposite effect and weakens the cancer from the inside, making it far more sensitive to harsh radiotherapy.

"Usually, cancer cells fight to survive, but the new treatment weakens them and makes them less resistant to treatment. Cancers with low oxygen levels are three times more resistant to radiotherapy. So, by restoring oxygen levels to those of a normal cell, the tumours become three times more sensitive to treatment. Additionally, a more stable blood supply in the tumour allows for better delivery of chemotherapy drugs.

"Research was carried out on breast, head and neck cancers as well as carcinomas that line the surface of the skin and organs. But it is hoped the treatment will be as effective in all radiotherapy-treated tumours, including those notoriously hard to treat, such as pancreatic cancer."

On the Cancer Research UK website, another article posted on March 1, 2012, has the headline, **"New clue to how cancer cells beat oxygen starvation"**. The article started with the declaration: **"We need oxygen to survive. Even the cells in the deepest, darkest parts of our bodies can't live without it. But some cancer cells adapt to survive in very low oxygen levels, and these end up being some of the most difficult to treat. Scientists in labs around the world are working to uncover the molecular machinery that allows cells to do this."** However, since the 2009 research demonstrated that cancer cells do not thrive in an oxygenated environment, does logic not suggest that they thrive in the opposite, in a low or non-oxygen environment, as Dr Warburg and others have demonstrated? So, why are they making a big deal about 'New clue to how cancer **cells** beat oxygen starvation', when the 2009 research already showed that cancer cells thrive in an oxygen-starved environment?

The 'how' they survive in such an environment was also stated by Dr Warburg: "Cancer, above all other diseases, has countless secondary causes. But, even for cancer, there is only one prime cause. Summarised in a few words, the prime cause of cancer is the replacement of the respiration of oxygen in normal body cells by a fermentation of sugar." So, cancer is the end product of the cell not being able to efficiently use oxygen to respire and create energy, but resorting to producing an inferior form of energy by the fermentation of sugar. Therefore, cancer doesn't 'beat oxygen starvation'; it is the by-product of oxygen starvation, which produces carbon dioxide and various acids. By-products of fermentation are ethanol (a colourless volatile flammable liquid), lactic acid, and carbon dioxide. So, perhaps they should conclude that cancer thrives in an acidic environment, which causes cells to utilise carbon dioxide to produce energy and survive.

"Every bootlegger knows that as sugars ferment, they bubble. The bubbles are the oxygen leaving. Cancer doesn't like oxygen too well, but it loves sugar. Starting to get the picture here? Fermentation means half-digested, oxygen-poor. This oxygen-deprived environment is perfect for cancer – it thrives in it. Fermentation creates an acidic environment and keeps oxygen away." – Dr Tim O'Shea.

Hopefully, the information above will show that our current approach to cancer treatment and cure can be questioned. The question about the validity of mastectomy and removal of ovaries as preventative measures against cancer is: how do these findings relate to such extreme actions? Most of us, who are not doctors, will feel awe towards them, and we will also trust them to varying degrees. Angelina Jolie's decision to undergo a preventive mastectomy and remove her ovaries indicates a strong trust in the medical advice she received. Like many facing similar risks, her choice may have been driven more by fear than by independent knowledge or reasoning. If we believe the headline that says, "Angelina Jolie reveals she had her ovaries removed over **cancer scare**," it suggests fear played a part. This highlights the significant influence and responsibility of the cancer industry. We should all understand that emotions, including fear, are not inherently bad. They can be positive if they motivate us to act in our own best interest or for the greater good.

It would take either a powerful belief or compelling benefits for any woman to remove two of the defining aspects of her womanhood – her breasts and ovaries. Simple reasoning can easily dismiss any notion of benefits, and no evidence has been presented that qualifies as scientific. Let's see if, through simple reasoning, we can agree that even without detailed knowledge of how cancer develops, basic logic and common sense can still help us evaluate whether specific medical procedures are genuinely effective. What follows is a combination of facts and reasoning:

Removing the breasts and ovaries as a preventative measure against cancer suggests **a *belief*** that these organs are more prone to cause cancer. This must be true, or else such action would be unnecessary and trivial. Triviality should have no place in such life-altering choices.

- There is no proof that the breasts and ovaries have any propensity to cause cancer. Common sense says that such drastic action can only be justified if there is incontrovertible proof. Yet, there is incontrovertible common-sense proof that cancer in the breast is not unique to the breast.

- Evidence from Cancer Research UK shows that cancers in the breast and other regions have responded positively to oxygen infusion. This strongly indicates that cancer, regardless of its location, shares standard features. When considered alongside Dr Otto Warburg's findings on oxygen's role in cellular health, there is at least a strong case for rethinking current strategies, particularly extreme treatments like chemotherapy or the preventative removal of breasts and ovaries.

- The following three bullet points prove this. Since there is no proof that women's breasts inherently 'attract' cancer, it makes no sense to remove them. We know this is not a universal truth because if it were, all women would need to remove their breasts to reduce their chance of getting cancer. This leaves us with the fact that there is no proof either that some women have inherited a 'breast-cancer gene'. There is no such thing as a breast cancer gene that causes cancer. At worst, there is a hereditary gene mutation linked to both breast and ovarian cancer. However, this is not the root cause of cancer, as demonstrated by Dr Warburg, nor does it explain how and why cancer spreads in the body. Cancer (cancer cells) is merely a symptom of the disease. The focus on the symptoms of cancer has led to over one hundred years of research, but no cure, and increasing cancer death rates.

- "Genetic mutations are not the primary cause of cancer but rather a secondary, downstream effect of dysfunctional cell respiration." – Dr Joseph Mercola quoting Thomas Seyfried, Ph.D., a professor of biology at Boston College and a leading expert and researcher in the field of cancer metabolism and nutritional ketosis.

- Since women can survive without their breasts or ovaries, it is not 'breast cancer' or 'ovarian cancer' that kills them. Is cancer found in the breast a type specific to that organ? What about prostate cancer or any other so-called 'type' of cancer? This point is worth emphasising: women do not die from either 'breast cancer' or 'ovarian cancer'. Why is this true? Two reasons support this, based on the fact that cancer found in the breast is not unique to this organ.

- For women suffering from the disease to die, cancer would have to metastasise to organs vital for their survival and necessary for their functioning. Typically, cancer causes death when it spreads from the breast or ovaries to critical organs such as the liver, kidneys, or pancreas. However, if death results from the failure of one of these vital organs, is it still called "breast cancer" or "ovarian cancer"? Or does the name change to indicate the organ affected? These questions highlight a deeper issue: do such cases imply that, regardless of where cancer begins, all cancers may share fundamental traits? If cancer in the breast were truly unique to that organ, how could it subsequently destroy other organs?

- Since there are many other parts of the body that cancer can manifest in, such as the lungs, bowel, skin, lymph, bladder, kidney, brain, pancreas, blood, oesophagus, stomach, mouth, liver, thyroid, and other sites, what is the compelling benefit that justifies the extreme measure of removing the ovaries or breasts?

- Should it be a criminal offence to bypass such simple logic and facilitate and perform this act on any member of the public?

- Are you aware that men can also be diagnosed with 'breast cancer'? How does this fit into the theory of removing breasts as a preventive measure against this 'type' of cancer for women? Since men do not have the same hormonal balance as women but still develop cancer in the breast, doesn't this suggest that this cancer is primarily a location issue and nothing more?

- Cancer cells or malignant tumours are symptoms of the disease, not the disease itself. They are the physical manifestation of the effect, and this effect has a cause. If this were not true, removing cancer cells or the malignant tumour would cure the disease entirely. However, this is not usually the case. In reality, people are often told they are in remission or given the 'all-clear', only for the disease to return. Remission means there are no visible signs of the disease. So, the numerous instances of the disease returning demonstrate the simple, logical, common-sense truth: the cause was not addressed, and you cannot resolve a problem without identifying and eliminating its root cause. Therefore, focusing solely on the symptoms of cancer does not make sense if your goal is to survive and be well. It also does not bring us any closer to a root-cause solution.

- Just in case you think that the description 'breast cancer' or 'prostate cancer' only indicates where cancer starts, this is not the case. The fact that donations are sought for research into these 'types' of cancers should dispel any such notion. Moreover, there are organisations explicitly dedicated to tackling these 'types' of cancers. For example, organisations like Breast Cancer UK state their goal as eliminating the causes of the disease so that fewer people die from it.

- The Prostate Cancer Research Centre describes their work as follows: *...they conduct research into the causes of and treatments for the UK's most frequently diagnosed male cancer.* Regarding their findings, they stated: "Prostate cancer is curable while it is confined to the prostate, but very difficult to treat once it spreads outside the prostate." This clearly states that even when cancer spreads outside of the prostate, it is still considered 'prostate cancer'. It also confirms that cancer found in the prostate is not unique to this organ, as it can spread. And it has long been understood that cancer must affect a vital organ for a person to die.

- Cancer Research UK states: "Prostate cancer is the most common cancer in men in the UK – 41,000 fathers, brothers, and sons are diagnosed with the disease each year. Although survival rates have significantly improved, the disease still claims 11,000 lives annually."

- Here's something you can be certain of: if a person dies from cancer in a vital organ like the liver, pancreas, or kidneys, but the cancer started in the breast or prostate without being recognised, they would be recorded as dying from cancer named after those organs or given a general cancer diagnosis. We know this because millions of people are reported to have died from breast and prostate cancer; however, the failure of these organs would not necessarily have caused their deaths.

A simple way to determine how effective cancer treatment is:

- ***Check the annual death rate from cancer in countries with free treatment. Nearly all European nations have universal health care. Still, 1.9 million people die from cancer each year. In the UK, the annual death toll is 165,000.***

- Since it is free, the vast majority of a large number of those who died would have been treated.

- When the effectiveness of cancer treatment is attributed to "catching it early," the claim can be misleading, particularly if chemotherapy was used. Why? Because early detection typically refers to identifying cancer cells before they multiply or metastasise, not to addressing the root cause of the disease.

- And according to Dr Dean Black, "Some original work was done by American Cancer Society researcher Robert Schimke in 1985, who discovered that the way cancer cells resist chemotherapy is to replicate even harder and faster… tumours seemed to come back with such a vengeance after chemotherapy."

Does it make sense for there to be a lack of checks and balances on the cancer industry?

The lengthy period during which the organisations entrusted with finding a cure for cancer have failed to do so should have prompted the question of why checks and balances were not established. There are several reasons why the progress of such organisations should have been closely monitored.

- Governments recognise naturopathic medicine, but because there is no system to scientifically test its effectiveness in curing cancer, this approach is not officially acknowledged as a legitimate alternative to allopathic medicine, which governments are legally obliged to validate. As a result, governments often rely solely on information from the allopathic medical perspective. Consequently, the system generally operates as if only one type of medicine deserves our time and resources. Relying exclusively on a single point of view for problem-solving, especially in the case of the cancer industry, is illogical.

- Millions of lives have been lost, and many more are at risk, including those in leadership. It should be common sense that any organisation generating tens of billions of pounds and mostly self-governing will have considerable self-interest. When such vast sums are involved, self-interest can become dangerously deceptive.

- Such a hugely profitable industry, which almost regulates itself and has never been prosecuted for its lack of tangible progress, would become rigid in its approach to testing and adopting any cure that isn't profitable.

- What if current approaches cannot find a cure? What if allopathic medicine isn't the answer? How can we assess whether alternative methods can provide a solution if there is no system to test them rigorously? Is saving millions of lives worth establishing such a system, or should we wait until the prediction that cancer rates will double by 2050 materialises?

The challenge of being human doesn't end after we learn how to survive. We also have to learn how to attain the universal quest for happiness.

CHAPTER SIX

The fourth major life issue to which Aristotelian syllogistic reasoning applies: **Common sense concerning old age, culture, and enduring happiness**

If you often feel bored, it might be because you are a boring person. Try to develop as many interests as you can. The more interests you explore, the more engaged you will be with life, and this will uncover more opportunities for you to fulfil your desires.

Happiness is the universal pursuit of life. You will never meet anyone who says they don't want to be happy. This is as certain as never meeting someone who would not want to be attractive.

Syllogistic logic on happiness

- Everyone wants enduring happiness, but not everyone knows how to achieve it.
- Happiness is a state of mind.
- We must learn what state of mind produces happiness.
- If we adopt such a state of mind, we will enjoy happiness.

The following account concerning happiness and the antidote to suicide is grounded in an understanding of introductory human psychology and straightforward logic, or simple syllogistic reasoning. How much insight do you have into how to attain *lasting* happiness? From the way this question is phrased, you would realise that it does not refer to simply knowing how to enjoy oneself. We all know how to do that, yet the world still has many unhappy people, some of whom are considered "successful".

As already mentioned, at each stage of our development, we can fall in love with or become comfortable with the person we are at that point. We may become at ease with being a cynic, expecting the worst in most situations. Yet paradoxically, even though happiness is a universal goal, adopting a cynical mindset ultimately works against it. This is because we often get what we expect. In effect, the cynic has unconsciously chosen not to be happy. Cynicism and optimism are incompatible attitudes. Optimism is a foundation for lasting happiness, and cynicism will only foster fleeting happiness at best. Due to life's inevitable trials, optimism is an essential attitude to counteract the power of disappointments. Without it, disappointments will overwhelm us. Nature serves as the greatest teacher of optimism. No matter how often a tree is damaged, it will regrow to its full capacity. If an animal loses its offspring, it will continue to reproduce. It seems as if it knows that life is meant to be *lived*. Nature is constantly regenerating, like a fountain of optimism. The best philosophy of optimism ever spoken is, *"Every day above ground is a good day!"* It is as if this person had read the book of life. This is precisely the philosophy of the tree.

Enduring happiness develops after designing a life based on our ability to create a mental picture of a future we eagerly anticipate — a future we can genuinely enjoy. The act of taking steps to turn this vision of the future into reality stimulates our senses. Many of us have experienced this while organising a holiday or a wedding. However, how many have applied this principle to designing and planning their lives? Happiness springs from cultivating a philosophy of contentment. It originates from being genuinely interested in things worth living for, or loving what you look forward to seeing or experiencing each day. It grows from feeling proud of the disciplined effort we've employed to navigate all of life's highs and lows. It's akin to the pride felt after completing a marathon, knowing the ordeal did not defeat you but strengthened you.

Happiness is a skill

We have the ability as humans to train ourselves to see many seemingly ordinary life moments as fascinating. Do you find it intriguing that when children meet for the first time, they often become instant friends? Even before they know each other's names, they could be hugging, laughing, and playing. They can do this because they have not yet developed the many hang-ups of adults. Isn't it fascinating that an ant can carry something bigger than itself? Someone once said, "The essence of intelligence is having the skill to extract meaning from everyday experiences."

A key skill for happiness is developing our emotional intelligence. Learning how to feel about different parts of life's experiences is crucial for achieving happiness. Did you know that the words we choose to describe life's events can significantly influence our sense of joy? For a more detailed explanation, I recommend Anthony Robbins' *"Awaken the Giant Within"*. In this book, he

provides a compelling example of how metaphors can impact our mindset. Imagine someone habitually describing their life experiences as: "I am struggling to keep my head above water". What image does this evoke in the subconscious mind? It suggests a person drowning. How confident and happy can someone be with such a mindset?

How many things in life bring you happiness? How about a good book? An engaging debate? How about sitting in a tree swaying in a cool summer breeze? Or feeling a gentle, not-too-cold wind on your face? Have you visited a Caribbean island and smelled the earth after rain? Have you been in a house and heard the wind rushing past while the rain plays music on the roof? These are just a few of life's experiences that can inspire happiness, but it depends on our emotional intelligence and ability to find joy in life. Do you ever *experience the rain*, or do you only get wet? Were you aware that there are two ways to experience this event? The more experiences in life from which you can draw joy, the happier you will be. Is a sunset a moment of beauty to savour, or a sign that it is getting late?

Imagine you're walking with someone and you stop to enjoy a beautiful sunset. The person merely glances at it, checks their watch, and says, "It's getting late, we should get going." Wow! What's the difference between the two of you? The difference is one sunset but two different emotions. The ability to find joy in the rain and Nature, in general, can be part of your formula for experiencing *lasting* happiness. Why? Because Nature is a constant presence in life that isn't temperamental, unlike many other human interactions that can change and disappoint us. **Should it not be common sense that we are meant to maximise our ability to enjoy the natural pleasures that surround and touch us? We can learn how to enjoy the rain instead of just getting wet!**

Antidote against suicide

"Murder is bad, suicide is sad." – Lt. Columbo (popular fictional detective)

Simple syllogistic logic against suicide:

- Irrespective of the state of our health, the body wants to live.
- We cannot hold our breath until life stops.
- The body will also resist being suffocated by another, even when in a poor state of health.

- Therefore, if the mind is in harmony with the body, there is no suicide.

Hope, anticipation, acceptance of life as it is, and confidence in our ability to influence changeable things are essential elements for our emotional well-being. Without these, despair, depression, and even suicide can occur. Even if you have never known a loved one who has taken their own life, understanding human psychology, perception, and the typical consequences of such tragedies indicates that coping with suicide is often more traumatic than dealing with death by accident or murder. Why is this true, despite each situation involving sadness and possibly anger?

- Murder and accidents can evoke anger, but in the case of suicide, whom can the survivors direct their fury towards? Inevitably, those closest to the deceased will agonise over whether they are to blame or if they could have done something to prevent it. They will often torment themselves with the question, "How come I hadn't noticed any signs?" In some cases, relationships may be shattered because blame was unjustly placed on a convenient 'victim(s)'.

- Those who have ever considered suicide should recognise that such an act would cause immense pain and suffering to those who love them. Could this realisation serve as a deterrent? I don't know, but I hope it might in some cases.

Here is a fascinating scenario to consider. It reveals how profound we are as human beings. On one hand, we have a situation where the World Health Organisation (WHO) has estimated that every forty seconds, someone takes their own life. On the other hand, there is Valeri Spidonov. He is a 30-year-old Russian man suffering from Werdnig-Hoffmann disease, which causes his muscles to waste away. This means his health is rapidly declining. He has volunteered to be the first person to undergo a body transplant. An Italian surgeon, Sergio Canavero, has claimed that he could transplant his head onto a donor's body. Spidonov has volunteered, even though one expert has warned that he could suffer something "a lot worse than death". China has agreed to facilitate this operation, with an expected date set for 2016. How do we account for such an extreme contrast in our attitude towards life? As human beings, we are usually afraid of the unknown—yet it's hard to imagine anything more unknown or frightening than this. Still, this man volunteered for a procedure that has never been performed, all for a chance, however uncertain, to preserve

his life. The point is this: some of us are willing to go to extraordinary lengths to stay alive.

The 'plot' thickens when we consider the professions that rank highest in suicide rates in America. These careers are among the most lucrative but are also regarded as highly stressful. The point is, these are non-disabled individuals with the 'world at their feet'. It's reasonable to question whether their lives are more stressful than those of someone like Valeri Spidonov or many poor and desperate people around the world. Here is a list of what is said to be the top ten professions with the highest suicide rates.

1. Doctors
2. Dentists
3. Financial workers
4. Lawyers
5. Police officers
6. Real estate agents
7. Electricians
8. Farmers
9. Pharmacists
10. Scientists

Life is meant to be a challenge to anticipate, instead of a series of problems to avoid

For suicide to occur, a person's reason for living must be significantly weaker than their problems or perceived problems. The accumulated pain has to outweigh the joy of being alive. Have you heard that a stressful situation is a matter of interpretation? This would not include situations where someone is holding a gun to your head or running towards you with a machete. Simple logic suggests that such situations should cause stress, and if possible, you should run! However, not everyone reacts to life's experiences in the same way. So, what makes the difference? Why do some of us have an unstoppable drive to live regardless of what life throws at us, while others do not? Common sense says it is an internal matter. It must relate to our twin driving forces – our philosophy and emotions. These forces are supposed to serve us in our pursuit of survival and happiness – they should be our equivalent of the usually successful instinct of animals. They should be the power that strengthens us against the poison of overwhelming hostile forces, enabling us to interpret events correctly and respond appropriately.

So, when should we begin cultivating this power or antidote? What if parents started with their children? What if they ensured that a child understands and accepts that life is not meant to be easy? What if they provided a perspective and a vocabulary of life that promotes the idea that *life is meant to be a challenge to anticipate, rather than a series of problems to avoid?* The mental and emotional growth resulting from this transformation will make them stronger and better, and thus worth the effort. Eliminating the possibility of suicide is not the only benefit that will arise from such personal growth. It will also evoke one of the immutable laws of Nature: we usually reap much more than we sow. This is because many of the antidotes against suicide are also the elixirs of happiness.

A gem cannot be polished without friction, nor a man perfected without trials. – Chinese proverb

---

"Winners develop mental toughness, which we commonly refer to as strength of character. Experiments have proven that adversities and failures in our lives, if adapted to and viewed as normal corrective feedback to use to get back on target, serve to develop in us an immunity against anxiety, depression and the adverse responses to stress." – Dr Denis Waitley (The Psychology of Winning)

Genuine learning happens when we consistently act on what we have seen, heard, or felt. The real question, then, is whether what we learn—and choose to act on—is truly in our best interest. And that, at times, is not easy to determine.

Having the right philosophy and attitude towards life eliminates the possibility of suicide. We have absolute control over only one thing: our thoughts. It is our responsibility to use this power to shape our emotions and attitudes. The more mastery we develop over this dynamic process, the more empowered we become. However, if we fail to take full ownership of this power, we may find ourselves overwhelmed by feelings of helplessness, frustration, futility, and even depression. This can contribute to the high rates of suicide. What if you interacted with life and lived in a way that made you feel awe-inspired? What if you became captivated by life's beauty, its mystery, and its challenges? What

if you viewed life's difficulties as challenges rather than problems, and looked forward to testing yourself against them? Here is the answer:

An awe-inspired life does not lead to suicide. A healthy mind and spirit are the driving force behind such a life. Such a mind will not constantly seek reasons to justify being alive; it is too engaged with life to entertain such a thought. Its attitude is one of, "I haven't got time to die right now, I've got too many things to do, see, and experience!" Such a mind is enthusiastic and connected to living. Nature can wow and enthral even the most indifferent among us. So, if we fall in love with Nature, it would be virtually impossible for suicide to become a reality because such a love will never be spurned. Nature has a way of engaging us and awakening indescribable feelings of wonderment that, once experienced and loved, never leave us and will always have us wanting more. Nature can be genuinely therapeutic. However, the life-enhancing benefits of living in a rural setting can be reduced if it leads to social isolation and less face-to-face contact with family and friends.

Urbanicity – the degree to which a geographical unit is urban

The term urbanism has signified several different ideas. Still, Louis Wirth was most influential in defining urbanism as a condition characterised by a loss of tradition and close family ties, and so much social and spatial mobility that people lose all of the virtues of the folk community. While some theorists challenged the negativity of this view, we all agree that urbanism is a way of life, one that is typical of the city, especially the larger city or metropolis. (www.urbanicity.us/Urbanicity.html)

Here is some food for thought related to stress and suicide: "Our bodies are made up of about 60 per cent water, which conducts electricity well. The Earth carries a negative ionic charge. Going barefoot grounds our bodies to that charge. Negative ions have been shown to detoxify, calm, reduce inflammation, synchronise your internal clocks, hormonal cycles, and physiological rhythms. The best places to absorb negative ions through your feet are near water. Everyone knows how soothing it is to be barefoot on the beach – now we understand why!" – Stephanie Slone (Reflexologist and Reiki practitioner)

Urbanicity can cause people's spirits to detach from reality. City living often involves a very artificial environment. We may have neighbours whom we rarely see, and people are usually less friendly than those in rural areas. Why is this? Common sense suggests that urban living—particularly the predominantly indoor lifestyle—plays a role. This way of life can diminish social interaction, and many homes lack even a porch where one might sit and watch the world go by. The artificial nature of city life often causes a disconnect from nature: many people never see how food is grown, encounter only a few trees, and live in skyscrapers without ever stepping on the ground that sustains and nourishes us. They live in an environment dominated by concrete, metal, and electromagnetic pollution. All of this can contribute to an unfriendly attitude.

These are some general thoughts on suicide that ought to be common sense:

- No child with a healthy mind imagines that they will someday commit suicide.
- No child with a healthy mind ever imagines that they will one day commit suicide for any reason. It must be the result of the absence of the right philosophy and emotions, and conversely, the accumulation of the wrong philosophy and emotions, where the mind becomes unhealthy.

The act of committing suicide contradicts the innate drive to survive. It thus highlights that the human mind is highly adaptable or programmable. This exemplifies the blank-slate principle. Common sense advises us to shield our minds from thoughts that threaten our survival or reduce our enjoyment of life.

Everybody needs to be programmed. A program is only bad if it is not in your best interest.

It is important to note that men are four times more likely to commit suicide than women. This shows that there are other strengths beyond the physical that we should respect. Simple logic indicates that stress and depression are not fixed experiences; rather, it is our interpretation of these events and feelings that creates mental and emotional strain. This fact is illustrated by the reality that many people can have the same experiences but react differently. Therefore, it is in your best interest to continuously develop your ability to handle potentially stressful situations. The wisdom of age, "This too shall pass," can serve as a mantra to diminish and neutralise situations that might become overwhelming.

"This too shall pass" is a truism from which we all can benefit. How many times have you heard someone express bemusement about a celebrity who ruined their career with drugs or committed suicide? They often point out that many are 'fighting' to be in their position, and many others can only dream of achieving what they have. They also claim they would love to be in these successful people's position, confident that they would handle it better. The question is, how can they be sure? Success and money are highly emotional. It therefore requires intellectual and emotional growth to manage them well. This means that if someone experiences success and wealth for the first time but hasn't grown enough to take control of it, they will end up being controlled by it. Those struggling to cope with the pressures of success and fame would benefit from recognising that the solution is always within. They must learn how to access it. Personal development, as we know, is the key. **It is that which inoculates against the *very fleeting* pleasures that drugs can bring. Personal development inoculates us against needing physical substances to produce a sense of well-being or 'happiness'. It is what inoculates against any thought of suicide.**

The song "Grooving Out on Life" pays homage to Nature. Nature, the extraordinary life and pleasure giver, can give to, and never disappoint, those who have developed the capacity to love and enjoy its gifts.

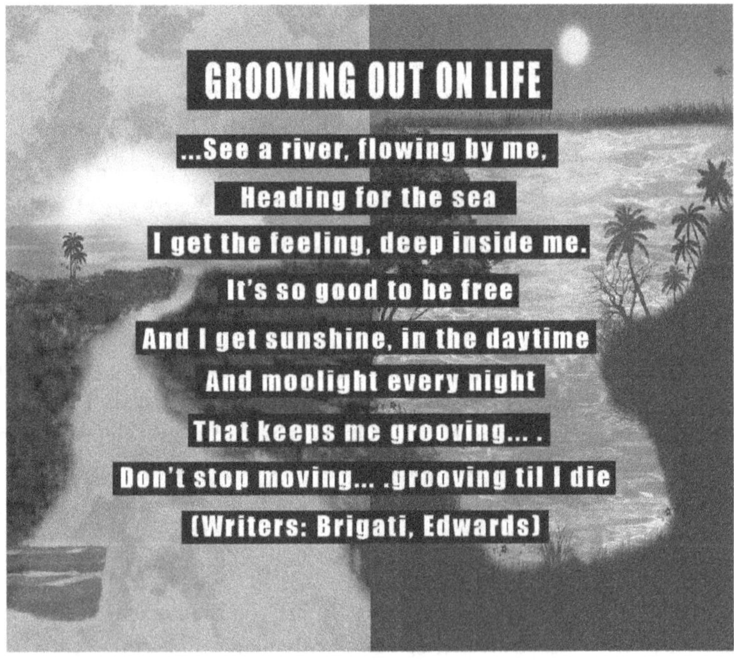

Who would volunteer to give up the above awesome experiences?

Simple wisdom that does not require much syllogistic reasoning – a variety of strengths

It takes strength to recognise our weaknesses and to ask for help. It's a mature, mental, and emotional philosophy that recognises that no one stands alone and that we can all use a little help sometimes. From this philosophical and emotional awakening, we can set aside our ego and seek out those who can help.

It takes strength to cry when it's appropriate. Crying is part of our emotional balance, just as laughing is. It helps reduce the body's stress levels.

It takes strength to admit when we are wrong and to apologise. This act can also help reduce our stress levels. Not apologising sends the message that you don't care about the other person's feelings. If you don't care, then it's a moot point.

Simple wisdom – an ode to being alive!

Today, I am adopting a philosophy and attitude that will protect me from failure, depression, and boredom.

I accept that life is complex and will always have its hardships. This is because the human mind and emotions are characterised by great diversity and contradictions.

I accept that life is not meant to be easy, so I am at peace with reality. If it were, the entire Earth would have fertile land, sufficient water, a welcoming climate, and abundant minerals and resources everywhere.

I acknowledge that I need to develop mentally and emotionally to handle life more effortlessly, and I am prepared for it.

I will find joy in facing and enjoying life's challenges. I will find joy in both my minor and major accomplishments.

I will find joy in all aspects of the Earth and the universe where I live.

I will always ask for another day, another taste of the rain; another taste of the sun, the moon, and stars, and other joys and challenges Nature offers because I relish this human experience, warts and all.

I am in control of my life. I endeavour not to worry about things I cannot change. Therefore, I choose how I respond to any of life's experiences and events. Some scientists claim the universe will end in five billion years. Just don't mention it to Tom—he'll start worrying. Do you know anyone who worries about many things they can do nothing about?

I will always aim to see unwanted experiences and events positively.

Common sense on growing old

Ageing is an inevitability. The culture we develop will dictate how we feel about it.

Growing old beats the alternative – dying young.

Basic syllogistic reasoning about ageing.

- A well-nourished mind does not feel ponderous or aged.

- The body can sustain health and fitness for over a hundred years.

- Katsusuke Yanagisawa, aged 71, ascended the world's highest mountain, Everest, at 29,035 feet (8,850 m).

- Hulda Crooks, aged 91, ascended Japan's highest mountain at 12,385 feet. She successfully scaled 14,505-foot (4,421 m) Mount Whitney 23 times between the ages of 65 and 91. During this period, she had also climbed 97 other peaks.

- Therefore, the fear of old age is not caused by a rational mind filled with accurate knowledge.

It is undoubtedly true that many fear growing old. At least, they do not look forward to it. Some individuals have declared that they would not want to live beyond a certain age they consider to be old. Such persons have not developed their understanding of how life and ageing work. Life and time accumulate through tiny increments of seconds that become days, and today does not feel different from yesterday. A mind filled with anticipation and joy does not want to end its human experience, which we call death. It's only a mind lacking anticipation of the future that may desire to end its earthly experiences. A person who arbitrarily sets an age they wouldn't want to exceed may not realise that the mind itself does not age. Therefore, whatever age we select, if the body and mind remain healthy, the mind will not want to die. If they understood this, they would not make such a statement. Here are some other reasons why they might choose a cut-off date for being alive.

- Some people believe that at a certain age, they will no longer be able to move freely or perform other physical activities. If sex is the focus of their life, they may also consider how long they want to live based on that. In this case, they have not broadened their sense of happiness and fail to see that life can contain joy beyond sexual pleasure.

- Many associate a certain age with looking decrepit. It is a fact that most people don't age very well. However, this is mainly due to diet and lifestyle and is, therefore, something within our control.

- Many associate various ages with debilitating illnesses, or 'old people's diseases' – they don't realise that good health can be preserved into a hundred years and beyond. If they paid attention, they would see that many so-called 'old people's diseases' are increasingly found among young people. Ageing is not an unavoidable precursor to diseases.

A wrinkled body does not necessarily indicate a poor life experience. Your mind is the centre of your existence. Being captivated by the endless mysteries and wonders of life can keep you in awe forever. A highly developed sense of reality will deposit in our emotional bank account the understanding that simply being alive is a joy in itself. The philosophy that states, "Every day above ground is a good day," belongs to those who have cultivated their senses to appreciate the wondrous brilliance of our existence. It's a mindset that recognises that death is unavoidable, and we will be dead much longer than we are alive. Therefore, we are compelled to extract joy from every moment of our earthly journey. This is a wise outlook because there is no definitive answer as to what happens after death.

Cause and effect… insight, our great potential

In today's complex world, the outcomes of our most vital actions should be widely understood. Here are a few examples:

- If you don't eat enough fruits and vegetables, what are the likely consequences or effects?

- If you eat junk food, what are the likely consequences or effects?

- If you don't save or invest money, what are the likely consequences or effects?

In the critical aspects of our lives, every action or inaction has consequences. The ability to identify the effect resulting from a given cause is based on syllogistic reasoning or common sense. We don't need to be geniuses to know the consequences of many of our actions. For example, most of us should be able to see the possible consequences of walking up to a policeman and

punching him in the face without provocation. Surely you should be able to foresee the following possibilities:

- You would, at the very least, envisage a future where you are in detention and facing the stigma of undergoing a psychiatric assessment.

- Or worse, you might find yourself on the floor with him asking you the reasonable question, "Are you crazy?!" while pummelling you into the ground.

- And even worse, you could be shot! (Depending on which country you are in).

One of the greatest strengths of insight is the ability to predict how our current actions will influence our future. Insight comes from accurate knowledge about life and people. Using it to assess our life in terms of scope, direction, and destination is the best way to utilise this personal development skill. Simple logic applied to the consequences of our actions or inactions can generate the common sense needed to help us steer life towards happiness.

Mavis embraced a philosophy that life should be lived to the fullest. Her mantra was, "Live full and die empty." While inspiring, this philosophy can be interpreted in both positive and negative ways, as the idea of "living life to the fullest" is highly subjective. For example, one day, a stranger in her neighbourhood saw her on her porch smoking a cigar. He approached her and said, "Excuse me, Ma'am, what is your secret for looking so happy?" She responded, "I smoke ten cigars a day, and before I go to bed, I smoke a big joint. I also drink a whole bottle of Jack Daniels every week and eat only junk food – no fruits, vegetables, or anything natural. On weekends, I pop pills, have sex, and I don't do any exercise." He exclaimed, "That is amazing! Do you mind telling me how old you are?" "Forty," she replied.

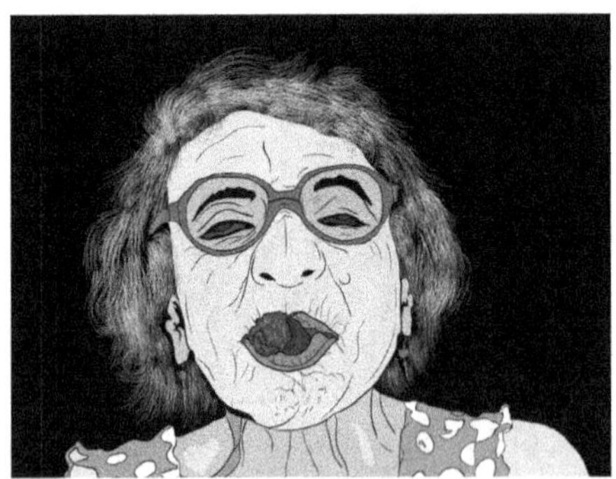

Common sense and culture, its effect on happiness – the story of Jeung Ling

Simple syllogistic reasoning:

- People are generally influenced by their culture.
- Culture offers rules meant to guide effective living.
- If a culture results in practices that limit survival and happiness, it must adapt.

Culture can be described as the ideas, customs, rules, and social behaviours of a particular people or society. It encompasses people's value systems and the methods they use to solve their problems. For example, arranged marriage—a cultural practice that was common worldwide until the 18th century—involves a third party, usually the parents, selecting the bride and groom instead of the individuals choosing for themselves. It is based on the belief that parents are better equipped to determine a suitable match for long-term happiness. This practice partly rests on the assumption that young people may prioritise immediate pleasure over long-term compatibility. Conversely, parents are thought to adopt a more analytical and future-oriented approach.

This is one of those cultural practices where it is not easy to determine if it is better, in terms of happiness and longevity, than other practices such as Western love marriages. While assessing happiness levels in arranged marriages is challenging, some cultural practices are undeniably harmful and cannot withstand rational scrutiny, whether based on common sense or other reasoning methods. One such practice is female circumcision, more accurately called female genital mutilation (FGM). What problem is this intended to solve? What benefit does it provide? The only lesson we can learn from this is what *to* avoid. It also emphasises that we are like blank slates, shaped by whatever is inscribed upon us. The effects of some cultural practices are clear, while others are more subtle. Often, we are simply products of the cultural beliefs and traditions we inherit.

China has cultural practices that have serious implications for its social and perhaps economic structure. For example, like many countries in the world, she has a male bias in terms of dominant roles within that culture. However, her particular application of this aspect of her cultural modality has had a devastating effect on my friend Jeung Ling. Jeung Ling retired to China from the UK after several decades of hard work building a business with his wife.

They have three daughters. While back in China, the cultural influences of his upbringing related to children began to tug at him.

China is the world's most populous country, and its population has been steadily rising. According to *Internet World Stats*, their population was 1,361,512,535 (1.362 billion) in 2015. This seems to support the need for the Chinese government's "one-child-per-couple " policy.

After settling back in China for a few years, Jeung Ling decided he wanted a son. However, his wife was past childbearing age, so he sought another woman who could have children. When his wife found out about the affair, she left him. The marriage ended in divorce, and she took half his assets, significantly reducing the quality of his retirement plans.

Over time, his girlfriend became pregnant. Sadly, due to misinformation claiming the foetus was female, she decided to have an abortion and blamed Jeung Ling for the situation. The loss was profoundly distressing for both of them, and ultimately, their relationship disintegrated. Now, Jeung Ling is an unhappy man. Was he a victim of cultural pressures or the architect of his misfortune? What are your thoughts?

Common sense laws for life and living: The story of Hershel Brown

There is a universal law of life that Hershel Brown and millions of others are unaware of. This should be one of the laws of life that is widely recognised and accepted. Essentially, this law should be common sense. Jim Rohn, the late great philosopher, promoted a universal principle that applies to all human life. Even when viewed from many perspectives, no weaknesses are apparent. It is like the unbreakable mathematical formula of 2 + 2 = 4. This is what he said:

- Philosophy = Attitude = Activity = Result, or from another point of view, it can also be explained this way:
- Culture = Attitude = Activity =Result

What we believe or hold as our personal philosophy and cultural outlook shapes our feelings (our attitude). Our emotions influence our choices of activities, which in turn determine our results. This demonstrates the universal law of **cause and effect**, a principle more essential to study and practise than any other law governing our existence. It is like a chain reaction, similar to the ripples caused when a pebble is dropped into a still pond. The *pebble represents the cause*, and each ripple indicates *one of the effects*. Our lives resemble this pattern, but crucially, we often fail to recognise the direct consequences of our thoughts and actions. Most of us rarely see a clear connection between our thoughts, our attitude, and the undesired results that follow.

In testing the strength of your emotional navigation system, here are some questions for you: How much would you sell one of your arms for? How about a leg? And a finger? Is your answer, "not at any price"? Not even your 'pinky' finger? I have often joked with people about these questions. The purpose is to emphasise the value of our billion-dollar bodies and to highlight the contradiction shown by our actions. Our actions often seem to suggest that we place very little value on our bodies. This provides the perfect backdrop for you to learn the story of Hershel Brown. Hershel epitomises millions of people who are unaware of the consequences of their thoughts and actions and, therefore, suffer the consequences as a result. They lack insight, a synonym for common sense.

Hershel Brown had a few flaws in his philosophy, attitude, and habits — one of which was a distinct sweet tooth. He loved sugary treats and often indulged. He also enjoyed baked goods, typically made with unhealthy, bleached white flour. He was frequently warned, "Man-made, concentrated sugar is not food because it has NO essential nutrients and is just empty calories."

The fact is, the human body does not respond well to concentrated sugars and empty calories. The evidence lies in the diseases linked to sugar consumption—diabetes, heart disease, high blood pressure, and obesity, to name a few. Hershel would listen and nod in agreement, but secretly, he was addicted. Sugar is one of the most harmful and addictive synthetic substances around. His cravings usually overrode any insight he gained from the advice he received, and the brief pleasure of the moment would outweigh any awareness of the long-term consequences.

Hershel had a longstanding relationship with his live-in girlfriend. Like many men shaped by a patriarchal system, he didn't treat his partner with the honour and respect that would naturally exist in a society where women are true equals. In many instances where he should have consulted her or sought her input, he chose to act unilaterally.

On one occasion, he made a decision that, in hindsight, should have been obvious: he should have discussed it with his partner first. However, he chose not to, justifying his silence by claiming that women are "too emotional." Later, he received advice intended to challenge this common misconception. He was taught something that ought to be common sense: women are not more emotional than men; they express certain emotions more openly.

He was once asked whether men are more aggressive than women, and he replied, "Yes." It was then pointed out that aggression comes from emotion, so wouldn't that imply men are more emotional than women? Should that have

been a "case closed" moment? Perhaps. Yet the original point remains valid: women may display certain emotions more than men, but that does not make them more emotional overall.

In truth, Hershel was very secretive with his partner. I once joked that the last time he told her anything was the time of day—and even then, only because she insisted. Logic rarely overrides emotional conditioning, and this understanding should be common sense. Still, the truth didn't change his attitude. Hershel wasn't entirely to blame for his views. For better or worse, we inherited a deeply flawed patriarchal culture—one famously captured in James Brown's song, *"It's a Man's World."* Hershel was, in many ways, a product and a victim of that worldview.

Hershel, like many others, had poor financial habits. Nonetheless, he was clever enough to buy a property and rent it out. However, at a certain point, he felt the need to sell it for reasons that seemed important at the time. He was advised to remortgage the property, extract some equity, and retain it. He was even given a piece of financial wisdom that should be obvious: properties in good locations tend to double in value every ten years. That's why banks are so eager to offer loans for real estate—property is one of the most stable and reliable investments.

As someone once said, "God will always make more people, but not more land." Needless to say, Hershel sold the property.

Sometime afterwards, he began driving an expensive, high-maintenance vehicle. A few years later, he lost his well-paid job and struggled to find another. Consequently, he bounced from one low-paid job to the next.

Do you think he would have found the rental valuable property at that time? Did buying the new car suggest he had exchanged an appreciating asset for a depreciating one? Unless it's a rare collector's item, a vehicle is not a true asset — it costs you money and gradually loses value. A car can depreciate so much that it eventually costs money to dispose of it. Shouldn't this be common sense?

All the actions we take—shaped by our philosophies and attitudes—tend to have a cumulative effect. Sometimes, what we do or don't do might seem trivial at first, but the consequences eventually become clear. Hershel's first significant consequence of poor dietary choices was diabetes. He lost a leg as a result.

He then fell behind on his mortgage and eventually lost his home. Because of his disability, the local council rehoused him. His failure to show proper care, respect, and attention to his partner also built up over time. The final blow was when she found out he had another woman. She left him.

Hershel didn't see this as a tragedy; he believed the other woman loved him and planned to move in with him. What he didn't realise was that she loved both of his legs, and one wasn't enough, so she left him too.

Now, based on your understanding of the human drama, what do you think the final years of Hershel's life are likely to be like?

Our survival and happiness are at risk if we do not use the proper knowledge to care for our food and the Earth, where we all live.

CHAPTER SEVEN

The fifth major life issue to which Aristotelian syllogistic reasoning applies: **Caring for Mother Earth, the environment, our food, and the absence of common sense**

Simple syllogistic logic:

The Earth's natural resources have sustained life for over 4 billion years, mainly through the natural process of decomposition, which produces what we call humus. It is the stable, fully decomposed organic matter that naturally forms in the soil over decades or centuries. It's the dark, nutrient-rich part of soil resulting from the complete breakdown of organic materials by soil organisms.

Humus or natural fertilisers are known to maintain and improve soil fertility.

- Unlike artificial fertilisers, humus enriches the soil without harmful side effects and supports long-term ecological balance.
- Food grown with natural fertiliser tends to be more wholesome and better suited to the natural needs of living organisms.
- Our bodies, like those of other living beings, are better suited to what is natural.
- Therefore, food grown with humus, a natural fertiliser, is best suited to support and sustain all forms of life.
- Compost is also a natural fertiliser we can produce. It's the decomposition of natural organic material that will eventually become humus over time. A dark, rich organic substance that enriches the soil.

What is the Earth?

Is the Earth simply a collection of dirt, rocks, minerals, and water—or is it also a living, breathing, and intelligent being? Could it be anything less and still possess the ability to support living, breathing, and intelligent life?

Even if you don't accept the idea that the Earth itself is alive, perhaps you can agree on this: it deserves the utmost care because it is currently the only home we have. Unfortunately, we are not doing a great job of caring for our planet. Alongside this neglect, the dominant mindset of subjugating nature—of bending it to fit our limited way of thinking—has become far too widespread.

Since nature's systems have supported life on Earth for over 4 billion years and sustained human existence for more than 190,000 years before the introduction of artificial fertilisers and pesticides, it is reasonable to assume that our role is to understand and adhere to the Earth's natural methods of production.

One of the clearest examples of a lack of common sense is the widespread use of unnatural chemical fertilisers to grow food. It is a typical case of mankind, motivated by profit, trying to outsmart and replace Nature. Because of this misguided philosophy, the natural way—Nature's way—has become a minority method of farming.

Food produced naturally is called organic, and ironically, it tends to be more costly. Can it be proven that organic foods are superior? Yes—and one of the clearest examples is bananas. Organic bananas ripen very quickly and, as a result, also rot faster. During ripening, they develop speckles on their skin, which is a natural sign of their maturity and freshness.

In contrast, non-organic bananas often take considerably longer to ripen and sometimes become less tasty or fail to ripen properly at all. This example highlights a broader issue: artificial fertilisers dominate global food production, leading to a significant deviation from what is natural and what is, arguably, common sense.

Historical background of the use of pesticides

The historical background of fertiliser use, coupled with advances in scientific understanding, can help develop a hypothesis using a *syllogistic reasoning framework*. This logical structure allows us to evaluate better and comprehend this critically important subject. In *The Secret Life of Plants*, authors Peter Tompkins and Christopher Bird share a compelling story related to the use of nitrogen-based fertilisers. The following are the key details of the case they presented.

- They cited the fact that George Washington Carver (1861–1943) had revitalised the soils of Alabama, USA, by **rotating crops** and fertilising the soil with **natural humus**. *This demonstrated what should be common sense: the soil is a living entity, and it prefers*

substances that are in harmony with its biochemistry. It also needs a break, so crops should be rotated. It is important to note that the principle of rotation also applies to fishing. Without it, fish populations become depleted. If fishers do not respect this, they could face hardship. This is common sense amongst fishers.

- Since Carver's death, farmers across Alabama and in every other state of the union have been attracted by the promise of large profits to treat the soil cheaply and artificially with chemical fertilisers, extracting every ounce of productivity from it.

- Rather than employing patient and considerate approaches to sustain the natural balance of their soils, as Carver did, many have opted to dominate nature instead of working with it.

- In 1966, in Decatur, Illinois, a farming community in the heart of the United States' Corn Belt had a promise of a bumper crop.

- In the twenty years since World War II, the farmers had doubled the land's corn yield by using nitrate fertilisers, unaware of the deadly danger they were risking.

- The amount of **nitrogen** applied exceeded what the corn could naturally absorb, and the surplus was washed out of the soil into local rivers: in the case of Decatur, all the way into the drinking cups of citizens.

- The following spring, someone noticed that a cup of drinking water from his kitchen tap tasted strange. He took it to the Decatur Health Department for testing. They were alarmed to discover that nitrate levels in the waters of Lake Decatur and the Sangamon River were not only excessive but potentially lethal.

- Nitrate, while harmless to the human body in itself, can become deadly when transformed by intestinal bacteria. These bacteria convert nitrate into methaemoglobin [methemoglobin] by combining it with the blood's haemoglobin, which blocks the natural transport of oxygen in the bloodstream. This can lead to a condition known as meth*ae*moglobin*ae*mia, which causes death by asphyxiation; infants are especially vulnerable to it. Many cases of the mysterious epidemics of "crib death" ["cot death"] are now believed to be caused by it.

- When certain strains of maize were harvested for silage, the nitrate levels were so high that the silos (structures used to store grain) exploded, and the runoff juice killed every cow, duck, and chicken unlucky enough to drink it. Even when silos did not burst, the nitrogen-rich maize inside became deadly, releasing nitrous oxide fumes sufficient to kill a person unsuspectingly inhaling it.

Why have artificial fertilisers become so popular in the world?

The popularity of artificial fertilisers can be traced to Justus von Liebig (1803–1873), a German chemist regarded as the founder of organic chemistry and the 'father of the fertiliser industry'. Liebig challenged common theories about the role of humus in plant nutrition, which suggested that natural, decayed plant matter was the main source of carbon for plants. Instead, he believed that inorganic materials could supply nutrients just as effectively as organic ones. He developed this 'genius' theory by incinerating plants and observing that all they needed was contained in the mineral salts found in their ashes. According to the authors of The Secret Life of Plants, "The visual results of the application of artificial fertilisers composed of nitrogen, phosphates, and potash, together with calcium oxide, or lime, seemed to prove Liebig's theory, and later resulted in the skyrocketing climb of fertiliser production by the chemical industry."

But can simple syllogistic reasoning produce the common sense necessary to see the bigger picture? Dr William Albrecht (1888–1974) was the head of the Department of Soils at the University of Missouri. He was a leading expert on the link between soil fertility and human health and earned four degrees from the University of Illinois. As emeritus Professor of Soils at the University of Missouri, he recognised a direct connection between soil quality, food quality, and human health. According to The Secret Life of Plants, "He described the sudden blind dependence upon nitrogen, phosphorus, and potassium, the main constituents of artificial fertilisers, as an 'ash mentality', since ashes suggest the idea of death rather than life." Now, since plants are living beings and they support the life of everything on this earth, including us, would analysing their ashes, as Justus von Liebig did, explain everything they need to be healthy?

If our bodies were burned and the ashes analysed, would that reveal everything we need to stay healthy? And where do the minerals in plant ashes originate? They come from the soil. So, where is the most natural and trustworthy source of plant nutrients? The answer is clear: the soil, unless you believe human reasoning can outmatch the 4.5 billion years of Earth's ecological development.

Do you think plants prefer to draw their nutrients from living, mineral-rich soil or from synthetic fertilisers? If you're genuinely interested in this topic, which concerns most of us, I highly recommend reading *The Secret Life of Plants* by Peter Tompkins and Christopher Bird.

Are artificial fertilisers necessary to feed the world?

If you believe that the problems caused by artificial fertilisers are necessary for feeding the world, consider this: According to theguardian.com, "Figures from the Institution of Mechanical Engineers show that between 30% to 50% or as much as 2 billion tonnes of food, never make it to a plate."

All of this remains highly relevant today, as nitrogen-based fertilisers are still widely used across the world. The main users include China, the United States, France, Germany, Brazil, Canada, Turkey, the United Kingdom, Mexico, Spain, and Argentina.

What common-sense lesson should we have learned from the event in Decatur, Illinois, as far back as 1966? Perhaps this: pouring chemicals into the soil is like pouring chemicals into our cooking pot.

The events in Decatur highlight a mindset that lacks basic common sense by valuing financial gain over human life. Unfortunately, prioritising profit above people remains a widespread attitude in our world today.

But did farmers have a safer, more sensible alternative source of nitrogen? According to *The Secret Life of Plants*, the authors addressed this very question, and the answer is well known to anyone familiar with agricultural science:

- Natural forms of nitrogen and other elements essential for plants are found in humus, which is decayed plant material. They can also be present in animal waste, such as cow dung and horse manure.

- Under *natural* conditions, nitrogen is stored in the soil as part of its humus, a brown-black material composed almost entirely of decayed vegetable matter.

- An almost limitless supply of such manure was accessible to Decatur in the nearby Sioux City, Iowa, America's heartland city on the Missouri River. A heap of steer manure had built up, stretching longer than a football pitch. This mound of organic waste, which created a significant disposal dilemma for the city officials, could be easily transformed into natural soil-enhancing products if anyone were interested in conserving the soil.

Based on the above scenario, who is more likely to apply common sense? It is probably the public. This is because our only genuine self-interest should be to stay healthy. Therefore, if we become sufficiently educated, we will begin demanding the use of natural fertilisers, making organic foods the norm rather than the exception. This is true because demand influences supply. Those profiting from the sale of chemical fertilisers have an apparent self-interest, one that is unlikely to be driven by public health concerns. History has shown that such interests cannot be trusted to act in the public's best interest, even before the incidents in Decatur, Illinois and according to *The Secret Life of Plants*, Dr Barry Commoner, Director of the Centre for the Biology of Natural Systems at Washington University in St. Louis, Missouri, presented a prophetic paper on the relationship between nitrogen fertiliser and nitrate levels in Midwestern rivers at the annual meeting of the American Association for the Advancement of Science. What do you think happened next? The authors explained:

- Two weeks later, a vice-president of the National Plant Food Institute, a lobby group aimed at protecting the interests of the $2-billion American fertiliser industry, sent copies of Commoner's paper for rebuttal to soil experts at nine major universities.

- Since they had spent most of their careers advising farmers that the best way to ensure bountiful crops is to apply artificial fertilisers to the land, many scientists in these centres of academic learning were as irritated by Commoner's allegations as the fertiliser lobby officials were. They, therefore, rushed to the defence of the lobbyists and themselves.

- Dr Daniel H. Kohl, an expert in the process of photosynthesis, stated that the issue of excess nitrogen in the soil was so severe that the future of the planet might be in jeopardy.

- His efforts were immediately and viciously criticised by his departmental colleagues on the grounds that such work was not a proper part of the department's goal of pure research.

Do the above examples demonstrate how self-interest can obstruct common sense? Considering the final point, how do you justify a "goal of pure research"? Does it make sense that research has any value beyond yielding practical conclusions? Why do you think Dr Kohl stated that the fate of the planet was at risk? Was he being melodramatic? Here is further information to help you consider whether our current fertiliser-driven agricultural practices are based on sound judgement.

- A website by the New South Wales Government (Australia) highlighted the benefits of earthworms: "By their activity in the soil, earthworms offer many benefits: increased nutrient availability,

- better drainage, and a more stable soil structure, all of which help improve farm productivity."

- Numerous studies have shown that earthworms enhance plant growth.

- **The Secret Life of Plants states that:** "With heavy application of chemical fertilisers and pesticides, a field can lose its entire earthworm population".

- Many scholarly articles discuss the adverse effects of artificial fertilisers on earthworm populations. For example, an article titled, **Long-term effects of nitrogenous fertilisers on grassland earthworms: Their relation to soil acidification,** authored by Wei-Chun Ma, L. Brussaard, and J.A. de Ridder, describes how Mineral Ammonium Sulphate (AS) — an inorganic salt with several commercial uses, most commonly as a soil fertiliser — contains 21% nitrogen and 24% sulphur. It significantly reduced earthworm numbers and biomass, and also lowered the soil's pH balance.

- With increased nutrient availability, earthworms generally attain higher biomass and populations (Edwards and Lofty, 1982; Hansen and Engelstad, 1999), although very high levels of fertilisation may suppress their proliferation (Haynes and Naidu, 1998).

- This is especially true when soils become acidic (Ma et al., 1990); earthworms are generally scarce in soils with a pH of 4.5 (Curry,2004).

- Numerous studies have demonstrated that organic fertilisers promote earthworms more effectively than inorganic fertilisers (Coindex and Ducommun, 1990; Estevez et al., 1996; Whalen et al., 1998).

Let's apply deductive reasoning to the above information:

- Earthworms enhance plant growth.

- Ammonium sulphate, a standard chemical fertiliser, is highly acidic and dramatically decreases the population of earthworms in the soil, showing that earthworms do not thrive in acidic conditions.

- Consequently, ammonium sulphate damages soil health.

- Earthworms are natural soil enhancers; they thrive in soils with a neutral to slightly alkaline pH and play a vital role in supporting healthy plant growth.

- While ammonium sulphate may temporarily boost crop yields, it is not a natural input and disrupts the long-term biological balance of the soil.

- Common sense suggests that soil rich in earthworms produces the best and healthiest plants because it's natural. This is true unless we know more than Nature. You can do some further reading to discover how earthworms improve soil fertility. Do you think there is a connection between the fact that our health favours a slightly alkaline pH, and the soil that produces the plants and food we (and animals) are compatible with also favours alkalinity?

Common sense on the use of pesticides

Another issue that calls for common sense is the widespread use of pesticides on plants. Why does this practice seem like a necessary evil? It looks so because artificial fertilisers produce weaker, less resilient plants, plants with limited natural defences against pests. As a result, we come to "need" pesticides. Paradoxically, the so-called solution to increasing food production ends up creating a new problem that demands even more chemical intervention.

Apply your reasoning to the following information and see if the conclusion makes sense. I am sure you have heard the saying, "You are what you eat." If you agree that this is true for humans, do you think it also applies to other living things, such as plants? So, if an inadequate diet leads to poorer health for us and makes us more susceptible to illnesses, does it likewise make sense that a deficient diet for plants would produce weaker plants that are less resistant to pests? In the book, *The Secret Life of Plants*, the authors mention these facts about Sir Albert Howard (8 December 1873 – 20 October 1947), who was a mycologist, agricultural lecturer, and regarded as one of the key founders of modern organic agriculture:

- He started to notice a fundamental flaw in the organisation of research into plant pathology. "I was an investigator of plant diseases," he wrote, "but I had no crops on which I could try out the remedies I advocated. It was borne in on me that there was a wide chasm between science in the laboratory and practice in the field."

- After noticing that crops cultivated by farmers around Pusa in India were free of pests, he decided to conduct a detailed study of Indian agricultural practices.

- By following the practices of the Indians, who used no pesticides or artificial fertilisers but returned to the land the carefully accumulated animal and vegetable wastes, Howard was so successful that by 1919 he had learned "how to grow healthy crops, practically free from disease, without the slightest help from mycologists, entomologists, bacteriologists, agricultural chemists, artificial manures, spraying machines, insecticides, fungicides, germicides, and all other expensive paraphernalia of the modern experimental station."

- His herd of work oxen, fed solely on the produce of his fertile land, never contracted foot-and-mouth disease, rinderpest, septicaemia, or other cattle diseases that frequently devastated herds at modern experimental stations.

- He wrote: "None of my animals were segregated; none were inoculated; they frequently came into contact with diseased stock. As my small farmyard at Pusa was only separated by a low hedge from one of the large cattle sheds on the Pusa estate, in which outbreaks of foot-and-mouth disease often occurred, I have several times seen my oxen rubbing noses with foot-and-mouth cases. Nothing happened. The healthy, well-fed animals failed to react to this disease exactly as suitable varieties of crops, when properly grown, do to insect and fungus pests—no infection took place."

- The authors also provided evidence from Glenn Gerber, who used natural seaweed fertilisers and other methods to eliminate some pests and significantly reduce others. While his neighbours lost more than half their crops to maggot flies, even after applying multiple insecticides, he experienced only a 10 per cent reduction in his onion yield.

Does the point about foot-and-mouth raise serious questions about the widespread burning of cattle, their segregation, the wearing of masks, and the sterilisation of everyone who came into contact with foot-and-mouth cattle during Britain's outbreak of the disease in 2001? What was responsible for this crisis that caused panic in British agriculture and tourism in 2001? Given the naturalness of organic farming, is it reasonable to blame the crisis on the fact that non-organic farming science dominates the world? What causes foot-and-mouth disease in cattle? Do you have enough information to apply common sense to this question? Just in case you do not, here is some additional information about pesticides.

- The Environmental Protection Agency (EPA) believes that the fruits and vegetables our children are consuming are safer than ever. Under FQPA (Food Quality Protection Act), the EPA assesses new and existing pesticides to ensure they can be used with a reasonable certainty of no harm to infants, children, and adults. EPA continuously reviews and enhances safety standards applicable to **pesticide residues on food**.

- It is important to realise, though, that just because a pesticide residue is detected on a fruit or vegetable, that does not mean it is unsafe. **Small amounts of pesticides that may remain in or on fruits, vegetables, grains, and other foods diminish significantly as crops are harvested, transported, exposed to light, washed, prepared, and cooked. The presence of a detectable pesticide residue does not indicate that the residue is at an unsafe level.** (Bold emphasis mine)

A safe level of pesticides that can be ingested?

Have you noticed that some are now claiming there is a "safe" level of pesticides in the human body? They even admit that pesticide residues can remain in food, even after it has been washed, prepared, and cooked! It is, therefore, indisputable that animals will consume much more pesticides than we humans. The following confirms that washing food is not enough to eliminate pesticides:

- According to Pesticide Action Network (PAN), an organisation aiming to promote alternatives to pesticides worldwide, *"Pesticides can have a cumulative 'toxic loading' effect both in the immediate and long term."* Could this explain why animals sometimes develop diseases? Since pesticides poison humans, as you'll see below, why wouldn't they also harm animals?

- 93% of Americans tested by the Centres for Disease Control and Prevention (CDC) had metabolites of chlorpyrifos — a neurotoxic insecticide — in their urine. Banned from household use because of its risks to children, chlorpyrifos is part of a family of pesticides (organophosphates) linked to ADHD – attention deficit hyperactivity disorder.

- According to the Centres for Disease Control and Prevention (CDC), "The Environmental Protection Agency (EPA) estimates that 10,000 - 20,000 physician-diagnosed pesticide poisonings occur each year among the approximately 2 million U.S. agricultural workers."

Since common sense relies on accurate information, is the above enough for it to be genuinely helpful in making the right decision? What about those with self-interest, profit motive, or political agenda? You have seen how a few of these interests influenced events in Decatur when Dr Barry Commoner predicted the overuse of nitrogenous fertilisers, and perhaps you've noticed how organisations and individuals often defend their positions regardless of the facts. Unfortunately, this tendency to protect positions or 'stand our ground' has led to many critical aspects of life being dominated by unfavourable interests. These interests often obscure the truth. Although common sense, our highest ideal, should guide us, it frequently struggles to shed light on many aspects of life that affect us all and determine the quality and duration of our lives. Common sense's ability to reveal the truth and expose pertinent information to the public is impeded because entrenched self-interests tend to block such disclosures.

It makes sense to know what's in your food

In our age of processed foods and corporate profit-driven pursuits, it is sensible to check the ingredients on packaging. Preservatives labelled as 'E' numbers are not real food, so the fewer you consume, the better. Look up the 'E' numbers listed and research their meanings.

A mother refused her son's request for some food, saying it wasn't good for him. His response was, "Why do they make it then?" Is this an example of pure wisdom that suggests we shouldn't sell harmful 'foods'?

Not understanding how to succeed and be effective within the system we have created for coexistence damages us both personally and as a group. It can lead to unhappiness, poverty, and despair.

CHAPTER EIGHT

The sixth significant life issue to which Aristotelian syllogistic reasoning applies: **Common sense about money, teamwork, and success**

Success in the broadest definition is not usually attained in a single, massive effort. Failure doesn't usually happen in one cataclysmic explosion. Both experiences are generally the cumulative effect of either repeated disciplined activities or repeated errors in judgement.

Money is not everything, but it ranks right up there with oxygen.
In the areas where money is necessary, there is no substitute.
– Zig Ziglar

Financial education

How much do you know about personal finance? What about protecting your financial future? Here are some of the rules:

The simple money formula

- Everyone desires enough money to live comfortably, but this aim is often too vague. A wish is not a goal.

- To turn "living comfortably" or "living in luxury" into a real goal, it must be quantified in terms of cost. Goals should be specific and measurable.

- If you're already living comfortably, calculate your current annual expenses. Then, add an estimated inflation rate. This will give you a projected yearly amount needed to sustain your lifestyle in retirement.

- If you're not yet living comfortably, calculate the annual cost needed to reach that level. Remember to include inflation in the yearly figure.

- Once you have that figure, determine which activity or activities could realistically produce that level of income. Then, identify the specific skills you'll need to develop or improve to succeed in those activities and reach your financial goal.

To succeed as a human being is not always the same as succeeding in your life's work, although they can go hand in hand. – Louis L'Amour

---

The simplest, but not the easiest, strategy for financial security is to set a goal to become a millionaire and develop a plan for achieving it.

- If you are already a millionaire, develop a plan to maintain your wealth. Many find it easier to achieve success than to retain it. It requires skill to both earn and preserve wealth. Transitioning from riches to poverty is challenging.

- "How can someone make ten thousand dollars per month and go broke? It's easy, spend eleven thousand dollars per month." – Jim Rohn.

Financial education needs to become a part of our national curriculum and scoring systems so that it's not just the rich kids that learn about money... It's all of us. – David Bach

---

The greatest good we can do for others is not just to share our riches, but to reveal to them their own. – Benjamin Disraeli

---

Jessie B. Rittenhouse 1869 - 1948

I bargained with Life for a penny,
And Life would pay no more,
However, I begged at evening
When I counted my scanty store;

For Life is just an employer,
He gives you what you ask,
But once you have set the wages,
why, you must bear the task.

I worked for a menial's hire,
only to learn, dismayed,
that any wage I had asked of Life,
Life would have paid.

The message in the above poem teaches about life's great wisdom regarding many aspects, including money. Our life experiences rarely surpass what we expect and are willing to accept. Since our mind is so powerful, and many of us recognise that we create our circumstances through our persistent dominant thoughts, we should be mindful of what we choose to think or believe about money. Here are some thoughts about money that should be considered common sense:

- There is nothing admirable about poverty or a lack of sufficient money. The only positive aspect of growing up poor was not being able to afford the cheap junk foods children eat today.

- Knives and guns are inanimate objects; therefore, they cannot be evil. They cannot make you do anything. Money is also an inanimate object. As a result of this truth, it cannot cause you to do anything evil, nor can it be evil itself. If a person kills for money, the money is not at fault. Blame the lack of a moral compass that would have prevented them from taking such drastic action for financial gain. Blame their neglect in not developing their ability to bring value to others' lives, and thus earn remuneration that aligns with their desires.

- Evil starts with a thought, so only thoughts and actions can be regarded as genuinely evil.

- If someone kills due to sexual jealousy, would you consider sex or love as something evil?

- Money is a valuable resource because, at its core, it represents access to food, clothing, and shelter.

- "A person cannot truly be free if he is bound to a routine job for most of his waking hours and only receives a subsistence in return.

If a person has to pay so much for existence, he is paying too high a price." – Dennis Kimbro.

- "The price of anything is the amount of life you exchange for it." –Thoreau.

- The money you earn reflects your life energy because you've exchanged your time for it, and time is a part of your energy.

- Given our natural abilities to dream, imagine, plan, organise, work, and build, isn't it a significant underuse of our potential if we settle for merely surviving rather than striving to thrive?

- Are we just equipped to survive or to thrive?

- We are compensated based on the value we contribute to the marketplace, not on the time we spend. That's why two people can work the same hours, but one can earn twice as much. Both wealthy and poor individuals have twenty-four hours each day. – Jim Rohn's philosophy.

- That which each of us calls our 'necessary expenses' will always grow to equal our income unless we protest to the contrary. – George S Clason (*The Richest Man in Babylon*)

- Without a clear vision of where money is meant to take us, we often give in to the emotional appeal of what we can buy. Having enough money to buy something does not necessarily mean we can afford it. For example, we might save or borrow money to buy a car but struggle to cover its ongoing costs. Additionally, such a habit, if repeated, could undermine the primary goal of earning money, which is the next point.

- Money is meant to be our 'magic carpet' that supports and delights us now, as well as when we no longer wish to work or are unable to work. It's called financial independence.

Who is responsible for our level of income?

- As previously quoted, one of Jim Rohn's key life lessons is, **"We get paid for bringing value to the marketplace."** So, the question is, who or what decides how valuable we become in the commercial world? We do. What if we presented a worthwhile business idea to the world and it wasn't given enough recognition? Should we spend a lot of time blaming the system? It's not the best option. Given the times we live in, developing multiple skills is not just recommended, it's essential for adaptability and long-term success. So, if we only possess one skill, we should acquire another, find a new idea, and implement a new plan. The classic book, *The Richest Man in Babylon*, includes a humorous story that highlights the misunderstanding many have about the link between personal development and income:

"Not long ago came to me a young man seeking to borrow. When I questioned him about the cause of his necessity, he complained that his earnings were insufficient to pay his expenses. Thereupon, I explained to him that, this being the case, he was a poor customer for the moneylender, as he possessed no surplus earning capacity to repay the loan. "'What you need, young man,' I told him, 'is to earn more coins. What dost thou to increase thy capacity to earn?' "'All that I can do,' he replied. 'Six times within two moons have I approached my master to request my pay be increased, but without success. No man can go oftener than that."

If we critically analyse George S. Clason's observation that our "necessary expenses" will always grow to match our income unless we actively resist, we uncover a valuable lesson. He highlights a common emotional tendency: the desire for increased comfort and convenience as income rises. To achieve financial success, this mindset must be challenged. The rational approach is to develop the discipline and skill to continually widen the gap between income and expenses, rather than allowing lifestyle inflation to close it.

This requires a strong sense of delayed gratification and a powerful desire for financial independence or freedom. What if we develop the habit of blaming everything and everyone for our economic circumstances and taking no responsibility? Where will we find the power to change any of our undesirable outcomes? Does it make sense that it is easier to change ourselves than to change others? If others truly were responsible for our financial situations, what chance would we have of ever changing them? The answer is slim to none. This is not to say people cannot be obstacles. The question is one of degree. Are they permanent obstacles? Should it be common sense that at each stage of life we have a choice in what we do, and that our choices will eventually produce a result? Should it be obvious that our lives are primarily governed by a series of decisions we make? Each decision or choice influences the next—the domino effect.

Money and time

If we are ambitious but do not master the skills necessary for earning money beyond the 'nine to five' system, we will be slaves to its pursuit. We should all learn on a deep emotional level that time is more valuable than money. Therefore, the ultimate key and strategy to earning money is to learn how to leverage our money through investing, so that our income increases without increasing our time input—or even better, it increases while we spend less time earning it. This is not to suggest that hard work should be avoided. We should learn how to work smart. A wise adage states: we will not reach the end of our lives and wish we had spent more time in the office or on the job. We might wish we had earned more money to enjoy life or provide greater comfort, but not that we had spent more time working to do it.

Who would not want to have financial independence so that they work only because they want to, and not because they must?

Common sense and teamwork

Any group or race of people is doomed to suffer if they don't embrace the power of teamwork. As you read the quote from Thomas Paine's pamphlet, Common Sense, the value of teamwork becomes clear from the outset when humans understand that they are entirely responsible for establishing themselves on this planet. Teamwork enhances the effectiveness of individuals within a team. Team sports are the best at demonstrating, in clear view, the power of the team concept. In 1998, Manchester United, one of the world's most famous football clubs, was managed by Sir Alex Ferguson. The club's legendary manager was praised for his tactical insight. However, his ability to get players to work in a coordinated way must be given significant credit. The partnership between two of his strikers, Teddy Sheringham and Andrew Cole, epitomised his team ethic and that of the players.

In 2010, Andrew Cole wrote an article for The Independent revealing that he had disliked Sheringham for 15 years because Sheringham snubbed him by refusing to shake his hand, as was customary when he walked onto the pitch to make his England debut. According to Cole, "… He actively snubs me, for no reason I was ever aware of then or since… I was embarrassed. I was confused."

"Two years later, in summer 1997… Sheringham arrived at Manchester United, and we played together for years…I never spoke a single word to him."

Despite the acrimony, the two players worked together on the pitch, and their teamwork largely contributed to Manchester United winning the Treble that year (the Premier League, the FA Cup, and the UEFA Champions League), marking the most successful season in the club's history. "People wonder how on earth we could function like that... I wouldn't ever cast aspersions on Sheringham's talent as a top-class footballer for his clubs and country." Cole and Sheringham scored 54 goals together for Manchester United, despite not sharing a close personal relationship. This illustrates an important principle: two people don't need to like each other personally to work effectively towards a shared goal—and, in doing so, contribute to the success of the whole team. By the same principle, even a team of the most talented individuals in any sport will lose consistently if they fail to perform as a united group.

Steve Jobs' parable of the rocks

"When I was a young kid, there was a widowed man who lived up the street. He was in his eighties...one day he said to me, 'Come on into my garage, I want to show you something.' And he pulled out this dusty old rock tumbler. It was a motor, a coffee can and a little band between them. And he said, 'Come with me.' We went out into the back and we got some rocks... some regular old ugly rocks. And we put them in the can with a little bit of liquid and a little bit of grit powder, and we closed the can, and he turned this motor on, and he said, "Come back tomorrow.' And this can was making a racket as the stones went around. And I came back the next day, and we opened the can. And we took out these amazingly beautiful polished rocks. The same common stones that had gone in, through rubbing against each other like this (Jobs clapped his hands), creating a little bit of friction, creating a little bit of noise, had come out as these beautiful polished rocks. That's always been in my mind, my metaphor for a team working hard on something they're passionate about."

Life often shows that a group of average individuals who are well-organised and dedicated to teamwork can overcome significant challenges, with each member contributing to a greater collective effect than more talented individuals who lack a strong team ethic. Teamwork frequently reflects cultural values. When people live together without a shared commitment to collaboration, that society can only be described as having a weak or poor culture because strong cultures are built on solid team values.

The benefits of teamwork are widely recognised, yet they are not always fully embraced. When individuals or groups see the importance of cooperation but do not put it into practice, the obstacle is often emotional rather than intellectual. In both developing and developed countries, people may

acknowledge the power of working together, but a lack of respect among socio-economic groups, combined with deep-seated self-interest, often prevents this understanding from being translated into action.

This is yet another aspect of life where emotion often overpowers common sense. The philosophy of teamwork is ultimately more beneficial than the philosophy of individualism, simply because together, we can accomplish far more than we can alone.

What if we embrace the following?

- It takes a whole village to raise a child. Would this help build stronger communities? Yes.

- What if we consistently surround ourselves with people who inspire us and act as sounding boards for good ideas?

- An average team will accomplish more than an average individual.

- A great team will achieve more than a great individual.

- The whole is greater than the sum of its parts.

"**Alone I can enjoy, but together we can celebrate Alone,
I can smile, but together we can laugh This is the beauty
of human relations We are nothing without each other.**" –
author unknown

CHAPTER NINE

The eighth major life issue to which Aristotelian syllogistic reasoning applies: **Common sense about sex and relationships**

Simple logic and common sense for sexual habits

- Animals that hunt during the day, eat and have sex during the day.

- Animals that hunt at night, eat and have sex during the night.

- We are not nocturnal creatures.

- At night, all our organs, including those related to sex, have the lowest energy levels. This is the time for detoxification and rejuvenation. Consequently, we draw energy from our sex organs when they are at their weakest.

- The best time to have sex is in the morning – this is after up to eight hours of body repair and rejuvenation, when the body is at its most relaxed and strongest.

- Consistently eating late at night is harmful to health, especially when the foods eaten are hard to digest and low in nutritional value, as they can drain the body's energy. It takes energy to digest food. Therefore, if the body is using energy to digest food when it is at its weakest and also using energy during sex at the same time, this creates an excessive energy demand on a weakened body.

- Sex places significant demands on the body's energy. When this energy is used at a time when the body is naturally winding down for sleep, it conflicts with the body's natural rhythm and energy cycle.

As social beings with intricate emotional and psychological needs, one of our biggest challenges is learning how to build and sustain happy, healthy relationships.

Simple Syllogistic Reasoning – common sense lessons for love and relationships

It is clear that humans must learn how to relate to each other. This involves understanding the basic needs we all share and how to satisfy those needs respectfully and meaningfully. Human relationships are uniquely complex compared to those of other living beings, mainly because of our ability to develop diverse philosophies, beliefs, and attitudes. This complexity is heightened by the variety of issues we must address: whether or not to have children, how many, how to raise and discipline them, how to manage domestic responsibilities, the roles each partner will assume in the relationship, and—especially in today's world—the financial realities of cohabiting in a sustainable, if not comfortable, way.

These and many other emotional issues can hinder us from having fulfilling and lasting relationships. It is for these reasons that we need more skills for successful relationships than any other beings.

If I don't like to spend time with myself, how can I ask someone else to enjoy spending time with me? – Gabrielle Union

---

The first lesson in building healthy relationships is that it starts with you. Are you clear about your philosophies, values, and priorities? If you're not, how can you genuinely assess whether someone you're attracted to is truly compatible with you? If both of you aim for a short-term relationship, it doesn't matter; and if both of you are content with just a physical relationship, it doesn't matter either. So, the starting point is you, and we will begin this discussion assuming that you are clear about your philosophies and values. We will also assume that these philosophies and values are not built on sand and, therefore, will not be shifted by the first strong wind.

When you meet someone for the first time and feel attracted to them, this initial stage is called infatuation. During this period, you might experience intense feelings about how desirable the person seems. They appear 'delicious', like something you would eat with a spoon! This is not love, and it is not expected to last forever. If it were, most people would stay in love, but infatuation is a common experience. If you have had more than one of those 'want to eat the person with a spoon' moments, you already know this to be true.

Emotional bank accounts and deposits

A fundamental wisdom in life is recognising that each person has an Emotional Bank Account, and like any bank account, it requires healthy deposits. The more deposits received, the healthier it remains. So, what are these emotional deposits that should become common knowledge? What are the essential things everyone should understand about the nature of being human, which are our core needs in relationships? Here they are, starting with one that should be obvious:

- Love is the most vital and healthiest of human experiences. Evidence of this can be seen in how children who are not nurtured with love often face difficulties in adulthood. The good news is that it doesn't have to be permanent. We humans can reset our minds and emotions from negative to positive. This change becomes possible when we adopt the right philosophy, one that encourages positive, empowering emotions and modes of thinking.

- Most of us need to be affirmed, receive the gift of attention, be emotionally supported, recognised, and shown genuine interest.

- There is a need for the gift of friendship, not only to be loved but also to be liked. I am sure you know that a person can love you but not necessarily like you very much. This is especially relevant in family relationships. For example, you might love a sibling but not always enjoy a close friendship.

- We have a need to be respected, understood, and admired.

- "Being heard is so close to being loved that for the average person, they are almost indistinguishable." – David W. Augsburger

Starting with yourself again, would you refuse any of the above emotional deposits? Do you think most people would? What people do is a strong indicator of how they think and feel—and, ultimately, of who they are. Common sense suggests you shouldn't expect a good outcome if, for example, you're interested in an artist but your behaviour indicates otherwise, like saying, "I'm interested in you, but I have no interest in what you do, so I don't even care to see your art." Similarly, if you were interested in a writer, you should not ignore their books. This principle applies to any profession or occupation that the person values. This discussion on emotional bank accounts and the idea of making emotional deposits provides insight into our shared human needs, desires, and the fundamentals of understanding others.

Millions of people are living in a state of deprivation or semi-deprivation of some or all of the above emotional deposits. Since emotional well-being is a vital factor in our overall quality of life, shouldn't this kind of understanding be regarded as common sense and standard practice? The more you learn about our psychological and emotional makeup, the more effective you become at responding to others' needs. And if you're genuinely interested in building strong relationships, or even experiencing an extraordinary love affair, the deeper your understanding, the greater your chances of success.

Here's a suggestion for improving any relationship: offer to meet a need or desire for someone without being asked. Why is this such a meaningful gesture? You might have heard the saying, "We are extras in each other's play." It reflects the truth that people often become secondary in our busy lives, which relates to the familiar saying, "Out of sight, out of mind." Therefore, when you take the initiative to support someone without prompting, you demonstrate that you not only think about them but also care about their well-being. It's a quiet yet powerful way to say, "You matter." Just be sure to do it sincerely. To love oneself is the beginning of a lifelong romance. - Oscar Wilde

You build an intense love affair first by having a healthy love for yourself, and this doesn't mean being narcissistic. Then, suppose your deepest intention is to find someone worthy of your deposits of care and affection into their emotional bank account. In that case, the infatuation stage of your relationship will naturally grow beyond the physical. These are some of the ideas that should become a common understanding of love. Are the experiences mentioned some of the basic needs and desires that most of us have? If these needs and desires apply to you, you're the right person for these ideas. Many of us would welcome love, friendship, and emotional support from our partners. However, the combination of these values usually requires deliberate intent. This is because most of us don't associate intimate relationships with friendship. A union of love and friendship is one of the greatest types of relationships. It is like a house built on a foundation of rock that doesn't shift with every slight or strong wind.

There are so many of us who expect to be close to those we have chosen not to share our goals and aspirations with. But does this make sense? Here is what makes sense: *"Remember, intimacy increases with honesty. Share less to keep people away and more to draw them closer."* – Martha Beck

---

Like a tree that bears fruit, love is not strong when it is static; it is strong when it grows. Relationship and love are action words. Too often, they are both put on autopilot, and relationships don't develop on autopilot. What a person looks like is important for a good relationship, but it should not be as important as compatibility.

'Family-ship' and friendship are not just based on bloodline and familiarity concepts that we hold in our heads. They only become meaningful if they are action-oriented.

A pearl of most crucial wisdom – emotional deposits are the key

It makes sense that, in a healthy relationship, we should aim to make more emotional deposits than withdrawals. Interestingly, the principles that govern strong relationships closely mirror the laws of nature. To thrive in our relationships, we must become like good farmers—patient, attentive, and consistent in our care. Here are some meaningful parallels:

- The fundamental principle of a successful relationship is to plant the seed of *caring* and *nurture it* with the partner of choice. Does the good farmer care for and nurture the soil in preparation for his crop to grow? Yes.

- The other fundamental principle of a good relationship is whether your seeds are compatible with the 'soil' you choose. The good farmer knows that not all soils are suitable for growing certain crops.

- Your 'seed' signifies the values you offer, whereas your 'soil' is the emotional bank account that requires the deposits mentioned earlier. Every person brings both soil and seed, or emotions and values, to a relationship. This demonstrates the ability to give and receive. Once you have developed your values and found someone confident in theirs, and they are compatible with yours, you can apply the suitable methods of *planting* and *nurturing* that suit both of you.

- We all try to deposit our values into our partner's emotional bank account. If our values are admired or loved by our partner and these values stay consistent in quality in all seasons, we have a much better chance of enduring love. We can understand this better by looking at what happens when we treat nature differently, when we fail to respect the soil as a living, breathing system and instead push growth with chemical fertilisers. The result is clear: exhausted soil, weaker plants, and ultimately, nutritionally poor food.

- We may produce abundant crops, but they are devoid of their natural value. Similarly, in relationships, this is much the same. You might spend considerable time with a partner, but if that time lacks genuine connection and emotional nourishment, it does little to strengthen the bond or promote the kind of spiritual growth that characterises a truly healthy relationship.

- Like Nature, relationships must undergo various stages of growth. As mentioned earlier, relationships begin with infatuation. For a relationship to produce lasting results, it needs a development process. This process requires a programme (DNA) that guides its direction and extent. This is akin to the DNA that Nature embeds in all things.

- For a relationship to yield *the fruit of our choice,* we need to obey one natural law that states, "Whatever you sow, you'll reap". So, plant what you want to receive.

- Nature teaches us to be very precise about what we seek. Like a good farmer, we must plan our sowing and harvesting carefully. We need to become adept at handling the unavoidable trials of love and life. Don't simply drift along with life's current. Once you know each other well, plan to experience the things that excite both of you.

- We notice that Nature produces more weeds than flowers. It teaches us that weeds represent life's trials and are inevitable. We can choose to develop skills to minimise the difficulties of love and life through personal growth, or we can simply hope for the best. The best choice is to become skilled captains of your love ship. **Nature reminds us:**

- Weeds will grow and take over a garden that is not well-maintained. Relationships, like a garden, will not flourish on autopilot; they require effort.

- The condition of all gardens reflects the character and personality of the tender; similarly, it is with the gardens of love. If the tenders are disciplined and nurturing, then a beautiful garden follows.

- This point cannot be emphasised enough: each tender should be clear about what they want from the garden of their relationship, and then proceed to give and to receive. In the world of relationships, many people enter with the mental attitude of "What can you give me?" "What can you give me?" The correct order is, "This is what I am giving you, to start the process of receiving." So, if each enters as a giver, then all will be receivers.

- What would happen if the farmer said to the soil, "I want a crop" before first investing time and energy? Fortunately, this is not the philosophy of the world's farmers, or we would all starve.

- Giving begins the cycle of receiving. If you have been giving without receiving, then you've been investing in the wrong soil. You are not compatible.

- Without a clear understanding of who we are and what we truly want, we often start to drift once the initial infatuation in a relationship fades. In pursuit of that excitement, we may try to repeat the cycle with someone new, never realising that the deeper, more fulfilling spiritual union we seek can only be achieved through commitment, self-awareness, and growth.

- It's the lack of growth that destroys many relationships. In the course of our lives, we are constantly adding new feelings and philosophies, both consciously and unconsciously. It is often said that people 'grow apart'. It is unique to humans that we can grow in any direction of our choosing, so if we grow apart, we either weren't on the same path to start with, or we changed at a certain point. In practice, most people *drift* into cultivating varying philosophies and feelings. This explains the high levels of separations, divorces, and short-term relationships.

- Like a well-planned garden that offers beauty, pleasure, enjoyment, contentment, and fruit, we must shape our relationships in the same way. Such a garden is cultivated by practising the skill of nurturing.

- Just as the rewards we gain from cultivating a beautiful garden, life will reward us with a lovely relationship, provided we are diligent and sincere in our efforts. If we do our part, Nature will do its part. This is the unspoken partnership between humanity and Nature. A beautiful garden is created by the laws that govern the sun, the rain, the soil, and the science of the seasons. Similarly, our relationships are governed by mental and emotional principles that require nurturing in the soil of thinking and activity.

Simple logical synopsis of common-sense tips on relationships

- Do not expect to be close to those you have chosen not to share your goals and aspirations with.

- A person's appearance is essential for a good relationship, but this should not be as important as compatibility.

- Compatibility starts with knowing who you are.

- Only after understanding who you are will you be able to identify who aligns with your values or peculiarities.

- History: it is unwise to begin a relationship with someone you do not know well. You must be aware of the significant events and influences from their past that have shaped them. When someone asks, *"How can you say you love me and you don't know me?"*, they are highlighting a gap between the love claimed and the lack of understanding of their *true self*, which includes: **their past experiences**, childhood, traumas, major life events, **influences**, people, environments, or events that have formed who they are, **along with struggles and growth**, the pain they have overcome, the lessons they have learned, **and core memories** — things that continue to influence how they feel and behave today.

- Love, in a profound and meaningful way, isn't just about how someone appears now. It's about honouring the journey that has shaped them into who they are. If that history is overlooked or unknown, the person might feel unseen, as if you're loving only the surface, not the core. So that phrase is a plea for genuine recognition: ***"Know what shaped me, the beautiful, the complicated, and then say you love me."***

- Similarly, if you do not know and understand the events and beliefs that shaped a country, your understanding of the people in that country will be lacking.

- A successful relationship requires understanding each other's needs and making regular deposits into each other's emotional bank accounts.

Since women make up half of the human experience, it should be our innate instinct to establish a system where they have equal status. It should be common sense that the whole is stronger when each half is equally empowered. In such a culture, sexism would be unlikely to occur.

CHAPTER TEN

The ninth major life issue to which Aristotelian syllogistic reasoning applies: **Common sense regarding women's rights and sexism**

Definition of sexism: Prejudice, stereotyping, or discrimination, typically against women, based on their gender.

Simple syllogistic logic on sexism and problem solving:

- Sexism remains a serious issue. Our male-dominated society does not benefit us much. While progress is evident, it is limited. However, if societal leaders do not directly address the root causes, their true commitment to eradicating it becomes questionable.

- Problems are solved by eliminating the root cause.

Make a list of the major problems in the world. If the root cause of any of these problems is not discussed, we have no intention of solving them, or we are deluded into thinking we are trying. If we want to solve a problem, the fundamental common-sense rule is to investigate the root cause. Have you ever heard a public discussion about why sexism exists? If so, how many times and by whom? Was it by the leaders and shapers of society?

The days of the goddess were over. The pendulum had swung. Mother Earth had become a man's world, and the gods of destruction and war were taking their toll. The male ego had spent two millennium running unchecked by its female counterpart ... this obliteration of the sacred feminine in modern life [has] caused what the Hopi Native Americans called koyanisquatsi – 'life out of balance' – an unstable situation marked by testosterone-fuelled wars, a plethora of misogynistic societies, and a growing disrespect for Mother Earth ... (From The Da Vinci Code, by Dan Brown)

> **Patriarchy couldn't be our dominant reality if goddess worship were the only representation of a creator we believe in. If it were God and Goddess, both genders would be equally represented, leading to a more balanced world, and we would all be happier.**

The disparity of gender curse words

Sexism in language is an offensive reminder of the way the culture sees women.

Let's begin with something that should be very obvious: generally, women tend to display more pro-social behaviour than men. A clear, measurable example can be seen in crime statistics, from minor offences to the most serious acts, where men vastly outnumber women. This isn't just anecdotal; it's a consistent, worldwide pattern. Global conflicts are usually started and planned by men. So, if this is true, why are there so many derogatory words and names used against women? Throughout history, different countries and cultures have had insulting words or phrases for women. How do we explain that our 'better half' still faces such disrespect? How can we justify the large difference in derogatory terms for women compared to men? Many of these derogatory words related to women have sexual implications, even though men tend to be more promiscuous than women. This list is by no means complete.

1. Bitch
2. Slut
3. Whore
4. Hussy
5. Town bike
6. Beef
7. Thing
8. Old Hag
9. Cow
10. Witch
11. Sketel (Caribbean term for slut)
12. Skirt

13. Heifer

14. Floozy

15. Jezebel

16. Belly warmer

17. Skank (woman who dates a married man)

18. Streetwalker

19. Bird

20. Chick

21. Mule

22. Bimbo

23. Piece of ass

24. Harlot

25. Flappers(used in the 1920s)

26. Sheng nu (leftover women – women who remain unmarried in their late twenties and beyond (China)

27. Swamp Donkey

28. Strumpet

29. Trollop

30. Wench

31. Thot

32. Nag

33. Shrew

34. Harridan

35. Battleaxe

36. Crone

37. Dog

38. Minger

39. Slapper

40. Trailer trash

The following male list is much smaller as the following indicates:

1. Bastard

2. Jerk

3. Asshole
4. Creep
5. Douchebag
6. Fag
7. Dog (can also be used as a term of endearment)
8. Cunt
9. Prick
10. Scumbag
11. Wanker
12. Son of a bitch (This insult is mostly derogatory to the mother)
13. Tosser
14. Dickhead
15. Perv
16. Manwhore
17. Loser
18. Deadbeat
19. Beta male

The issue of sexism goes beyond merely a disparity in derogatory names for women compared to men, as I am sure you recognise. Yet, how deeply are you aware of this anomaly? A mere scratch on its surface reveals that it makes no sense, whether common or otherwise. Every subject can benefit from considering a historical perspective.

"According to ancient superstition, women, 'whores' or otherwise, were not permitted on board ship: they were regarded as unlucky and any unfortunate woman who found herself on board would have been thrown overboard to drown." (Catharine Arnold, *City of Sin: London and its Vices,* page 23) (fix on board)

- "…until recently [relatively speaking] the lives of women were not considered worth recording." (Catharine Arnold, *City of Sin: London and its Vices,* page 45)

- "… the Visigoths ruled that whores must be publicly whipped and their noses split open, whilst one early Aryan form of Christianity practised among the German tribes saw promiscuous girls and women put to death…the conditions for 'respectable' women were little better: regarded as the property of their husbands and fathers, they were traded like horses and sold into wedlock for financial or political gain." (Catharine Arnold, *City of Sin: London and its Vices,* page 24).

The following historical perspectives demonstrate how much progress we have made, but they also raise the question: How did we regress to this extent? It also shows that we are like a blank slate on which anything can be written.

Some of the ways in which someone could be accused of being a witch (16th to 18th centuries). [Since belief in witches is linked to belief in Satan, it is inseparable from religion.]

Taken from separate articles written by D.G. Hewitt and Leah Beckmann

- Just being a woman –"For thousands of years, people have believed women to be more susceptible to sins than men, and sinning is a clear indication of devil worship. In Salem, of the 19 people hanged for witchcraft, five were men and 14 were women. Historically, the numbers dramatically favour accused women over men."

- You are poor/cannot support yourself financially.

- You are rich/financially independent – do not need help or supervision from a man.

- You have one or more female friends. A gathering of women without a male chaperone was considered a "coven meeting to worship the Devil."

- You are very old. Older women were treated with suspicion, especially if they lived alone.

- You are a healer.

- You are a midwife. Wise women used their knowledge of herbal medicine to help others give birth safely, but it left them open to accusations of witchcraft…if a woman gave birth to a healthy baby and lived, the midwife would be accused of having used magic or making a deal with the Devil. Or if the baby or mother died, the midwife might also be blamed and accused of cursing the birth… by the late-17th century, the persecution of innocent midwives had largely stopped. As men started to take over the medical professions, including midwifery, the effectiveness of herbal remedies and natural medicines became increasingly accepted." This is indisputable evidence of sexism.

- You are married with too few (or no) children; the Devil cursed your unholy womb with infertility. Furthermore, if your neighbours and their several children are suffering in any way, they almost certainly believe the jealous crone living next to them has hexed their home.

- You have exhibited "stubborn," "strange," or "forward" behaviour.

- You have a reputation for being argumentative. Nobody liked or trusted an assertive woman back in the 16th and 17th centuries.

- You 'look the part'; you have a mole, birthmark, limp or have a hunched back (usually women). Prosecutors were always on the lookout for tell-tale 'signs of a witch' (almost any physical imperfection or skin blemish), especially on female bodies.

- You have a third nipple. They thought that Satan himself would suckle on the nipple…

- You have had sex out of wedlock – women were expected to follow strict sexual rules.

- You have broken virtually any rule in the Bible and thus entered into a pact with the devil.

- You talk to yourself: As the Salem Witch Trials (1692/93) showed, simply muttering under your breath could be seen as a sign of black magic.

- You don't dress smartly enough: In some witch trials, an individual's refusal to dress like everyone else was seen as something distinctly sinister - women who were expected to follow strict dress codes.

- You are left-handed. According to many traditions, there was something 'sinister' about being left-handed, and it was seen as one obvious sign that someone was a witch.

- You have a cat. For centuries, people really did believe that women who lived alone with cats for company were probably in league with the Devil…pet snakes, even pet dogs, might also be seen as witches' companions and could get their owners in serious trouble.

- Failure to quote fluently from the Bible might be seen as a sign of being possessed by evil.

- Having curdled milk in your house. Many believed that witches were able to make milk go bad just by walking by.

> **We need to go after and uproot ignorance and superstitions with the intensity of science and facts.**

> **The great Empress of soul music, Gladys Knight, sang the plaintive words from the song, *The Need to Be*: "To fulfil the need to be who I am in this world is all I ask…there is a need to be something more than just the reflection of a man. I can't survive in someone's shadow. I need my own little spot to stand…"**

The discriminatory idea that women need to prove themselves

A radio call-in programme moderator argued in favour of women being allowed to be ordained as pastors in the Adventist church. He proclaimed that women have "proven" themselves over the years.

The very act of using the word *"proven"* in the context of doing something that doesn't require muscle is, in itself, a revelation, a signal that many of us have been unconsciously conditioned into irrational, sexist thinking. What did these women do to "prove" themselves that we didn't already believe they were capable of doing? Why have we reached a point where women must "prove themselves" to occupy certain roles?

Since the roles in question do not require physical strength, we are left with questions of mental and emotional competence. However, in today's world, we should have no doubts about women's capabilities in either regard. The persistence of such doubts must therefore be, at least in part, a result of deeply rooted social conditioning passed down through generations.

We all should recognise by now that women have the same mental and emotional capacities as men. So if they are not being excluded due to physical limitations, nor because of intellectual or emotional inadequacy, the only remaining explanation is one that history makes painfully clear: the current status of women has been socially constructed.

Social engineering result: women had/have to fight for many rights

As a result of this social engineering, women have had to struggle for many rights that should be inalienable for all human beings. These rights include the right to equal education, to own property, and to vote, among others.

Sexism has persisted with us for so long that it has become the norm, and in some cases, it is practised unconsciously. It is an emotionally charged dilemma that both men and women can unknowingly become entangled in. The almost universal lack of genuine equality between men and women stems from our deepest underdevelopment in emotional intelligence. And emotional intelligence, in turn, plays a crucial role in nurturing common sense.

In some cases, sexism is deeply embedded in institutions to such an extent that gender bias has become a cultural norm for much of the world's population. The 'good news' is that it used to be worse, as you have already seen — and will see shortly. For example, you'll encounter advertisements that show a level of disrespect towards women that would be unthinkable today. So yes, we've made progress, but we still have a long way to go.

This isn't always obvious, however, because our current world has never genuinely experienced a different relationship dynamic between men and women. Consequently, what we deem "normal" has fostered an illusion of progress. In some areas, the normalisation of sexism has been so effective that many of us — myself included — fail to recognise its more subtle manifestations.

One such example can be found in the acting profession. Chris Rock, the comedian and host of the 88th Academy Awards, referred to this when he said: **'There is no real reason for there to be a men and women category in acting… It's not track and field [athletics]… Robert DeNiro has never said, 'I better slow this acting down so Meryl Streep can catch up.'"**

Cost of sexism 1: the human experience out of balance

In 1914, the physician Agnes Elizabeth Lloyd Bennett publicly opposed Sir Frederic Truby King's view that higher education for women was harmful to their maternal functions and thus to the human race. This exemplifies many distorted philosophies that have led to limited access for women to vital aspects of human activity. Such a lack of common sense has contributed to a world disproportionately influenced by male dominance. Consequently, female energy and creativity tend to be underused. This contradicts the natural order of life and the universe. All life comprises both male and female elements. Life cannot exist without these energies, yet for various reasons, we have established cultures where women lack equality in the governance of human affairs. The reasons for this are complex and rooted in deep historical causes.

The topic of this book does not allow for a lengthy historical discussion, but a short historical background and examples of severe sexism will be provided.

Those of you who see the different unfair treatments of women as a strange anomaly, something that contradicts common sense, should investigate this further. You might be surprised by what you discover.

I cannot begin to describe how much I despise the cultural practice of sexism. Part of my reason is self-interest. It's one of life's great tragedies that I will never experience a world where women are treated as truly equal.

A world where governance benefits equally from both male and female energies would be vastly different. Recognising the importance of our psychology and emotions suggests that such a world would be far more enjoyable to live in than our current reality, as the latter diminishes the quality of the human experience.

If women had equal influence in governing the world, there would be fewer wars. This should be common sense. Those who want to challenge this might do so due to a mistaken or shallow understanding. A deeper insight reveals a crucial wisdom:

A world where women are truly considered equals would nurture both women and men with mental and emotional qualities that reduce conflict. This harmony could only be achieved if both genders recognise and value the importance of balancing masculine and feminine energies—energies that promote ease, cooperation, and harmony, much like the principle of yin and yang. Such a balance is seen as ideal for resolving conflicts and problems.

This male-dominated world often forces women to suppress their feminine instincts to survive and succeed in "a man's world." In politics, for example, they frequently have to become the "iron lady," adopting a tough persona to contend with the dominant, aggressive male energy that prevails in that sphere.

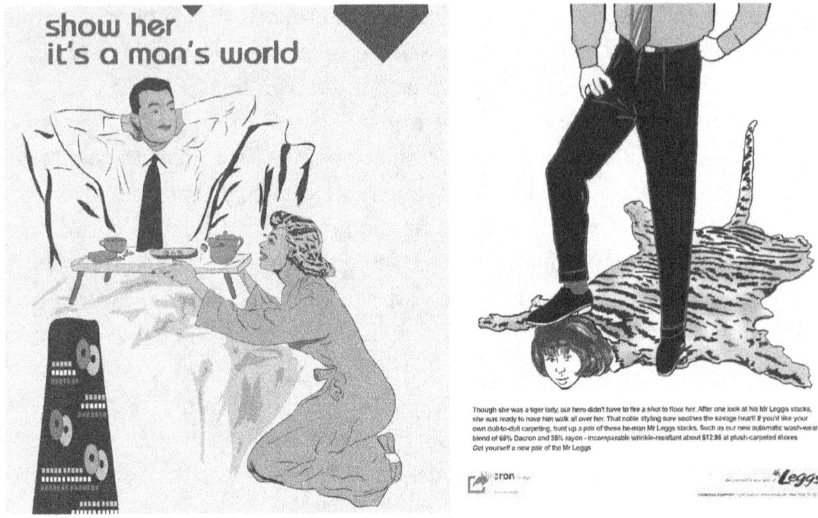

Cost of sexism 2: a male-dominated world (1951 and 1970 adverts)

Our basic ability to perceive should inform us that there is something very unnatural about the cultural and social fabric of the world today. What sense can we make of a situation where every **major** aspect of human endeavour is dominated by men, except for childbirth and child-rearing? Even some aspects of life that seem to be a woman's domain are dominated by men. Here is a list of major human endeavours for you to decide which ones seem to be a woman's domain, or, at least, ones in which she should have an equal say and participation.

- Men dominate all governments.
- Men dominate all churches, mosques, and synagogues in leadership positions.
- The fashion industry is dominated by men – most big designers are men.
- Men dominate the cooking industry – most celebrated chefs are men.
- Men dominate the movie industry.
- Men dominate the banking and commercial worlds.
- Men dominate farming and agriculture.

This system lacks common sense because, at the very least, it underutilises at least half of the human population. Women are just as intelligent as men and can provide a valuable perspective. Therefore, if men make most decisions, we are using less than half of our mental capacity. We are also making choices that affect everyone based on an unbalanced, male-dominated viewpoint.

Physical analogies for male-female balance:

- The Earth and the universe operate because there is balance.

- Life functions **and exists** because there are male and female (a balance), and this is Nature's unwritten instruction of how our society should function.

- In a car, there must be balance. The man is like the accelerator, and the woman is like the brake. Both are equally important. If the brake is missing, there will be a crash. If the accelerator is missing, the car cannot move unless you push it, which defeats the purpose of having a car. The world is crashing because of the imbalance between male and female input.

Should you separate the Yin from the Yang? If you did, what would it become?

Common sense suggests that the world would operate more smoothly if there was balance, especially between the masculine and feminine energies that influence our societies.

Cost of sexism 3: women were like men's property

Sexism is not an accidental attitude; societies shaped it, and it was also codified in law, and still is. This has been passed down through generations. Here is an example from Harvard Business School:

> "During most of American history, women's lives in most states were circumscribed by common law brought to North America by English colonists. These marriage and property laws, or 'coverture,' stipulated that a married woman did not have a separate legal existence from her husband. A married woman or *feme covert* was a dependent, like an underage child or a slave, and could not own property in her name or control her earnings, except under specific circumstances."

Sexist adverts from 1959 and 1953

After the rise [start] of the women's rights movement in the mid-19th century [1848], coverture came under increasing criticism as oppressive towards women, hindering them from exercising ordinary property rights and entering professions. Coverture was first substantially modified by the late 19th century, when the Married Women's Property Acts were passed in various common-

law legal jurisdictions. It was weakened and eventually eliminated by subsequent reforms. Certain aspects of coverture (mainly concerned with preventing a wife from unilaterally incurring significant financial obligations for which her husband would be liable) survived as late as the 1960s in some states of the United States.– Wikipedia on Coverture

During the era when coverture law was in force, no one would object to the statement, "If he had common sense, he would never have signed a contract with a married woman." This shows how common sense can be specific to its time. The law of **coverture** was partly based on the false belief that men were more intelligent than women. Therefore, if a shared communal understanding cannot be based on truth, should we still call it common **sense? Or is it more accurate to call it common nonsense?** Is this a case of prejudice preventing common sense, or is it an example of the fundamental blank slate principle, where we can be conditioned to accept almost anything?

Was an aspect of our highest ideal — good sense — absent during the period when coverture was the law? It is clear that while this law was in effect, both our emotional and rational minds experienced significant downturns. And honestly, we have not yet fully recovered from them.

How did men come to be in charge and so dominant? In Western civilisation, this dominance can be traced back to the division of survival roles. Men were the primary hunters — the food gatherers — while women played what was considered a minimal role in survival. However, that perception is deeply flawed.

Historical evidence indicates that women invented agriculture. This positioned them at the centre of human survival in ancient times. Despite this, the story of male dominance became widespread, and it has endured ever since.

The dominant male role persists because, at a certain point in history, men created a dangerous, unstable world and then appointed themselves as the solution. We cause the problem and present ourselves as the answer. We shaped a world that became increasingly militarised, which in turn increased the value placed on physical strength and thus reinforced male importance.

But a better world, a more balanced and humane one, would not be so militarised. In such a world, physical strength would diminish in importance. A more peaceful, cooperative society would value different human qualities, like patience, empathy, and nurturing.

And yes, those are strengths. Can women compete in these areas? Absolutely. One might argue they lead. Why else do you suppose that, in nine out of ten cases where a relationship breaks down, the woman keeps the children?

Is there any role more essential to the continuation of human life than caring for and developing children? Surely not. Yet we still tend to undervalue these contributions, not because they are insignificant, but because they do not fit the outdated standards of power we've long upheld.

Is the occasional omission of the word 'obey' from the traditional marriage vow an indication that we are diminishing the male-dominated mindset? I hope so.

Cost of sexism 4: Cruelty to women

During a period when Europe imposed extremely harsh punishments for crimes, the distorted attitude that governed male and female relationships was displayed in the most grotesque ways within the 'justice system'. The reality of a husband being regarded as a **lawful superior to his wife** was at its cruellest during this era. For example, in 1726, Catherine Hayes was executed for murdering her husband. These are the facts about this reality:

- Murder was a capital offence. However, if you were convicted of treason, the punishment would be much worse than a simple hanging. A man would be drawn, hanged, and quartered. Yet, this was deemed inappropriate for a woman because of the nudity involved, so she was burned instead.

- A man was guilty of treason if he had transgressed against the king or queen, the state, the church, and committed other crimes.

- A woman was guilty of petty treason if she killed her husband. Why would killing her husband warrant a harsher punishment than other capital offences? What was the thought process behind the inhumane punishment of being drawn, hanged, and quartered in the case of men, or being burnt in the case of women?

- It began with the belief that kings were divinely appointed. Therefore, crimes against the king were considered crimes against God. Such offences were punished with the most brutal methods.

- Why was the punishment for a woman who killed her husband the same as for crimes against the king or God? According to Catharine Arnold in her book, *Underworld London*, a husband's standing regarding his wife was akin to the king's status among his subjects. Consider the significance of this. A more severe punishment was meted out for an offence against the king because he was believed to be divinely appointed, and similarly, a woman who killed her husband, "a lawful superior,' was punished more harshly, given that he held a similar position of authority as a divinely appointed king does to his subjects. This excessively severe punishment for women was not limited to killing her husband or crimes against the king. According to Catharine Arnold, she could also be burned if she was convicted of killing a woman to whom she was an indentured servant.

- I found no evidence of a man suffering a harsher punishment for killing his wife. From the above, it's hard to imagine a worse consequence of poor emotional intelligence, which has led to a lack of common sense (fairness, sound judgement, sophistication, enlightenment or sensitivity). Besides the extreme barbaric nature of the punishment for crime, the fact that it was practised for a long time, even though it was not a deterrent, indicates an extreme lack of insight into human nature at that time.

Nature's rules on sexism

Interestingly, despite the world being dominated by men, nature has revealed some insightful truths. For example, according to Joseph Chilton Pearce in his book, *Magical Child*, a male foetus is more likely to be aborted. Elizabeth Pennisi also wrote on *sciencemag.org* an article titled, **"Why women's bodies abort males during tough times"**. The article stated, **"In times of trouble, multiple studies have shown, more girls are born than boys... Males are more likely to die than females while in the womb... Females are thought to have a better chance of reproducing than males in tough times, so aborting them doesn't make as much evolutionary sense."** Isn't this information fascinating and profound? Does it raise deep questions in your mind about life? What about the role women are meant to play in our human affairs? Here is something to consider: based on the role that nature has assigned women in reproduction, it suggests that they play a greater role, and in practice, they do. They provide the birthing chamber (the womb), the egg, the nourishment to sustain and bring the baby into this world, and nourishment after birth, while we men merely supply the sperm. There is nothing in this arrangement that suggests she should have a lesser say about the life and welfare of humanity, a humanity she plays such a critical role in fostering.

> *Those of you who study history will recognise that life was not always like this – we men have socially constructed this current reality. For over one hundred thousand years, women were considered genuine equals.*

A highly condensed version of the start of human procreation based on simple logic

Our imagination can help us reasonably understand what happened after the first couple had sex and pregnancy occurred. Simple common-sense reasoning suggests that it was our sex drive that came before the initial act. Or, as Count Volney says, "By attraction of a powerful pleasure, he approached a being like himself, and perpetuated his kind."

Having never seen a pregnant animal or one giving birth, and with no one around at the time with the experience to explain what might happen after their needs were satisfied, they had no idea of the possible consequences. Initially, they thought the woman was getting fat due to overeating. So, our mind can lead us to imagine, perhaps, the world's first comedic moment. This occurred when the baby emerged. The man, unprepared, said something like, "What the…H?!" or another popular expression.

Historical reverence for female fertility

This might have marked the beginning of the historical reverence for female fertility and the idea that the woman is the ultimate giver of life. The start of this reverence for women reflected the limited scientific understanding of procreation at the time. Therefore, this 'miracle' performed by women led to females being held in awe. Over time, people conceptualised the creator as a Goddess, often represented as being akin to the earth, which provides life to everything. Hence, she was called Mother Earth or the Earth Mother. Is 'Father Earth' a common expression? No. We still use an expression that recalls a period when man's fertility and role in procreation were not understood.

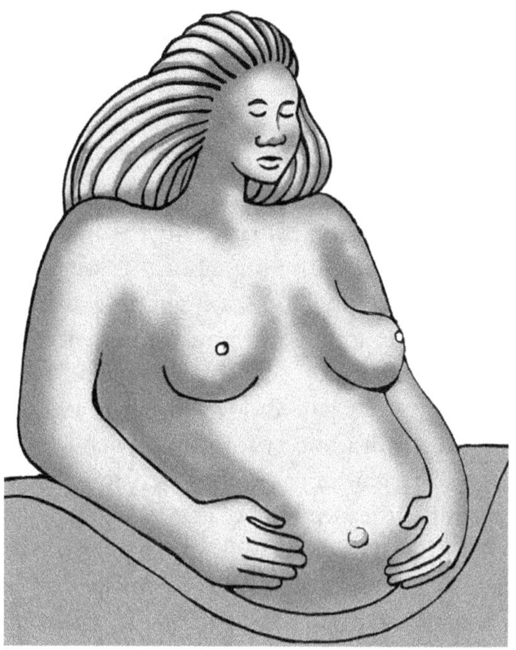

This Mother Goddess is depicted holding her creation tenderly

It is instructive to note that the scale of justice is depicted as a woman. The above images serve as reminders of a time when life was different.

A world dominated by beliefs, at the expense of knowledge, is a world that will not function at its best.

The historical mistreatment of women is fundamentally linked to a lack of common sense. Wisdom, which is often seen as a synonym for common sense, reflects our instinct as parents to treat our daughters equally to our sons, in terms of love and respect. However, there exists a contradiction to this innate parental love and the absence of gender discrimination. As we grow into adulthood, most of us are ultimately socialised into harbouring at least unconscious beliefs that men are better suited to lead than women. In essence, we are conditioned to accept the idea that men are more capable than women.

This conditioning is easily passed down through each generation because we already have secular institutions that exhibit a gender bias, which is often accepted as normal. Most significantly, we have religious institutions, and we are encouraged to respect their leadership because they are regarded as having the highest moral and spiritual authority. With such a powerful institutionalisation of gender bias, each generation, born into the world with limited awareness, will accept this contradiction to our parental instinct unless we become conscious of it and actively challenge it. Through insight and reflection, we can begin to question this imbalance by examining our historical journey—from worshipping both gods and goddesses to ultimately embracing a single, male-centred concept of God.

Based on deductions from the research of historian Professor Charles Finch, the worship of God as the primary deity, rather than the Goddess, began around eight thousand years ago. However, the earliest representation of a deity was created by the ancient Egyptians. It is an image of a pregnant Hippopotamus named Ta-Urt, symbolising Great Mother Earth, and the depiction references a tradition that predates them. Given that humans have been on Earth for approximately 200,000 years, the worship of goddesses, or female representations of the divine, could date back over 190,000 years.

There is no written history of how women were treated during the period when goddesses were worshipped earnestly. However, it is easy for us to make a reasonable guess about their treatment. The answer lies in our understanding of how deeply held religious beliefs are known to influence human behaviour. Here is an example, expanding on the practice of Hinduism, as previously mentioned:

Simple common-sense deduction

- In India, where people follow Hinduism, the cow is regarded as sacred, and killing a cow is illegal. In 2017, the new government increased the sentence for cow killing from seven years to lifetime imprisonment. The penalty for transporting beef was also raised to a maximum of 10 years from three. There have been cases of vigilante violence against those accused of eating beef or slaughtering cows.

- The cow is not regarded as a god or a representation of God. However, in the Vedas (the oldest Hindu scriptures), the cow holds great significance and is linked to Aditi, who is described as 'the mother of all gods'. Could this be the subconscious reason for the severe punishment? Is the cow connected to a goddess with such a revered title?

- Humans are generally seen as a higher form of life than animals. However, in many cultures throughout history, humans have faced harsh punishment for harming certain animals, not because of the harm itself, but because the animal was regarded as sacred. This illustrates the powerful role of ***sacredness*** as a social and moral force.

- If sacredness has the power to elevate an animal above harm, then consider its implications when applied to a human being.

- It follows, then, that if the human female were regarded as special — even sacred — because she gives birth, creating life in a manner that mirrors the creator, how would she be treated? What kind of reverence, protection, and respect would naturally develop in a society that genuinely sees her in this light?

- The answer is clear. From the above, we can easily conclude that when we wholeheartedly worshipped goddesses instead of gods, we would not have discriminated against women at the very least. It is more likely that women were considered superior to men when they embodied the likeness of people's concept of their creator. However, as we now have a global culture of 'God (male) worship', the opposite is now true. This is worsened by men writing in religious texts that **humans were created in God's image.** And since God is always depicted and referred to as male, it is obvious that men would be viewed more favourably, especially in terms of power and ability.

- The fact that humanity is both male and female (who create life together), yet the 'image' of God is only male, does not seem to register as a contradiction in the minds of those who accept this anthropomorphic characterisation of God.

- Finally, if we recognise that our acceptance of sacredness greatly influences our behaviour, it becomes clear that attributing gender to a creator gives that gender an advantage. Nothing could be more sacred than the image or concept of whoever or whatever we accept the creator to be. If humanity viewed the creator as gender-neutral, it would eliminate the basis for discrimination against females as described in religious texts.

- The only sensible basis for assigning value to gender should be the obvious: one cannot survive without the other. It is a matter of recognising the complementary traits, akin to yin and yang. An all-knowing God would not assign gender to itself because an all-knowing God would understand the psychological impact of the bias it would create on human behaviour, just as belief in a male creator has encouraged bias against females. Religious dogma has legitimised female oppression and discrimination.

Culture and sexism

No one can reasonably deny that we now have a male-dominated culture. Here is a definition of culture by the late Dr Amos Wilson that you may find enlightening: ***"Culture is a set of rules and procedures to meet needs. The ultimate thing culture should do is to solve problems. When a culture no longer meets the needs or solves the problems of a people, that culture must be transformed. There is nothing sacred about a culture."*** The rules and procedures of a culture can be lacking in sound judgement.

What need does this currently male-dominated culture address? What problem does it resolve? If you agree that this male-dominated culture is irrelevant to our current needs and has never solved any of our problems, does it make sense for it to be transformed to foster a more balanced society? Should women continue to fight for equality or fairness, or would it be better to channel that fighting spirit into a creative one, utilised in a situation of equal partnership that benefits us all, male and female? If the logical mind were dominant, sexism would not have persisted for centuries.

Cost of sexism 5: unequal pay

Isn't it fascinating that we have strict anti-competition laws to promote fairness in business, and yet, in 2015, the headline in The Independent read, ***"Gender pay gap: Firms who pay men more than women to be 'named and shamed'"*** by the government of England? It went on to say, ***"Writing in the Times, he [Prime Minister, David Cameron] said the government was making a 'really big move' by forcing companies to reveal the pay gap between the sexes.*** He said: ***"That will cast sunlight on the discrepancies and create the pressure we need for change, driving women's wages up."*** So, we have strict anti-competition laws, but the best we can do to address wage discrimination against women is 'name and shame the offenders'? This is incredible.

How profound is this sexism, then? It must be very deep if the government feels compelled to publicly acknowledge that a solution is necessary. That kind of admission alone highlights the seriousness of the problem.

However, the proposed solution, ***naming and shaming***, borders on absurdity. It suggests that the issue is recognised but not genuinely addressed. In reality, *naming and shaming* have become a coded language for *doing nothing of substance*. It creates the illusion of accountability without any real consequence or structural change.

So we must ask: Is the absence of strong action against the gender pay gap because, in this male-dominated society, it's regarded as a minor issue? An inconvenience rather than an injustice? Something not worth too much fuss?

If so, it reveals not only the extent of sexism but also the indifference that allows it to continue. What about 'gender-ageism'? Well, according to the British Broadcasting Corporation (BBC) website (23 July 2017), "Andrew Marr, [of The Andrew Marr Show] who is paid between £400,000 and £449,999 a year by the BBC, said if he was a woman he would have been removed from the TV '10 years ago'. 'There's a real lack of older women on the screen,' the 57-year-old said."

The online medium reported that "The salaries, **published in the corporation's annual report**, revealed two-thirds of its stars earning more than £150,000 are male, with Radio 2 DJ Chris Evans the top-paid on between £2.2m and £2.25m," while, "Claudia Winkleman, Strictly Come Dancing co-host and Radio 2 presenter… was the highest-paid female celebrity, earning between £450,000 and £500,000 last year."

Is pay inequality equivalent to the oppression of women? Shouldn't this be illegal and at least warrant a fine? Do you think oppression is too strong a term? Isn't our time our most valuable resource because we can never get it back?

Therefore, a woman spending her time and energy and being paid less than a man is effectively robbed of her most valuable resource.

Isn't the ultimate term for not being paid for your time and effort 'slavery'? So, does a lesser degree of this amount to oppression? Does the Prime Minister's response, at a minimum, reflect a lack of strong empathy towards sexism affecting women? As a remedy to this deeply rooted issue, naming and shaming companies is nearly as ineffective as men's nipples.

A direct link exists between the software of our minds –our formal and informal education, such as common sense, determines the direction, scope, and destination of our lives.

CHAPTER ELEVEN

The tenth major life issue to which Aristotelian syllogistic reasoning applies: **Common sense concerning education**

"The illiterate of the 21st century will not be those who cannot read and write, but those who cannot learn, unlearn, and relearn." Alvin Toffler

---

If we don't know how to look after our health, how can we legitimately claim to be fully educated? What better purpose should education serve? Should we know more about maintaining our car than our own body?

Since people are a country's greatest asset, and nurturing and developing this asset requires teachers, they should be well-trained and paid well.

Real education is knowledge that helps us understand and interpret the subtleties of life accurately.

Simple syllogistic logic – common sense:

- We are not born instinctively skilled in economic productivity and the ability to fulfil and attain some of our fundamental needs and desires, such as survival and happiness.

- If our formal and informal education does not meet this necessity, it is of limited value.

- Therefore, a blueprint must be put in place to precisely navigate the complexities of life in order to become effective human beings.

The value of knowledge lies in its ability to be applied for meaningful purposes. Beyond economic utility, this includes fostering mental and emotional growth, enhancing our capacity for happiness, improving survival and longevity, and enriching the quality of our relationships—whether intimate, familial, or platonic.

> **It is possible to store the mind with a million facts and still be entirely uneducated." – Alec Bourne**

Common sense on education

What should be the purpose of our education system? Should it merely serve as a factory to train and prepare us as workers? Should its main focus be on teaching us how to understand and manage ideas (abstract intelligence), or should it emphasise how to understand and handle physical objects (mechanical intelligence)? Should it simply aim to stimulate our ability to learn and reason? Considering how our lives are influenced by government, politics, and the media, should our education system also inform us of their roles and our responsibilities? It makes sense to have an education system that ensures we all develop a keen interest in politics, the administration of our affairs, and our country. Why? Because the people we elect, the decisions they make, and the policies they implement can have life-or-death consequences for us; they can determine war or peace. Additionally, their policies influence all the topics discussed in this book. Views on how our active interest should influence governance and politics will be examined further in Chapter Twelve.

What about **social intelligence**, a term attributed to both John Dewey and E.L. Thorndike in 1920? Thorndike described social intelligence as ***"the ability to understand and manage men and women, boys and girls – to act wisely in human relations."*** How could anyone argue against its value, given how challenging it is for many of us to maintain good relationships, which are a crucial part of the success and happiness formula? Could it be taught in schools? E.L. Thorndike remarked that: ***"Convenient tests of social intelligence are hard to devise... Social intelligence shows itself abundantly in the nursery, on the playground, in barracks and factories and salesroom (sic), but it eludes the formal standardised conditions of the testing laboratory."***

Syllogistic reasoning = common sense

Wisdom is integral to the definition of social intelligence. It is a synonym for common sense, and no capacity for understanding surpasses wisdom. Therefore, social intelligence should be the primary focus of education. Although Thorndike claimed that measuring social intelligence formally is challenging, there is a school that has been promoting this essential personal development skill in children aged between 2.9 and 7 years. Eliot-Pearson Children's School in Medford, Massachusetts, at Tufts University, USA, is one such institution. Given that these ages are critical periods for development, consider reviewing the school's philosophy and programmes to decide if such practices should be standard in all pre- and primary schools.

- Our programme centres on activities that foster cooperative problem-solving and self-confidence through individual and group challenges.

- Through spontaneous, structured, and integrated play opportunities, teachers and children foster problem-solving, creativity, and learning. This play environment encourages children to actively interact with materials, peers, and teachers. These hands-on, constructive experiences nurture and enhance children's self-esteem, confidence, sense of wonder, and natural passion for learning. Our focus remains on the whole child.

- Children should be offered a range of materials, strategies, and approaches because children learn in different ways.

This point is re-emphasised with this statement:

- Because variation in young children's development is normal, at the Children's School, standardised evaluations are not part of the routine assessment process.

- Through social interactions with peers, children learn to collaborate, cooperate, and understand others' points of view. Children who engage actively in their learning make sense of the world around them and develop their own ideas. By having choices and making decisions, children learn to take control of their learning and become independent thinkers.

The school's method and philosophy aim to foster emotional development, social intelligence, and other skills that lay the groundwork for common sense in adult life. Even in childhood, common sense remains relevant. For instance, children sometimes inadvertently act cruelly towards others in ways that can impact their self-esteem. This is evident from my earlier confession of referring to a tall girl as 'crane'. The school offers a programme that encourages respect for individual differences. It is called anti-bias education.

- Anti-bias education is a stance that encourages children and their families as they develop a sense of personal and group identity within a complex and multicultural society. This approach helps teach children to be proud of themselves and their families, to respect a range of human differences, to recognise unfairness and bias, and to speak up for what is right. (Derman- Sparks & Olsen,2010)
- Helps children and adults listen to each other with an open mind.

Is it common sense that schools should not focus solely on academia? What about life skills: the knowledge, attitude, and temperament necessary for success in life? Considering the common-sense approach of the Eliot-Pearson School, should this model become standard practice? Because the human mind is like a blank slate that can be shaped with a wide range of information and impressions, it should be obvious that the fight for our minds begins in infancy. If the programme implanted is thorough but not in our best interest, reversing it can sometimes be impossible. We are all vulnerable, and many are prone to manipulate others. Therefore, we should all be aware of the following, which ought to be common sense.

Intellectual and emotional miseducation

We can be miseducated both intellectually and emotionally. Intellectual miseducation is straightforward: it's simply a matter of receiving incorrect information. Emotional miseducation, however, is somewhat more complex. We may be presented with images and sounds that evoke feelings unrelated to logic and truth. Advertisers excel at persuading us to buy products and connect with certain brands. Essentially, they manipulate our feelings. Many of our misguided emotions are shaped by stimuli and impressions we absorb from our life experiences. In most cases, these emotions are never properly examined or questioned. I trust you now see that it is logical to accept that our emotions are the main drivers of our behaviour. Here are some key emotions that significantly influence our lives:

- How we perceive history – should we forget about it and focus on the present and the future, or should it guide us on how to live now? Today feels more meaningful because we understand what happened yesterday.

- How we feel about ourselves, groups of people, different races and ethnicities – such feelings are the foundation of many of the world's problems.

- Our attitudes towards different religions – this is the foundation of many of the world's conflicts, divisions, and issues.

Learning from our experiences

- **"Not by age but by capacity is wisdom acquired."** – Titus Maccius Plautus (Roman comic dramatist (254 BC - 184 BC))

- It is false that age automatically brings wisdom. We must have enough sense to understand that acquiring knowledge and wisdom is not an automatic process as we grow older. A few things are natural consequences, and wrinkles are one of them. On the other hand, a phenomenon related to this is the issue of ageism. Ageism has fostered a stupid attitude among many that, at some arbitrary age, a person's skill or value has diminished. This is supported by a cultural attitude that says appearance is everything. No sense, whether common or otherwise, is usually involved in these deep-rooted emotional issues. This emotional behaviour has led to a lot of human resources being wasted. We see the impact of ageism in our visual communication industry, television, and Hollywood, and it affects women the most. When was the last time you saw an

older female newscaster? How many older women get lead roles in blockbuster films?

- We should adopt a maxim stating: a person should be judged by their ability to perform, not by their age. When people discriminate or act unkindly towards others because of their age, one wonders if they expect to become older themselves. Those who do this should have enough sense to realise that they will likely reach the age of the person they discriminated against or treated unfairly. And unless they plan to die before that age, they could find themselves in the same situation.

- But too often youth believes that age only knows the wisdom of days gone by and thus gains no benefit. Remember this: the sun that shines today is the same sun that shone when thy father was born and will still be shining when thy last grandchild passes into darkness. The wisdom of age is like the fixed stars, shining so steadily that the sailor ***can rely on them to guide his course.*** – George S Clason (The Richest Man in Babylon)

- **Perceptiveness = common sense**

- Common sense, if we acquire it, would guide us to learn from our experiences, yet many of us fail to do so. Consequently, we often repeat the same mistakes. Therefore, as Jim Rohn eloquently states, ***"We all have recorded memories of past deeds and of the subsequent rewards or consequences of those deeds. The key is to make the memories of past events our servants, lest the repetition of those events makes us their slaves."***

- We learn things simply by the process of growing older, some more than others. The amount we remember from growing older depends on how much we examine and reflect on our life events. However, thinking about and reflecting on experiences is not all that is needed for us to gain accurate knowledge from each experience. It mainly depends on the understanding we apply to each event. Did we observe events with wise eyes? Did we bring wisdom or an improved understanding and application of the collective truths of human experience to each of our life events?

- The above might seem like the dilemma of whether the egg comes before the chicken or vice versa. However, each life experience presents itself for us to understand, and we will grasp it if we can identify its root cause. If we do this, we can then apply this insight to the next experience. This process will continually enhance our navigational system. Moreover, if we combine this with extensive research and contemplation, we will be fully equipped to understand the world and life's events. Our research must include an accurate knowledge of history. One of the best ways to improve our navigational system is to discuss and debate life's events and experiences with others.

- Imagination, empathy, and sensitivity are central to the common-sense formula. Imagination acts as a skill we must develop, much like any other muscle. Empathy arises from caring about people or things beyond our own interests. It also results from seeking to understand others. How can we possess much common sense in our dealings with people if we only understand them on a superficial level?

- If a person lacks sensitivity, meaning they do not have a quick and delicate appreciation of others' feelings, are they not more likely to say the wrong thing at the wrong time? Would this 'lack' influence their ability to demonstrate common sense? Therefore, we should work on our sensitivity by developing the ability to see and understand things from others' points of view.

- No one can tell us why or how to care; we must find our reasons. If we invest knowledge, imagination, and empathy into everyone we meet, including others on this life journey, our ability to develop and gain common sense will improve. Are you able to see life from the perspective of people of different races, ethnicities, cultures, backgrounds, and environments? Do you only understand those who are like you? Are you so preoccupied with your own affairs that you have scarcely taken a moment to understand others?

- Politicians are often criticised for being out of touch with working-class people, the common man, or other social phenomena. This is another way of saying they are absorbed in their world and not particularly interested or involved in the worlds of others. They have, in effect, been minding their own business. People who strictly mind their own business contribute significantly to the idea that common sense is not common, because common sense is gained chiefly through a genuine interest in life and people. Political parties have lost elections because they failed to apply common sense.

Simple syllogistic reasoning (common sense) points to

The importance of reading, possessing a good vocabulary, and broad general knowledge

The incorrect choice of words can produce the opposite of the intended effect. Being sensitive and understanding the impact of words can be useful in our communication. With this skill, we can be tactful and use common sense by avoiding the unintentional use of the wrong words. If someone feels a bit down, it's better to ask, "What's troubling you?" rather than, "What's wrong with you?" Words are the tools we use to see. Therefore, a limited vocabulary equals a limited vision. Common sense tells us we cannot interpret what we do not see. It also shows that limited knowledge restricts our opportunities and, consequently, our success. We have all been presented with opportunities. How many of these did you turn down because you didn't understand them? Many business leaders have concluded that most people reject business opportunities because they either don't understand them, fail to see their potential, or are afraid to take a chance.

Here is a simple illustration of how a lack of knowledge can rob us of opportunity:

John attended an event and struck up a conversation with an elderly man. During their chat, the man revealed he was facing financial difficulties and needed to sell his car. John agreed to have a look at the car in the car park.

So, what did he *see*? He saw an outdated-looking car being sold by an old man and thought the price was too high for what seemed to be just an old vehicle. He politely declined the man, giving the false excuse that he didn't have the money.

Later that day, John bumped into a friend who looked particularly excited about something. The friend told him he had just bought a car at a bargain price. Curious, John followed him out to the car park, only to see the very same car he had declined.

Surprised, John asked his friend why he would pay so much for a car that looked so old. His friend smiled and told him the car was a **Morgan**.

At that moment, it became clear: John had never heard of a Morgan, let alone appreciated its value. His rejection of the car exposed his lack of knowledge, and that lack had cost him a rare opportunity.

His friend went on to explain that the car was worth more than **ten times** what he had paid for it. So, what was John's reply? He shrugged and said his friend was just lucky.

But was it really luck? No — his friend took the chance because he *recognised* what he saw. John failed, not because he lacked money, but because he lacked the **knowledge**, the *words*, to see the opportunity before him.

He had no words for what he saw.

Taken from my book – *"For the Love of Money: Root of All Evil?"*

Common sense on reading and comprehension

- Do you know how many people refuse to read books that could set them free, improve their finances, health, relationships, and help them reach their goals? While adopting this attitude of not reading, many complain about their circumstances. Jim Rohn wisely observed, "They curse the effects, but nourish the cause."

We are living in the information age. Never before has it been this easy to acquire knowledge. Why is this the case? Because, as previously mentioned, the Internet is the greatest library ever created and is accessible in billions of homes. So, here is the good news: information is just a click away. The bad news is that we will not learn what we don't seek.

- A book must be the axe for the frozen sea within us. – Franz Kafka
- *"There is definitely a relationship between vocabulary and behaviour. The more limited the vocabulary the more there is a tendency to poor behaviour. If you think about it for a while, it makes sense. Vocabulary is a way of seeing; one reason for vocabulary is to interpret what we see and hear. The vocabulary of the mind grapples with the words and the images that come to our minds. If you have a poor set of words, skills, and tools with which to interpret, you can imagine the errors and the mistakes you will make in judgement. And since vocabulary is a way of seeing, if you can't see well, you can imagine the errors you can make and how they will compound as life unfolds."* – Jim Rohn.
- All major breakthroughs come as a result of taking new information. – Dennis Kimbro
- Saying you're too busy to read many books is like driving down the motorway, running out of petrol, and deciding that you were in such a hurry that you couldn't stop.

Common sense or wisdom urges us to read, learn, grow, and develop so that we can take actions that lead us to a place of our deliberate choosing.

As we add new knowledge, we will begin to refine our philosophy. As our beliefs change, so too will our choices. And from better choices come better results. – Jim Rohn

Suppose governments desire to raise the performance of their countries. In that case, those who design and control our school system should elevate reading and comprehension to a more rigorous application.

What is the best choice: a bag of knowledge or a bag of gold?

I'll have a bag of gold, please!

One of the most insightful questions ever asked is, "If you were offered the choice of a bag of gold or a bag of knowledge, which one would you choose?" Some chose the bag of gold, claiming they would use the gold to gain knowledge. Many, recognising that it's a trick question, chose the bag of knowledge. However, chances are, if this were a real-life situation, the vast majority would choose the bag of gold. In their minds, they would be thinking that they could always acquire knowledge later. On this matter, this is what our **perception** should teach us:

If we are not currently in the *habit* of acquiring extensive knowledge, it is because this activity is not a high priority for us. Therefore, after receiving the 'bag of gold' and satisfying all our financial needs, we would have even fewer reasons to pursue knowledge. Our best option would be to choose the bag of knowledge, and here is why: it takes wisdom to keep money. Most importantly, perceptiveness (common sense) tells us that it can be a devastating and depressing experience to enjoy a life of financial freedom, then lose it, and have no knowledge or skill to regain it. It's indeed better to have loved and lost than never to have loved at all, but this sentiment does not apply to losing a fortune.

An investment in knowledge pays the best interest. —
Benjamin Franklin

Two key features of our increasingly complex societies are **politics** and the **media**. Whether we engage with them actively or not, whether we vote or follow the news, they continue to influence our lives in significant ways. That's exactly why we *should* pay attention to them. But paying attention isn't enough. To engage meaningfully, we need more than just awareness; we need **critical thinking** and **common sense**. These are the tools that help us interpret what we see, question what we're told, and make informed decisions.

CHAPTER TWELVE

The tenth major life issue to apply Aristotelian syllogistic reasoning to **is understanding common sense about the core issues in politics, including government, economic policies, the role of the media, and how to select politicians**

Basic common sense about the role of governments

In a democratic system, governments are groups of people elected through a voting process to act on behalf of everyone. So, how did this principle originate, and what was its usual focus? Here is an example of how a Western country began: before America became a country, when establishing a typical town, the people's priorities were demonstrated by their first collective act—hiring someone to represent everyone. The main goal was usually to teach their children. Employing someone to maintain order, such as a sheriff, only became necessary with population growth and signs of criminal activity. Self-employed individuals provided other services. Apart from this, people generally managed their own affairs. As the town's population increased, more people were employed to make decisions and work on behalf of the community. This essential trend continued and expanded significantly, leading to the development of a complex society known as the United States of America.

A system in which a few manage the affairs of everyone by the authority of the whole **is essential** for large populations to coexist with a good level of cohesion and prosperity. The question now is, with government employees in place, what should we prioritise? Was the instinct to collectively hire a teacher as the first employee based on wisdom? *Since knowledge is the foundation of all human progress*, the answer is yes. Consequently, all current governments should prioritise the use of our taxes similarly. In our modern context, this priority translates to free higher education for all. In democratic countries where this is not the case and people aren't demanding it as a priority, perhaps they suffer from a loss of sense of what truly matters, or they do not realise it is necessary for fair coexistence. People must remember that governments are public servants; they work for the people. Therefore, we have every right to demand that they prioritise education for everyone and hold them accountable when they do not.

Democratic power is taken from the people

In every country with democratic political systems, power should rest with the people, who entrust the government to act in their best interests. Power being in the hands of the people is not meant to be an abstract idea or limited to voting during elections. Currently, a common situation exists where government mechanisms allow them to easily bypass the wishes of the people and act against their best interests. As a result, many times, the people do not have control over how their tax money is spent. Additionally, politicians can, and have, enacted laws that enable their own enrichment at the expense of good governance. To some, it now appears that many are working for the privileged few. Essentially, the original purpose of democratic governments has been turned upside down. The majority should not be working for the increasing benefit of the privileged few. Employers should not, in effect, become employees. This is a clear abuse of the fundamental principles upon which governments were meant to function.

Three ways in which democratic governments and politicians typically abuse the principle of governance, by not acting in the best interest of the people and habitually getting away with it, are to:

- Keep their actions a secret or lie to their employers, we the people. They often hide unfavourable information under the guise of 'national security'. And they can punish any employer who exposes any of their secrets, even if the secret is criminal.

- Implement policies that mainly enrich or advantage a privileged minority rather than the majority.

- Use psychology to manipulate people's ignorance, prejudice, and bigotry, causing them to vote against their best interests. They also foster divisions and conflicts, which can be seen as appealing to people's worst instincts and are often achieved through lies, propaganda, and fear-mongering.

Why did the change occur

A key reason why democratic governments and politicians often get away with acting against the interests of the people is that most of us do not consciously think from a position of power. We forget that *we* are the government's employers, and they are supposed to act in *our* best interests.

In essence, our attitude towards them is that of 'public rulers' rather than public servants. If we consciously regarded them as our employees and

had a clear sense of what is in our best interest, we would consistently have governments that prioritise our taxes to ensure that we all have free access to higher education. We would demand that they provide us with this basic option, or face losing their jobs.

Why do political parties stay relevant and keep winning elections, even though they repeatedly fail to act in the best interests of the majority?

Apart from the tactics already mentioned, various other factors also play a role in this phenomenon.

- One significant factor is the **increase in intense partisanship**. Many voters have become so devoted to their political party that they will not change allegiance, even when their own interests are at risk. For example, someone who cannot afford higher education may still refuse to vote for an opposition party that promises free or affordable access, simply because of deep-seated partisan loyalty.

- In this way, **rabid partisanship overrules rational decision-making**, keeping voters loyal to parties that may not serve their best interests, and enabling those parties to remain in power with limited accountability.

- Inadequate intergenerational education has hindered many people's understanding of how governments function and prevented them from gaining an *accurate* awareness of what is happening in their country.

- The 'historical instinct' to promote equality through education appears to have been eroded in many by misinformation about what our governments and officials should prioritise when spending our taxes. Some of us are conditioned to accept that taxes are mainly spent on arms, 'security', and conflicts, rather than ensuring free access to higher education for all. It is also true that many remain unaware of how governments allocate their tax revenues.

- Many of us have, at least unconsciously, accepted the concept of **class and privilege**. This silent acceptance explains why, in some democracies, elite universities and colleges remain priced far beyond the reach of ordinary citizens, yet there is little public protest. The system benefits a few while excluding many, and the majority has become accustomed to it.

- People also lack effective **methods** to convert their collective efforts and contributions into shared benefits. This issue is worsened by a lack of **collective awareness**. In a genuine democratic system, the people should hold the most power, not just during elections, but continuously. However, for many, democracy has become reduced to voting every few years, rather than actively shaping the systems that govern their lives.

How should a democracy maintain power in the hands of the populace?

Returning to our model start-up town in America, the first employee was often a school teacher, despite the limited practical value of formal education, which demonstrates an ingrained appreciation of its worth. They recognised it as the fundamental starting point of all progress. Since most, if not all, of us agree that education is linked to success, we will only oppose equal opportunities for higher education if we are prejudiced against certain people because of classism or other reasons.

Our initial instinct to employ a teacher was both sensible and rooted in common sense. It demonstrated a clear understanding that learning is vital for both personal and shared development.

The modern equivalent of that instinct, in our more advanced and complex societies, is to prioritise the use of public funds, our taxes, to provide **free higher education** for all. Just as it was then, the extent of one's educational opportunities today should **not** be determined by the socially engineered barriers of class and privilege.

Perhaps this innate instinct to elevate oneself through education inspired the following poem, one that has been recited by children worldwide and across generations.

Labour for learning before you grow old;

For learning is better than silver or gold.

Silver and gold will vanish away,

But a good education will never decay.

Key ways a well-educated, critical-thinking population would transform politics

- They would prohibit politicians from deliberately, with malicious intent, making foolish or outrageous comments or speeches to deceive. The politicians would realise that the public would find it

offensive, and they would face negative consequences such as losing an election. Therefore, they would feel compelled to deliver speeches of the same standard as those they give in their private clubs.

- They would ensure politicians avoided the tactic of 'repeat a lie often enough, and it becomes true for many.'

- They would not elect politicians whose self-promotion was of a low moral or intellectual standard. This would improve the quality of political candidates, and as a result, we would have more capable employees.

- They would diminish media bias and propaganda, ultimately compelling the media to deliver accurate information within the correct context.

- They would require stronger public proof of the necessity for going to war. This would result in fewer or no unjustified wars due to the assured political repercussions. Ultimately, more conflicts would be resolved through diplomacy and justice.

- They would keep the founding democratic principles and ideals alive and instil them in the minds of the population to guard against political excesses.

Education is the most powerful weapon which you can use to change the world. – Nelson Mandela

---

The function of education is to teach one to think intensively and to think critically... Intelligence plus character – that is the goal of true education. – Martin Luther King Jr.

Dissatisfaction with democracy within developed countries is at its highest level in almost 25 years, according to University of Cambridge researchers. Academics have analysed what they say is the biggest global dataset on attitudes towards democracy, based on four million people in 3,500 surveys. The UK and the United States had particularly high levels of discontent...the figures for 2019

> **showed the proportion dissatisfied rising from 48% to 58%, the highest recorded level. By Sean Coughlan, BBC News family and education correspondent, 29 January 2020**

The diminishing value of interdependence in democracy

> **We are social beings. We would not survive or thrive if we never formed bonds with others. Interdependence is a vital part of human progress. Without interdependence, there would have been no growth in the human population and civilisation.**

Remembering the power of interdependency

In Chapter Two, *The Birth of Common Sense*, the obvious was articulated by Thomas Paine regarding our interdependent nature: "**The strength of one man is so unequal to his wants... that he is soon obliged to seek assistance and relief of another, who in turn requires the same.**" Paine understood a key truth: **we rely on one another**. Interdependence is not a sign of weakness — it's the bedrock of civilisation.

However, the **value and strength of interdependence** have been diminished over time. This decline mainly results from the **unfair, biased, and harmful misuse of education and privilege to segregate people**. Instead of using education to bring people together and uplift them, societies have too often weaponised it to create division.

The more educated a population becomes, the more influential it can be, not just economically, but socially and politically. If a highly educated and skilled populace **united in its appreciation for interdependence** and was supported by **effective, people-centred governance**, the outcome could be transformative.

Such an arrangement would offer the **majority** a genuine chance to experience what we all seek: **success, happiness, and the everyday comforts** that should be reward for an organised, modern society, far surpassing what was accessible in nomadic life.

So why, then, have some countries chosen to restrict access to higher education? **The answer lies in the acceptance of a flawed political and social philosophy** — one that prioritises individualism, elitism, and control over fairness, unity, and shared human dignity.

Elitism, unequal opportunity, lack of vision, the **misallocation of public funds,** and the **segregation of education** all contribute to eroding the benefits we should gain from our interdependence as a society. Consequently, many people now live in a state of constant struggle and unhealthy stress, conditions that entirely oppose the original aim of settling into organised, interdependent communities. Humans moved from a nomadic existence to a structured society to reduce hardship, increase stability, and improve well-being, not to swap one form of suffering for another.

Widespread access to advanced education was meant to be a key part of that solution. It aimed to empower individuals, lessen societal struggles, and enable everyone to succeed in a complex, modern world. And when the system inevitably encounters setbacks, when people slip through the gaps and require support, we should be ready and willing to provide it. After all, when we lived as nomads, we didn't abandon our injured, sick, or struggling members. We lifted them. We shared our resources. We survived together. A more advanced system, with all its resources, infrastructure, and knowledge, should never offer **less** protection for human dignity, survival, and happiness than a simple, nomadic way of life.

In some wealthy, democratic capitalist countries, this ideal is not reflected in their policies. The government neglects its citizens, and those who suffer most are often the **poorly educated and underpaid**. These individuals face limited opportunities, a diminished quality of life, and little social mobility.

In contrast, other democracies make a **very different calculation**. They recognise that it's *more cost-effective*, both economically and socially, to invest in **public well-being**. They understand that nurturing the population results in fewer health issues, lower crime rates, increased productivity, and a happier, more stable society.

These countries opt for the more intelligent, **more humane choice**: free advanced education, fair wages, access to healthcare, reasonably long paid holidays, freedom of conscience, and social systems designed to keep people well, not just alive. They view the people not as a burden, but as the most significant **national resource**, one worth protecting and empowering.

So, after humans transitioned from a nomadic lifestyle, did they expect to be **dominated by a minority**, dictated to, or treated unfairly? Did they envision a society where the benefits of cooperation were **unjustly distributed**? **Certainly not.** What they would have expected was **collective prosperity**.

With settled life came immediate advantages, **greater security**, safety in numbers, and a shared commitment to helping one another within the group.

As with all human groups, leadership appeared, and over time, those leaders became what we now call the government.

As discussed in Chapter Two, the passage of time led to the development of **classes, cultures, and royalty**, all of which are human inventions, not divine mandates. Yet their **validity was gradually accepted and normalised**. Eventually, this acceptance laid the groundwork for more dangerous ideas: the belief in **inherent superiority or inferiority based on birth or bloodline**. Although much of this outdated perspective has been challenged and discarded in modern times, the harm persists. A persistent **disregard for the masses** still exists, rooted in classist and elitist mentalities.

What worsens this situation is that many people remain **unaware** of it. They are often misled by **elitist politicians** who pose as allies of the working class while supporting systems that maintain inequality. Equally concerning is the fact that the **masses often fail to recognise their own collective power—** the power to hold their governments (their employees) accountable, to demand transparency about how their taxes are utilised, and to **reshape the system** through democratic means. They forget that in a democracy, **the people should lead the government**, not the other way around.

Accountability of the servants of the people is paramount.

In many democracies, the public has allowed **excessive, unchecked power** to accumulate in the hands of their government and its officials. A prominent example of this is the **imbalance in legal accountability**. Politicians and public officials, who are meant to serve the people, have often **elevated their roles** to shield themselves from the same legal consequences that apply to ordinary citizens. Consequently, we now see instances where these individuals enjoy **greater protection against prosecution**, even when they commit obvious violations of the law.

This is not only **illogical** but also **very unwise**. At the very least, public officials, especially those in leadership roles, should be held to **the same level** of accountability as the citizens who granted them power. In fact, considering the trust and responsibility they bear, they should arguably face an even **higher** standard. Ask yourself this: if you owned a company, would you allow your employees to write rules that let them **break your policies without consequence**? Would you permit them to **commit crimes against you**, the owner, with legal immunity? Of course not. That would be a glaring loophole, and in many democracies, it's a loophole that persists.

This imbalance of power has escalated to the point where, in some cases, **citizens fear their employees**, including law enforcement officers who are

supposed to protect and serve, not intimidate and dominate. What kind of democracy permits its **public servants to break the law openly,** without facing consequences, while ordinary citizens, **their employers,** are swiftly punished for far lesser actions? In many democracies, government officials, our **employees**, have become corrupted by power and need to be **forcefully reminded** of their proper role. **Being elected is not a licence to deceive, exploit, or oppress.** It is a mandate to **serve**, to protect the people, and to implement and manage policies that reflect the **public good**, not personal or political gain.

Here is a more detailed explanation of how and why a social and economic system, **supposed** to be driven by the will of the people, has moved in the wrong direction. Instead of collective progress, we now observe a significant gap between the **'haves' and the 'have-nots'**. The *'haves'*, who constitute the **minority**, hold most of the power and enjoy the greatest benefits. Meanwhile, the *'have-nots'*, who form the **majority**, have the **least power** and receive the **fewest benefits.**

- Some of the earliest leaders eventually became part of a self-interested elite. Over time, **power tempted them**, and **corruption took hold**. These leaders, our employees, took control of setting the rules that govern how national resources, including taxes, are allocated. And when those in power are **corrupt** or **lack empathy** for the masses, they almost always write the rules **to benefit themselves.**

- As a population increases, it often **loses the homogeneity** that smaller communities tend to have, especially in terms of **shared values and priorities**. With that loss comes a weakened sense of what the **common good** truly is. When people no longer share a clear set of common causes, it becomes much harder to **mobilise collective action** that pressures governments to alter policies for the **benefit of the majority.**

- Over time, the importance **of education for all has diminished, as it slipped from being a top priority,** and people lost sight of its **vital role in promoting equality and narrowing the wealth gap**. Perhaps the masses became **distracted by fierce partisanship** and the increasing complexities of daily life. Later in this discussion, the way some Western democracies have managed to **distribute their national resources more fairly among their populations** is examined.

- **The public has not been adequately educated or socialised** to understand the actual power dynamics that should define a democracy. Consequently, many people **do not see the status quo as something they can change**, or even believe it is their right to do so.

- **Partisan loyalty has become deeply ingrained**, often to the point that it overrides both **collective interests** and even **personal self-interest**. This form of conditioning creates a rigid mindset, making it **difficult to change views** or foster unity around shared causes.

- **Political apathy and disengagement** are becoming more common, resulting in **low voter turnout**. Ironically, this lack of participation **diminishes the power of the majority**, allowing a smaller, often more elite group to retain control.

Why voter apathy is widespread in democracies, why it reduces people's power and is dangerous

Low voter turnout is often blamed on apathy, but the deeper issue is usually **disillusionment** — a feeling of futility. Many believe that **no party truly represents their interests** and that **nothing will change**, so they think their vote doesn't matter. Ironically, the fewer people who vote, the **smaller the group politicians need to win over**. In such cases, the party with the most **devoted or loyal base**, often indifferent to policy, decides the result.

The public does not perceive itself as a unified group of employers wielding power in a democracy. Disillusionment exists **only because people have not exercised their democratic rights**. They have failed to demand that their **political representatives** act in their interests.

Many people do not realise that **government decisions can determine life-and-death matters**, such as going to war. Whether or not citizens participate in shaping policy, **they still face the consequences**. Usually, it is **ordinary people or their children who go to war**, even when the war is **unjust** and only benefits a small, elite minority. Meanwhile, the politicians who make those decisions face **no personal risk**. The days when a king or his sons fought in the wars they started are long gone.

People also fail to recognise a key truth supported by political science: **"Democracies perform better when more people vote,"** as noted by Stanford University's Adam Bonica and Michael McFaul. However, this is especially true when people vote because they **understand their role as stakeholders** in a **collective enterprise**, choosing government representatives to **manage the country's affairs** on their behalf.

This truth is **less significant** when voter turnout only rises during crises. If people only engage when the system seems to be falling apart, it indicates that

disaster, not civic duty, prompts participation. In a healthy democracy, **high voter turnout should be normal**, even during quiet periods, because voting involves **choosing how to manage the country**, not just reacting to chaos.

The solution begins

The People's Information Service (PIS) and the People's Empowerment Movement (PEM)

- **So, how do people address the widening social and economic divide, particularly in wealthy democracies?**
- How can they, when a powerful minority is **entrenched in greed and power**, and has **little interest in the advancement of the masses**?
  How can they, when **most people remain unaware of their collective power**, or do not **instinctively grasp it**?
- A significant obstacle is **rabid partisanship**. Many citizens have been **socialised into blind political loyalty**, often without realising that their allegiance is **working against their own best interests**. This deep division complicates the problem **and makes it more challenging to resolve**.
- One of the most harmful effects of this hyper-partisanship is that it **shields underperforming political representatives**. These politicians face **little risk of being voted out**, not because they serve the people well, but because the electorate is too divided or too loyal to hold them accountable.

So, what actions should people take to restore democracy and maximise its advantages?

The People's empowerment movement (PEM)

This group of people, who would effectively serve as guardians of their democracy, would establish public funding to organise and employ the most practical and necessary tool for empowering the masses, which is their watchdog media. The larger a country's population, the more essential this type of media becomes.

> The role of a watchdog media is to act as a protector or
> guardian of democracy, and therefore the people's or
> employers' best interests. Its function as a guardian is to
> provide citizens with the information they need "to prevent
> the abuse of power" and to "warn citizens about those that
> are doing them harm".

The Role of the PIS and the PEM: Institutionalising People Power

To be effective, the **People's Information Service (PIS)** must be **entirely independent**, funded and managed by the people themselves, not corporate sponsors, political parties, or wealthy donors. Its name reflects its purpose: to promote **public empowerment through reliable information, education, and accountability**.

The PIS would fulfil two core roles:

1. **Provide a credible, public-interest source of information** to counter the surge of propaganda, false news, and distortion by professional political operatives.

2. **Work with its founders, the People's Empowerment Movement (PEM)** — a structured, non-partisan civic organisation that promotes greater political engagement (voter turnout) and ensures government accountability.

Objectives of the People's Empowerment Movement (PEM)

The PEM aims to **redefine democracy as a year-round civic engagement** rather than merely a four-year voting ritual. Its goals will include:

- **Collaborate with the PIS to pursue a campaign to educate the masses about the need for constitutional reforms** that legally establish the true power of the people, not just in words.

- **Persuade the populace of the need for establishing a legal framework for public-led removals** of elected officials, including the head of state, under exceptional circumstances, ensuring justice through a well-informed, bipartisan public jury.

- **Ensuring that unlawful orders by leaders are disregarded without consequence**, and making such actions grounds for impeachment.

- **Banning obstruction of justice by government officials**, especially in cases where they are under investigation. Complicity will lead to immediate prosecution.

- **Making it compulsory for political candidates to demonstrate knowledge of the Constitution** or its equivalent in other democracies, ensuring a minimum standard of legal and cognitive competence.

- **Enforcing majority-driven policy-making** within the bounds of human rights and international law.

- **Vigorously defending the democratic process**, considering voter suppression and election tampering as direct attacks on democracy, with a bipartisan response and legal consequences.

Objectives of the People's Information Service (PIS)

The PIS would act as the **informational backbone of democracy**, dedicated to transparency, education, and critical oversight. It would:

- **Working with the PEM, it would also boost voter turnout through persuasive campaigns**, reminding citizens that political decisions can have a significant impact on everyone, sometimes affecting lives as a matter of life or death.

- **Scrutinise all candidates and public officials**, guarding against the corrupting influence of power.

- **Alert the public to breaches of ethics, law, or democratic principles**, with real-time consequences for those in office.

- **Keep citizens updated** on national and global issues, particularly conflicts and policy changes.

- **Oversee judicial fairness**, guaranteeing that legal systems are not weaponised against the public.

- **Evaluate economic policies for fairness**, emphasising unjust wealth concentration or systemic poverty.

- **Examine corporate malpractice**, particularly when public health or safety is at risk.

- **Perform relentless fact-checking**, exposing lies by politicians or public figures, and offering evidence-based rebuttals.

- **Always provide context**, balancing perspectives, but grounded in verifiable truth. No manipulation, no blind neutrality—just informed, deliberate balance.

A New Approach to Partisan and Bipartisan Politics

So, what is this **new approach to political activism** that the PIS should promote through the PEM?

What **core philosophy** should underpin this reimagined engagement with democracy?

It is a **redefinition of both partisanship and bipartisanship**, shifting away from blind party loyalty and towards **allegiance to principles, policies, and people**.

It encourages citizens to:

- Vote according to values and results, not identity or party branding.

- Call for cross-party collaboration when it serves the public interest.

- View political representatives as **replaceable employees**, not celebrities or saviours.

- Recognise that **uncritical partisanship is anti-democratic**, and that bipartisanship, when it benefits elites at the expense of the people, is just as harmful.

The world faces problems when the uninformed greatly surpass the informed, particularly in an era where the desire for profit and power exceeds moral considerations.

A new philosophy and approach to politics and political activism – the People's Empowerment Movement (PEM):

Simple syllogistic reasoning

- For the public to make good judgements when voting, they must be fully equipped with accurate information and able to analyse that information critically.

- This is crucial to elect the people who will act in their best interests.

- An educated and well-informed public is therefore essential for this process.

- If the masses are not well educated, they must demand that this change be made for their children and future generations.
- In the meantime, they must be street smart enough to utilise their media to act as a watchdog, analyse and break down complex issues for them, and keep them well-informed.

For people to be truly empowered and have political leverage, they must agree on bipartisan rules to hold their government and politicians accountable. The leverage depends on the ability to exert bipartisan pressure on the government or politicians. This power can be twofold: pressure to enact policies and pressure to impeach when politicians break rules. In sufficient numbers, the government will heed the wishes of the people, especially if they are certain that the consequence of inaction is losing their jobs in the next election or, worse, depending on the type of transgression. Therefore, the public should agree on some rules of conduct for politicians and other holders of high office, which should eventually be incorporated into their constitution or other legal guardrails.

Simple logic: for the masses to hold power, they must recognise a shared objective and understand that only the strength of bipartisanship will secure its realisation.

It isn't easy to find a politician whose party or self-interest does not outweigh that of the people.

A common-sense framework for people's empowerment

The PIS should promote the following framework, which would be the core strategy of the PEM: to maintain a healthy democracy that works for the public, the people should have two clear agreements; they are partisan when they elect their government, but they should be bipartisan when their government or politicians transgress on rules or policies that the public should determine. It is not in the people's best interest for politicians' transgressions to be tolerated due to partisanship, as this would effectively undermine their power. The power of the people is only effective when it is united on principles that transcend partisanship. We need to be educated and socialised into understanding that the individual is strong because they are part of a large employer group. **We can only maintain a fair balance of power if there is unity in disciplining our employees when they violate *our rules*, which should be codified into a constitution.**

Here are suggestions for some of the rules, and they should be based on what actions the public feels comfortable with governments taking on their behalf, and their vision of the societal values they wish to uphold. There should also be a list of the core benefits they expect from their collective taxation, which they perceive as facilitating their success and happiness.

1. Governments and employees are not allowed to participate in wars that do not serve our national security interests. They must be wholly transparent and avoid secretive actions in other countries that could incite conflicts. In military conflicts, it is the children of us, the employers, who often end up fighting and dying, not the politicians we hire or their children. It is worth repeating: Gone are the days when the king and his sons would fight in the war he initiated.

2. *All people should have equal access to the highest levels of education. The public should share and uphold this core value, which they held from the beginning before the nation was formed – education for all children. This should be the highest priority, because higher education and training are the most certain and reliable paths to prosperity and security, which is why nations were established in the first place. The more people who achieve higher education and training, the better off the country will be—having a populace that is highly educated (especially if the education fosters critical thinking and common sense) and well-trained makes it easier for us to collectively agree on what additional benefits should be financed through our collective efforts and taxes.*

3. The government should not favour a privileged few, as this leads to social and economic injustice and discrimination. A country that is so divided is not as strong as it could be. In effect, the government should avoid practising crony capitalism.

4. Everyone should receive equal protection under the law. This provision must be monitored to ensure it is upheld in practice.

5. Provision should be made for a dedicated task force to fast-track solutions to recurring societal issues that cost lives. For example, if a country faces a problem with gun violence that results in many deaths, and the government has failed to address it, a set percentage of the population could trigger a hearing where a solution must be identified and implemented.

6. Political campaigns should be publicly funded. Special interests, such as corporations or the wealthy, should not finance them. This aims to prevent undue influence on politicians, which can lead to corruption.

It should be common sense that for rules three and four to be effective, we must defend each other when our government or employees break these rules. If left unchecked, this situation could become normalised and create fertile ground for seeds of discontent, deep-seated anger, and further hostility to grow. Widespread popular anger, resentment, and discontent are significant causes of revolutions, including the American Revolution (1775–1783). The French Revolution (1789–1799) can serve as a valuable lesson from history on how fragile a country divided by class and resentment can become. The following seven causes of the French Revolution share some uncanny resemblances with aspects of our current societies. They have been adopted from **"_10 Major Causes of the French Revolution_"** by writer and educationist, Anirudh, **posted on the website,** https://learnodo-newtonic.com/french-revolution-causes,

- **Social inequality in France stemmed from the Estates System** [a three-tier social division based on social estate or class].

- The First Estate, the Roman Catholic clergy, made up about 0.5 per cent of the population. The Second Estate, the nobility or aristocracy, comprised around 1.5 per cent. The Third Estate, [the lower classes], consisting of merchants, lawyers, labourers, and peasants, accounted for approximately 98 per cent of the population. They were excluded from positions of honour and political power and were looked down upon by the other estates, which caused significant anger and resentment within society.

- **Tax burden on the Third Estate**

   The clergy (the First Estate), although comprising only 0.5 per cent of the population, owned 10 per cent of the land. They were highly privileged and wealthy, yet they collected tithes or one-tenth of the annual produce or earnings from the lower-class masses to support the Church, while paying no taxes. The nobility (the Second Estate) owned 25 per cent of the land. They were exempt from paying many taxes and were permitted to collect dues from the peasants. The Third Estate [The under classes], by contrast, was compelled to pay heavy taxes while the other two estates were exempt. This extra burden provoked significant resentment among them.

- **The rise of the Bourgeoisie**

  The bourgeoisie were the wealthy members of the Third Estate who began to gain influence in the years leading up to the revolution. They resented the status of the First and Second Estates, which they believed was earned through their efforts, and they sought political equality with them.

- **Ideas put forward by Enlightenment philosophers.**

  Enlightenment philosophers like John Locke, Jean-Jacques Rousseau, and Baron de Montesquieu questioned the traditional absolute authority of the monarch and divisions of society such as the Estates System… Locke argued that a leader may only govern a society if he has the consent of those he governs; Rousseau was against all class divisions, and Montesquieu advocated for a system of government based on the separation of powers.

- **The financial crisis caused by costly wars**

  Having fought in the Seven Years' War (which it lost in 1763) against Britain, and subsequently becoming involved in the American War of Independence from Britain (1775-1783), France incurred significant costs. It accumulated a vast debt that pushed it towards bankruptcy.

- **The rise in the cost of bread**

  Poor grain harvests cause a significant rise in bread prices – the staple food in France and historical estimates indicate that the impoverished working class spent over 90 per cent of their daily income solely on bread. Once again, they bore the burden.

If people genuinely want to build societies that maximise their potential by nurturing their citizens, they should consider the new bipartisan philosophy proposed. And if they believe it has merit, they should include it in compulsory civic lessons in our school systems to ensure society is socialised into this new

philosophy, which should become part of the country's political culture. These measures are necessary because after so many years of 'democracy', it is clear that it is not just communism and other forms of political ideology that corrupt or make those who seek to serve power-drunk.

Why should access to free higher education be enshrined in the people's constitution? Since common sense suggests that a country's greatest asset is its people, it is in the best interest of any nation to maintain a highly trained and educated population. The more educated a society is, the more effective it becomes, especially if this education includes a significant amount of common sense and critical thinking.

Education is the most dependable tool for empowerment known to humanity. To reiterate, it is reasonably sure that most people would support access to free education up to the highest level. To break the vicious cycle of too few attaining higher education, society should enshrine in law that tax revenue must be allocated primarily to a system where everyone can access higher education. The education system should reflect the fundamental values and rules for coexistence held by the people. Such an education system would also instil in those who choose to become government officials or employees a deeper understanding of civic responsibility. If, in educating children for life, the personal development skill of social intelligence—like that offered by the Eliot-Pearson School in Medford, Massachusetts (see chapter eleven)—were universally applied, there would likely be an increase in individuals receptive to higher education. This approach to education boosts children's intelligence and social skills.

In any country, the greater the number of people with higher education, the more capable they are of solving problems and ensuring prosperity. This includes reducing crime, especially violent crime. Free, widespread higher education would ensure that not only could the privileged few afford it. But also in some countries where education is not a top priority, and caring for their most significant asset is not standard practice, many parents cannot afford to send their children to primary or secondary schools. A country with a high percentage of its people educated in common sense and basic skills would find it difficult for the government to manipulate the many for the benefit of a few. Everyone would benefit from a nation with a highly empowered population. One significant benefit of increasing the number of highly educated individuals is higher taxation, as they tend to earn more through employment or entrepreneurship, which also creates more jobs.

Many Western democracies have societies where a privileged few are descendants of an elite class. It is from this group that the 'ruling class' (those born into privilege and power) typically originates. By making higher education freely available to all, societies would gradually expand the pool of qualified candidates for governance. As this pool grows, the chances increase that leaders will better represent society rather than just the minority elites. The benefit would be a population with leaders more likely to empathise with them and act in their best interests.

> **The forest was shrinking, but the trees kept voting for the axe, for the axe was clever and convinced the trees that because his handle was made of wood, he was one of them. Turkish proverb**

The realisation of the bipartisan political philosophy that has been promoted would require deliberate social engineering to eliminate extreme partisanship. It would take time, but the intellectual and emotional development gained would make it worthwhile. Free access to higher education, which includes sufficient civic lessons, would support this growth. The PIS would have led this transformation by raising awareness of this new philosophy. Political propaganda is typical in today's world, so the best way to protect ourselves from it is through accurate political and economic knowledge. Here is some information that can help to develop a precise view on governance, political philosophies or systems, and the role of the media. The discussion on mainstream media will demonstrate how it differs from the independent People's Information Service (PIS).

Common sense regarding systems of government and their economic policies

The first common-sense lesson about systems of government is that no system is perfect. This is because we are not perfect. So, with this in mind, how do we decide which of the current economic and political-ideological systems is best suited to govern us, imperfect humans? It must be the system that aligns most closely with our nature as humans. So, what aspects of our nature are relevant when choosing which economic and political system suits us best?

- We value free will, the ability to choose and to alter our minds about how our lives are arranged.

- Our seemingly boundless imagination works best when it is free from restrictions, and it is rewarded with material and lifestyle comforts when it creates something of value for others.

- We dislike being corralled and restricted, like having oppressive parents.

So, which political and economic system best fits these human characteristics? First, we need to understand the differences and nuances of various government economic systems. This is because politicians often use scare tactics, exploit people's lack of knowledge, and deceive voters to gain support. A widespread understanding of the fundamental aspects of different political and economic systems would prevent this. People would also be better able to choose political parties wisely. Here is a simple breakdown of the various systems and their nuances.

Communism

Definition: At its core, it is an economic and political system with an ideology of equality where private property is eliminated, and the government, not the people, primarily controls the means of production and trade.

Noted disadvantages of communism for the people

- In general, they have limited options for material and lifestyle choices or advancement.
- They are unable to select the government or its policies.
- Limited competition *can* hinder or restrict innovation.
- The quality of products may decline due to reduced competition.

Noted advantages of communism for the people

- Low crime rate.
- Economic safety net – Basic food and shelter are provided for everyone, noand there is homelessness.
- Because it has a centrally planned economy, it can rapidly mobilise economic resources on a large scale, implement massive projects, and establish industrial strength.
- All levels of education and healthcare are free, provided by the government.

This system addresses the *essential* and most vital needs of the greatest and most valuable asset of every country, the people. Common sense suggests that there is no better use of a country's resources than to meet such needs. **However, humans tend to prefer satisfying more than just our basic needs.**

Capitalism

Definitions: At its core, it is an economic and political system where the means of production are mainly controlled by the people, not by the government. It is an economic and political system in which a country's trade and industry are controlled by private owners for profit, rather than the state.

Noted negatives of capitalism for the people

- Fewer economic safety nets, so homelessness and hunger can become widespread.

- Generally, it experiences more crime – its prevalence *can* be horrendous.

- Higher education can be too costly for many and may impose heavy debt burdens on those who pursue it, potentially limiting the advantages of higher qualifications for years.

- The practice of crony capitalism. To illustrate why this is problematic, here are two definitions:

  1. Crony capitalism is an economic system where businesses succeed not through risk-taking but through profits gained from close links between the business and political classes. This is often achieved by leveraging state power instead of competition, such as managing permits, government grants, tax breaks, or other forms of government intervention.

  2. An economy that appears to be free-market but permits preferential regulation and other favourable government interventions based on personal relationships. In such a system, the false image of "pure" capitalism is maintained publicly to uphold the exclusive influence of well-connected individuals.

Ironically, one of our first common-sense lessons at the start of civilisation was that we needed more than one person to build a tolerable dwelling, yet, as soon as civilisations developed, some of us adopted the philosophy of "every man for himself – the fittest of the fittest shall survive". Tolerable dwellings in advanced civilisation are more complex and require more skills and specialised knowledge. Therefore, a consequence of our decision to abandon nomadic life is that we must have a system to manage this complexity effectively. So, now more than ever, it is true that "the strength of one man is unequal to his wants", and it can take more than five men to "Raise a tolerable dwelling". Consequently, in our current reality, interdependence is far more essential. It would thus be a regression in human evolution from a nomadic lifestyle if our combined resources were sufficient to meet our basic need for shelter. Still, we chose not to provide it for those who cannot provide it for themselves. Are they not some of the links in the chain of previous generations who contributed to building this country? Our original social being, or socialist instinct, that ensured our survival on Earth, has diminished as a result of our invention of divisive concepts and practices such as classism, snobbery, and privilege.

Noted positives of capitalism for the people

- Almost unlimited material or lifestyle choices, though this can be tainted by the practice of crony capitalism as described above. This practice can unfairly prevent many from having a genuine chance to enjoy all the benefits, including opportunities to rise to the top.

- The people can mainly control the means of production and services.

- Generally, competition leads to the production of higher-quality goods and services.

- People, in general, can select who they wish to employ on their behalf – in effect, they *can* choose government policies.

Based on the characteristics of the political and economic systems examined, the one that has fostered our unlimited imagination and love of choice is the one with capitalism *as its foundation*. The evidence of this is that most technological inventions occur in democratic capitalist societies. The question is, does this suffice for our wellbeing and happiness, the ultimate purpose of organised societies? No.

Socialism

> **The term socialism[6] refers to any system in which the production and distribution of goods and services is a shared responsibility of a group of people. Socialism is based on economic and political theories that advocate for collectivism. In a state of socialism, there is no privately owned property.**

No country practices a form of capitalism where everything is operated solely by private owners for profit. In reality, almost all countries that adopt capitalism provide some level of 'free' services, which are characteristic of socialist and communist principles; the extent of these services varies. Essentially, all developed countries implement some degree of socialism. If this were common knowledge, disingenuous or ignorant politicians and television pundits would not be able to frighten people about 'socialism'. The debate should focus on which system offers the best quality of life for the majority who make a country function. Even the USA, often regarded as "the great bastion of capitalism," incorporates elements of socialism; it has six major welfare programmes, which are considered 'socialist' programmes.

TANF, Medicaid, CHIP, SNAP, EITC, Supplemental Security Income, and housing assistance.

> **When we talk about the word 'socialism,' I think what it really means is just democratic participation in our economic dignity and our economic, social, and racial dignity. It is about direct representation and people actually having power and stake over their economic and social wellness, at the end of the day.** – Alexandria Ocasio-Cortez, US Congresswoman

---

[6] There is no country that practices socialism that totally fits this definition. Some countries practice a degree of collectivism where workers in some companies have equal representatives among the board of directors. Socialism also refers to a philosophy and practice of caring and sharing – that is, the masses enjoy many social benefits or services.

American pioneers' instinctive action of pooling their collective resources to hire a teacher for the benefit of all in their first town indicates that when we see ourselves as part of a team, we come together for the common good. Everyone, regardless of their means, was educated. This suggests that we are inherently socialist in our thinking.

Socialism etymology (origin of) = social + system/action = we are social beings[7] = 2 + 2 = 4

In one respect, democratic countries can operate like a communist country where people *cannot choose what they want*. Democracy may appear to offer choice because people vote. Still, people can consistently vote but *not receive* what is in their best interest. This remains true even though democracy is meant to reflect the will of the people more than any other system. Repeatedly not getting what benefits us can be facilitated by the system being manipulated through voting and election rules, as well as media propaganda.

A sensible examination of two capitalist economic policies

These two economic policies are intended to stimulate and boost the society's economic growth. Take a look and determine which one benefits everyone more.

Even if it's never called by name, the trickle-down theory of economics is often implemented in major democratic capitalist countries. This is a practice where taxes are frequently reduced for businesses and the wealthy, with the suggestion that it will stimulate business investment in the short term and benefit society at large in the long term.

Trickle-down theory of economics

Syllogistic common-sense reasoning regarding the trickle-down theory of economics.

---

[7]   A **social being** is a creature (human or animal) that interacts regularly with their fellows and cooperates with others to achieve common goals.

- **Theory:** Tax cuts or giveaways for corporations and the wealthy are the most effective way to stimulate economic growth.

- **Fact:** In the short term, economic growth is driven by an increase in aggregate demand (AD) for goods and services. Therefore, giving a tax cut to the wealthy and large corporations does not boost aggregate demand for goods and services for two reasons: 1) the rich do not have many unmet needs for goods and services, so they would not use the money to buy a broad range of goods and services; 2) a person or company will not expand their business and hire more people unless there is unmet demand.

- Demand for goods and services will not rise unless those with unmet needs have more money to spend, and they are usually people with low incomes and the middle class, who did not receive a tax cut and have no increase in disposable income.

Trickle-up theory of economics

A contrast to the trickle-down theory is the trickle-up theory, which is based on the idea that policies that directly benefit the middle class will improve society's overall productivity. These benefits will "trickle up" to the wealthy.

- **Fact:** Higher wages, a tax cut, or a 'give-away' to those who are not wealthy can boost economic growth because these individuals often have many unmet needs. Consequently, they will demand goods and services across a wide range of economic sectors. This can improve their sense of well-being and potentially stimulate short-term economic growth—a win-win situation.

- **Fact:** Much of the goods purchased by the middle and working classes will be supplied by the wealthy.

- **Fact:** When the economy has room to grow, the wealthy *can* use this extra revenue to expand.

It's easier to become rich if you are part of a large population. The population needed to produce a billionaire would be larger than that required for a millionaire. It is the recognition of their interdependence with the public that motivates some of the wealthy to give back and want

to pay their fair share of taxes. The masses should wake up and agree: implicit in their agreement to have a democratic capitalist society, those who benefit the most should always pay their fair share of taxes.

You cannot succeed by yourself. It's hard to find a rich hermit. – Jim Rohn

---

Here is a valuable piece of common sense for schools: No matter our political or ideological differences, we share a commonality. It takes all of us to make each of us successful.

Examples of countries whose basic economic structure is capitalism, but have mixed (capitalist and socialist) economies

Brief listings and descriptions of their social programmes and other indicators of their social condition.

It is reasonable to conclude that a country's social and economic policies influence life experiences, including the quality of life of its residents. We understand that quality of life affects people's behaviour. Therefore, we can deduce that policies which lessen people's stress and anxieties and promote their enjoyment and happiness would decrease the occurrence of life's inevitable negatives. There should be a link between the number of lifestyle benefits provided by the state (as listed by different countries) and the number of unavoidable negatives. Let us compare a country regarded as very capitalist with one considered very socialist. Is there anything concerning about the lifestyle offered to its citizens? Are these benefits the ones that should result from the power of interdependence?

How countries' resources can be shared Norway vs. the USA		
	Norway- Social democracy[8]	**United States of America – Capitalism**
Population	5.328 million (2019)	327.2 million (2018)
GDP	98.8 billion USD (2017)	19.39 trillion USD (2017)
Average workweek	37– 38 hours	47– 50 hours
Life expectancy	82.3	78.7
Workers protected by unions	57%	10.7%
Homeownership	81%	64%
>	Free universal health care	>
>	Free higher education	expensive higher education
>	Financial security for seniors	no security for elders no paid vacation per year
>	35 days paid vacation per year	no paid parental leave
>	35 weeks paid parental leave[9]	37%
Average personal income tax	38%	>
Inevitable negatives:	>	5.748 per 1000
Infant mortality:	1.993 per 1000	5.00 (2018)
Murder rate	0.53	

Is there anything scary about the lifestyle provided by these other countries with many social programs? (Source: Where to Invade Next (2015) – Michael Moore)

---

[8] A political, social and economic philosophy that supports economic and social interventions to promote social justice within the framework of a liberal democratic polity and a capitalist-oriented economy. – Wikipedia

[9] Mothers can take 35 weeks at full **pay** or 45 weeks at 80% pay, and fathers can take between zero and 10 weeks depending on their wives' income. Together, parents can receive an additional 46 weeks at full pay or 56 weeks at 80% of their income. https://www.businessinsider.com/countries-with-best-parental-leave-2016-8?r=US&IR=T

Italy (social policies in brief)

Population 60.48 million (2018) murder rate 0.9 per 100,000 GDP 1.935 trillion USD (2017)

Life expectancy 82.54 (2016)

Infant mortality rate 2.517 (2019)

15 days paid honeymoon - entitled to 4 weeks paid vacation, equal to a minimum of 20 vacation days

10 national paid holidays – workers receive extra pay even when these holidays are not on workdays.

39 hours work week on average

Five months of paid maternity leave.

Two months' wages are paid in December, and holiday leaves can be accumulated.

One employer's philosophy: "We have to take vacations to relieve our stress and return to work." 39 hours work week on average

Five months of paid maternity leave.

Two months' wages paid in December. Holiday leave can be accumulated.

One employer's philosophy: "We have to take vacations to relieve our stress and return to work relaxed."

Lunch break, two hours – employees can go home for lunch

Ducati CEO – "There is no clash between the profit of the company and the well-being of the people. By paying a good wage with good benefits, the company still makes a healthy profit."

Public education in Italy is not free, but university is markedly cheaper than in the UK, averaging between €850 (£720) and €1000 (£840) per year in tuition fees.

Not all the benefits Italians enjoy were 'handed over'. Unions nudged them, but now that the employers are used to it, they prefer working with happy people.

France (social policies in brief)

Population: 66.99 million (2019) Murder rate: 1.3 per 1000 GDP: 2.583 trillion

Life expectancy: 82.59 (2019)

Infant mortality rate: 3.124 (2017)

Vacation: 30 days per year, Workweek: 35 hours, Maternity leave: up to sixteen weeks. Six before and ten after.

Lunch break: Many French businesses close down for two to four hours every afternoon

College: tuition around $200 per annum at public universities.

Fun facts about France's first graders from Michael Moore's documentary, 'Where to Invade Next'

A description of the first graders' school lunch, which is standard in the country. It was interesting and heart-warming to see children, some of whom look like toddlers, hurrying to wash their hands before heading to the cafeteria. The film shows that:

- Their food is prepared in a three- or four-star kitchen.

- They sit and wait at tables, being served by chefs who bring the food to them. They eat with cutlery and drink from glasses. They enjoy four-course meals, and interestingly, the school was not located in a wealthy neighbourhood. This is said to be standard practice nationwide.

- The school regards lunch as a class, a learning experience. "It is a full hour, where you learn how to eat in a civilised manner, enjoy healthy foods, and serve each other."

The documentary puts this in context:

- Once a month, the school chef meets with city and school officials, and a dietitian to review the daily menus.

- Michael Moore asked an official, "Why is the mayor's office concerned with what is being served in the children's cafeteria?" The official responded, "Because the children will learn, over time, what a balanced diet is, and to pay attention to what they eat."

- "How do they afford it? Pay a little extra tax."

- France's taxes in 2019 are as follows: earnings up to €9,964: pay 0%; €9,964–€27,519: 14%; €27,519–€73,779: 30%

Slovenia (higher education policy in brief)

GDP 48.77 billion USD (2017)

Population 2.084 million (2018)

Unlike many other European countries, higher education in Slovenia is mostly free. The three largest state-funded universities in Slovenia are the University of Ljubljana, the University of Primorska, and the University of Maribor.

Denmark (social policies in brief)

The Danish welfare system includes the following benefits:

- Health insurance.
- Free education and healthcare for all.
- Child allowance.
- Maternity benefit.
- Holiday pay.
- Disability benefits.
- Sickness benefits.

Finland (economic and social policies)

In recognition of social and economic class issues, Finland acted wisely. Wikipedia states: "In the last years of the nineteenth century, Finnish social policy had as its goal a lessening of class friction." As a result, "Finland had one of the world's most advanced welfare systems, one that guaranteed decent living conditions for all Finns." "The social security system was an outgrowth of the traditional Nordic belief that the state was not inherently hostile to the well-being of its citizens, but could intervene benevolently on their behalf. According to some social historians, the basis of this belief was a relatively benign history that had allowed the gradual emergence of a free and independent peasantry in the Nordic countries and had curtailed the dominance of the nobility and the subsequent formation of a powerful right-wing."

According to Finnish sociologist Erik Allardt, the defining feature of the Nordic welfare system was its comprehensiveness. Unlike the welfare systems of the United States or most Western European countries, those of the Nordic nations cover the entire population. They are not limited to groups unable to care for themselves. Examples of this universal coverage include national flat-rate pensions available to all once they reach a certain age, regardless of their contributions to the plan, and national health schemes based on medical needs rather than financial means. Additionally, citizens of the Nordic countries have a legal right to the benefits provided by their welfare systems, whose provisions are designed to meet what was perceived as a collective responsibility to ensure everyone a decent standard of living.

Has this practice caused their development to suffer or fail? - It certainly doesn't seem that way. Take a look at these statistics and facts:

- Finland was a relatively late entrant to industrialisation, remaining largely an agrarian society until the 1950s. After World War II, the Soviet Union demanded war reparations from Finland not only in money but also in material goods, such as ships and machinery. This compelled Finland to industrialise. It quickly developed an advanced economy while establishing an extensive welfare state based on the Nordic model, leading to widespread prosperity and one of the highest per capita incomes globally. Finland ranks highly in numerous metrics of national performance, including education, economic competitiveness, civil liberties, quality of life, and human development. In 2015, Finland was ranked among the top in the world in the Human Capital Index and the Press Freedom Index, and as the most stable country during 2011–2016, according to the Fragile States Index, while being second in the Global Gender Gap Report. It also ranked first in the World Happiness Report for 2018 and 2019.

- **Finland has the lowest level of organised crime in the world.** *World Economic Forum, The Global Competitiveness Report 2018: Organised crime.* [Yet, per capita, they have the fourth most firearms in the world.]

- **Finland's judicial system is the most independent in the world.** *World Economic Forum, The Global Competitiveness Report 2018: Judicial independence.*

- **"Next to Norwegians and Icelanders, Finns feel the second least insecure in the world.** *Gallup, Law and Order Index, 2018. "*

- **Finland has the third-highest level of personal freedom and choice in the world.** *The Social Progress Imperative, 2018 Social Progress Index: Finland. "*

> **When we conceived the idea of governance, it stemmed from recognising the practical value of having dedicated workers to uphold and maintain law and order, and organise and regulate our economic activities.**

Common sense on how to assess and select a political leader

Definitions
Character: the mental and moral qualities that are distinctive to an individual
Personality: the outer appearance and behaviour of a person

For many people, their political decision about which party to vote for is heavily influenced by party loyalty and/or the personality of the leader. However, before considering the reasons that should guide our choice of a leader, let's dismiss the idea of choosing a political leader based solely on charisma. Although this quality can help a politician, it is probably more helpful for a game show host. By the time we reach adulthood, we should all recognise that some unscrupulous individuals possess an abundance of charisma and are skilled at pretending to be what they are not. Acting is not solely the preserve of Hollywood. We should also be aware that charismatic world leaders have made decisions resulting in the unjustified deaths of millions of people, and such decisions should have led to them being tried as war criminals. Voting based on charisma and personality is not suitable for those with common sense. Having a charismatic and dynamic personality does not necessarily mean possessing good character, which is a vital trait for effective leadership. Here are the common-sense reasons that should guide our choice of political leaders.

- **They have a practical plan that benefits the people.**

  Crucial among these is the implementation or consolidation of the most basic and effective strategy for prosperity – free education for all the people, who are the country's greatest assets.

- We believe that other aspects of their economic plan could foster prosperity and security for everyone, not just a select few. Prosperity that benefits only a few often breeds widespread discontent in society, which can lead to high crime rates. A high crime rate will also affect the privileged few, who may have to live with an increased sense of danger, prompting them to adopt additional security measures, including arming themselves.

- They hold a political ideology that is compassionate and dedicated to ensuring equal opportunities for all. A caring society experiences less crime.

- We believe they are capable of executing their plans.

- We connect with their sincerity of purpose – the most important reason of all. For our perception of their sincerity to be accurate, we need the ability to assess a person's character. This is crucial because it is not in our best interest to choose a glib, charismatic leader who tells us what we want to hear to gain power but has no intention of fulfilling their promises. Be prepared by gathering good information about the person's history. If they have been in politics for a few years, review the policies they have supported. If they are a first-time politician, learn as much as you can about their public life or any controversies they have been involved in – in particular, whether they have been involved in crimes or civil lawsuits.

If people feel a strong connection to a party's ideology unrelated to economics, this emotional bond can cause them to overlook the absence of economic benefits. Consequently, it may lead the government to neglect its essential role of governing the country for the prosperity of all citizens.

It's easy for the government of a democratic nation not to act in the best interests of the people – they simply under-educate a large section of the population and socialise them into bigotry and violence. Bigoted politicians can then exploit these intense emotions, galvanise this significant minority, and repeatedly sway elections in their favour.

Simple logic/common sense

Some indicators that it should be evident that politicians are not suited for public office:

- They habitually lie! It's remarkable to see people ignoring this trait of a politician. This might be because they have an emotional connection to the person. In business, a company or individuals will not hire someone and tolerate them engaging in misconduct such as lying, deception, corruption, and oppression. To assume that a habitual liar won't lie to win votes is the height of foolishness. **Common sense indicates that a person who habitually lies and deceives should not be trusted.** A compulsive or pathological liar lacks empathy. Empathy should be a crucial and essential trait of the political leaders we choose. Someone whose words influence people's lives will not habitually lie to those they care about unless they have a mental disorder, which would also disqualify them from leadership. Habitual liars do so for self-serving reasons. The role of a political leader is far too important for such behaviour to be tolerated. People with an emotional bond to such a politician should realise there is a great chance they will not deliver on their promises; therefore, they should not accept this abuse from them.

- They habitually practise hypocrisy; they do what they advise their listeners not to do.

- They repeatedly apply a double standard in political debate. This implies they lack principles.

- They continually change their stance on important issues in a short period. This suggests they may have a conflict of interest or lack clear principles, values, or vision.

Common sense about our current mainstream media and its role in politics

Initially, the press had a long history of censorship, partisanship, and withholding information from ordinary people due to control by the monarchy and government. However, freedom of the press is now protected by law in democratic countries. This freedom grants them the right to broadcast or circulate opinions and information without government censorship. The question is, whose viewpoint does mainstream media represent? It would be inaccurate to broadly state that mainstream media do not serve the public interest. They undertake significant journalistic and broadcasting work that benefits public understanding. So, why can't they serve as the People's Information Service (PIS)? Here are some reasons:

- They are driven by profit motives or influenced by special interests. The media's entire ethos must prioritise the interests of the public. Just as a company's employees strive for the success of the organisation, so too should the media's primary aim be for the benefit of the public.

- Compared to the proposed PIS, mainstream or corporate media cannot be described as being preoccupied with acting as a watchdog.

- The media is so influential that governments can commit numerous crimes, and their popularity polls won't reflect this. This remains true whether special interests sway them or if they simply are not vigilant watchdogs. This wouldn't happen if the people had a PIS that they actively paid attention to.

- They would not speak against their owners' interests, even if those interests conflict with the people's. Suppose the owner is among the wealthy elites heavily invested in For-Profit Colleges. Making college education free does not serve his best interests. What if his connections with political policymakers give him confidence they will not pass legislation for free college for all? Would his media inform the public about this? Unlikely. Would such media advocate for free college? Or, if the owner is fiercely partisan, would his media be balanced and fair on political issues? At best, there might be one or two broadcasters who occasionally challenge the status quo. The people's business is too important for this to be enough.

- The business and ratings-driven nature of many mass media, especially visual mass media, seems to have shaped them into a form of neutrality in how they present political information. Moreover, they often invite opposing political advocates or hacks onto their platforms and give them free rein to say whatever they like. In this scenario, viewers lack *the benefit of fact-checking or context and may either be swayed by the speaker with the most emotional impact or tune out.* Suppose visual or electronic media are meant to educate the public more quickly and *efficiently* than reading. In that case, they fail when they present information that falls far below the standard of a well-researched and constructive book. They also do not bridge

the gap for those who lack the time to read or do their research to form accurate opinions. So, who benefits from this format? Indeed, not the public.

- Many news segments on broadcasting media recite what each political adversary says, offering no context or conclusion about which side is accurate or truthful. Propaganda in politics is known to cost lives. It is perhaps out of frustration with this kind of lazy 'journalism' that someone unknown wrote: "If someone says it's raining, and another person says it's dry, it's not your job to quote them both. Your job is to look out the #?%#&* window and find out which is true."

- In this era of television ratings, some news outlets often prioritise creating drama over providing genuine education to the public. This increases their profit margins because it entertains.

- It is quite common for some stations to regularly interview representatives of political parties who often misrepresent the facts. Yet they rarely challenge or verify their claims, leaving the public once again in the difficult position of processing information without context. Therefore, whether they accept the information as true will depend on their level of knowledge and their deductive reasoning skills.

Undoubtedly, it will take time for society to evolve into a system where democracy functions as it should, with power in the hands of the people. People resist change, even those who stand to benefit from it. Like beliefs, social conditioning is difficult to alter. Nevertheless, the proposed changes are worth pursuing.

Calling the people to action

The common-sense attitude towards the climate change crisis in six sentences

Even if climate change is not real, wouldn't we be better off if we eliminated pollution? According to Independent.co.uk, "Globally, nine million people died in 2015 as a result of air pollution." According to the WHO, "Air pollution kills an estimated seven million people worldwide every year." Is this enough reason for it to be classified as an existential crisis that requires urgent action? Why then should this issue be controversial? Why would any government have an anti-climate change policy unless it's rooted in a 'money over morality' philosophy? This is a typical stance, so it would be unwise to dismiss it as a reason.

> **If pollution or climate change poses an existential threat to our success, happiness, and survival, it should be a deal-breaker when electing any politician who does not prioritise it.**

The destruction and suffering of countless lives, the immense strain on human and financial resources (prisons), and the absence of a practical solution compel us to consider the next life issue from a different perspective.

CHAPTER THIRTEEN

The eleventh major life issue to which Aristotelian syllogistic reasoning applies: **Common sense regarding the consequences of the illegality and criminalisation of drugs**

Simple syllogistic logic:

- If criminalising drugs causes seven major problems, and legalising the same drugs reduces these issues to two, then legalisation is the better choice. It's preferable to have two issues rather than seven.

- History and understanding of human psychology indicate that people will always use drugs, whether legal or illegal.

- The consequences of prohibition demonstrated this.

Those who do not learn from history are doomed to repeat it.– unknown

---

We can say with reasonable certainty that the earliest humans, dating back 200,000 years, did not have a drug problem. History suggests that this behaviour emerged alongside the development of an increasingly complex world and society. Since drugs can destroy lives, and the instinct for self-preservation generally drives every form of life, any deliberate action that opposes this drive must be influenced by emotions that have been programmed to override our self-interest. This is because, if **syllogistic reasoning**, which can produce sound judgement (**common sense**), were the dominant force, it would not consciously lead us to self-harm. Once again, we observe the pattern of simple logic or common sense in all our sound judgements.

- I want to be healthy and fully in charge of my life.

- Taking drugs can damage my health and cause me to lose control of my life.

- Therefore, taking drugs can be counterproductive to my desired life outcome.
- Therefore, I will not take any drugs.

We recognise that the growth of the human population has led to organised societies and a more complex world. This has required an improvement in our problem-solving ability. The difference between a few people, then, and millions of people now, living in the same space, inevitably results in more issues to address. An emotional response is the least effective way to resolve such complex challenges. A clear understanding of human psychology and emotions, combined with syllogistic reasoning, will produce the sound judgement and common sense needed to tackle problems such as the desire for drugs and the criminal activities that stem from it.

Mint Press News March 30, 2017

" 'Hospitalisation rates for opioid painkiller dependence and abuse dropped on average 23 per cent in states after marijuana was permitted for medical purposes, the analysis found. Hospitalisation rates for opioid overdoses dropped 13 per cent on average.'

"The study, published in *Drug and Alcohol Dependence*, was authored by Yuyan Shi, a public health professor at the University of California in San Diego. According to *Reuters*, Shi's study is the fifth in recent years to demonstrate declines in opioid dependence in states where medical weed is legal…

"One 2014 study showed opioid deaths dropped an average of 25 per cent in states where medical marijuana is permitted…"

"It is becoming increasingly clear that battling the opioid epidemic will require a multi-pronged approach and a good deal of creativity… Could increased liberalisation of marijuana be part of the solution? It seems plausible."– Dr Esther Choo.

Laws are not supposed to create more problems than they solve!

After analysing the facts about drug use, common sense shows the futility and harmful effects of its illegalisation. It reveals that we are worse off because drugs remain illegal. Our emotional reactions and political manoeuvres have

kept us in this unhealthy situation. Because of the strong emotions involved in this issue, it needs careful examination. You will see that the illegality of drugs has caused at least five major problems for society, and laws should not create more issues than they solve. They should not add difficulties while trying to resolve other problems. And this is precisely the situation we face today.

Snapshots of the consequences of drug laws

Colombia

- It is estimated that drug-related violence currently makes up a significant portion of the country's 30,000 annual murders, one of the highest homicide rates outside a war zone and more than twice the number of murders recorded in the United States during 1998. Politically, the impact has been widespread corruption, undermining both governmental legitimacy and executive authority. The emergence of several powerful and violent drug cartels in the 80s and 90s, notably the Medellin Cartel under Pablo Escobar and the Cali Cartel, exerted considerable political, economic, and social influence in Colombia during this period. These cartels also financed and influenced various illegal armed groups across the political spectrum.

- "Where are the voices of the development community? Prohibition is putting money in the pockets of criminals and armed groups. Profits from the illegal trade in drugs are not only used to buy guns, they also to buy police chiefs and judges. Corruption is off the scale and, as it grows, democratic accountability, the key plank necessary for poor people to access and defend their rights, is progressively eroded...The families caught up in this nightmare are the victims of an unworkable 'war on drugs'."– Jonathan Glennie, ODI Research Fellow, former Head of Christian Aid's Colombia Programme, 2010.

America and globally

- M A Zahn and M Bencivengo, authors of the journal, *Violent Death: A Comparison Between Drugs Users and Non-Drug Users*, reported that, in Philadelphia, in 1972, *homicide* was the leading cause of death among drug users, even surpassing deaths caused by adverse effects of drugs; and drugs accounted for more than 31 percent of the deaths in Philadelphia.

- The "war on drugs" is facing unprecedented scrutiny. It aimed to establish a "drug-free world." However, despite spending more than a trillion dollars fighting the war, according to the UNODC [United Nations Office on Drugs and Crime], an estimated 270 million people use illegal drugs, and organised crime profits from a trade with an annual turnover of over $330 billion—the world's largest illegaicitrket.

Business Insider: 32 reasons why we need to end the war on drugs, by Matthew Boesler and Ashley Lutz

- "The global war on drugs began in 1961 when the UN Single Convention on Narcotic Drugs was established to create a 'drug-free world." The United Nations Office on Drugs and Crime puts out an annual "World Drug Report," wherein they examine trends in drug use and production. However, the report **never cares to assess the costs created by the war on drugs itself, which are the real problem, to begin with.** [The term, 'The war on drugs' was popularised by the media shortly after a press conference given on June 18, 1971, by President Richard Nixon – the day after publication of a special report from President Nixon to Congress – during which he declared drug abuse, "public enemy number one".]

- "A new organization, Count the Costs, has decided it's time for an assessment. To this end, they have compiled a comprehensive report detailing the death and destruction the war on drugs has directly caused around the world over the past 50 years. Unfortunately, as Count the Costs points out, the saddest effect of the war on drugs is that "the centrality of criminalising users means that **in reality, a war on drugs is to a significant degree, a war on drug users –** *a war on people."*

- *Count the Costs is a timely initiative. The failed war on drugs has empowered organised crime, destabilised governments, violated human rights and devastated human lives everywhere.* – Fernando Henrique Cardoso, former President of Brazil.

- "Count the Cost [of the war on drugs] is a collaborative project between a range of organisations that, while representing a diverse range of expertise and viewpoints, share a desire to reduce the unintended costs of the war on drugs."
  – http://www.countthecosts.org/about-count-costs

Globally, more than $100 billion a year is spent on fighting the 'war on drugs'.

Lessons from the unlearnt consequences of prohibition

Common sense should guide us to make practical and workable decisions. When these decisions involve people, history, and an understanding of human emotions and psychology, these principles ought to steer them. So, when in 1920 Prohibition was introduced under the Eighteenth Amendment to the U.S. Constitution, it was not based on any of these principles. Prohibition was a nationwide constitutional ban on the sale, production, importation, and transportation of alcoholic beverages that lasted from 1920 to 1933. It was championed by the "dry" crusaders, a movement led by rural Protestants and social Progressives in the Democratic and Republican parties. It was organised by the Anti-Saloon League and the Woman's Christian Temperance Union. Below are lessons from history that could have helped guide them against prohibition.

Michael Lerner, the historian, explained:

- When a Massachusetts town banned the sale of alcohol in 1844, an enterprising tavern owner devised a clever way to evade the law. He started charging patrons to see a *striped pig*—the drinks came free with the price of admission.

  So, he was not breaking the law since he was not selling alcohol. Furthermore, no one could dispute how valuable and intellectually stimulating it was to sit and look at a striped pig.

- "When Maine passed a strict prohibition law in 1851, the result was not temperance, but resentment among the city's working-class and Irish immigrant population. A deadly riot in Portland in 1855 led to the law's repeal."

  We appear to have a talent for not learning from history. So, despite the powerful lessons that could have been learnt above, sixty-five years later, prohibition was enshrined in America's constitution.

What was expected from prohibition?

When the law came into force, they anticipated:

- Clothing and household goods sales are set to soar.
- Real estate developers and landlords expected rents to increase as saloons shut and neighbourhoods improve.

- Chewing gum, grape juice, and soft drink companies all anticipated growth.
- Theatre producers anticipated new audiences as Americans sought new means to entertain themselves without alcohol.

This is what they got instead

- A decline across the amusement and entertainment industries as a whole.
- Restaurants failed because they could no longer make a profit without legal liquor sales.
- Theatre revenues fell rather than rose, and few of the other economic benefits that had been forecasted materialised.
- The closure of breweries, distilleries, and saloons resulted in the loss of thousands of jobs, which in turn led to the loss of even more jobs for barrel makers, truckers, waiters, and other related trades.
- One of the most notable impacts of Prohibition was on government tax revenue. Before Prohibition, many states relied heavily on excise taxes from alcohol sales to fund their budgets. In New York, nearly 75% of the state's income was generated from liquor taxes. Once Prohibition was enacted, that income was lost immediately.
- At the national level, Prohibition resulted in the federal government losing a total of £11 billion in tax revenue, while enforcement costs exceeded £300 million. The most enduring consequence was that many states and the federal government would come to depend on income tax revenue to fund their budgets in the future.

  http://www.pbs.org/kenburns/prohibition/
  unintended-consequences/

Peter McWilliams' book, *Ain't Nobody's Business If You Do*, lists more points:

- Disrespect for the law – If everyone breaks the law, it loses respect. Nearly everyone broke the law of Prohibition, turning everyone into criminals.
- "Prohibition goes beyond the bounds of reason in that it attempts to control a man's appetite by legislation and makes crimes out of things that are not crimes." – Abraham Lincoln

- Prohibition encouraged people to see the law as whimsical and unimportant, instead of something good and protective. It did nothing to promote the respect and obedience the law deserves.

- *Prohibition made the gangster not just well paid, but well-liked.*

- It required a large organisation to smuggle the quantities of alcohol people wanted. The result was organised crime, which didn't distinguish between petty crimes like transporting liquor and serious crimes such as violence, murder, and theft.

- Prohibition corrupted law enforcement, the court system, and politics.

- Organised crime was huge, and it had a lot of money and influence.

- Policemen and politicians were bribed and blackmailed: When mobsters couldn't buy or threaten someone in a powerful position, they either "wiped them out" or, following more democratic principles, ran a candidate against the incumbent in the next election. They funded their candidate, stuffed the ballot box, or leaked scandals about the incumbent just before the election (or all three). The main goal was winning, and more often than not, someone beholden to organised crime rose to a position of power.

- Prohibition burdened the police, courts, and penal system. In 1923, for example, the US District Attorneys spent *44% of their time* on Prohibition cases. This takes time away from the real purpose of police and courts: to protect people and their belongings, not impose a religious group's morals.

- Because alcohol was illegal, its purity was not regulated. While fruit, vegetable, and grain alcohol are usually safe, alcohol made from wood is not, but it is difficult to tell the difference until it is too late. Over 10,000 people died during Prohibition from drinking wood alcohol. Others who were not killed went permanently blind or suffered severe organ damage.

- Prohibition altered the drinking habits of our country, for the worse. Instead of going out to drink, people mainly drank at home. When they did go out, it was often to get drunk – you couldn't be seen with a bottle, so they finished it quickly. As a result, prohibition also led to more people drinking.

- An explosion of immorality. Men and women began drinking together – they were partners in crime, and they became bed partners. Unmarried sexual activity increased, and the decade became known as the "Roaring 20s."

- Prohibition was a massive failure at legislating morality.
- The primary issue with prohibition was that it never led to people drinking less, which was its main aim.

Other credits for prohibition info:
https://www.patheos.com/blogs/unreasonablefaith/2009/03/12-bad-effects-of-prohibition-you-should-know/–Daniel Florien https://wandervogeldiary.wordpress.com2014/05/11/

Common sense indicates that we should learn from the consequences of prohibition and apply these lessons when contemplating other victimless crimes, such as soft and hard drugs, gambling, and prostitution. A victimless crime refers to an action, often consensual or solitary, that is made illegal but does not directly infringe upon or threaten the rights of another person. Understandably, our emotional reactions to this provocative statement might vary: the sale of cocaine, heroin, and other hard drugs, including alcohol, is a victimless crime. If the sale of cocaine and heroin is not victimless, then neither is the sale of cigarettes and alcohol. In reality, they are all victimless crimes, as no one is forced to use them.

Yet, cigarettes and alcohol are legal, while cocaine and heroin are not. All these substances can cause death, but cigarettes and alcohol are particularly known for causing millions of deaths, including those from cancer. Despite this, what is most people's emotional response regarding the sale and use of cocaine and heroin compared to cigarettes and alcohol? Many of us strongly oppose cocaine and heroin and feel indifferent towards cigarettes and alcohol. This is partly due to the criminal nature of illegal drugs.

Attitudes towards drugs are time-specific

History shows us that attitudes towards drugs are specific to their era and influenced by governments and religious groups. There was a time when cocaine was an ingredient in Coca-Cola. In 1839, the United Kingdom went to war with China because the Daoguang Emperor, alarmed by the increasing number of opium addicts caused by the trade activities of the British East India Company, rejected proposals to legalise and tax opium, and appointed Lin Zexu to solve the problem by ending the trade. Lin confiscated around 20,000 chests of opium (about 1210 tonnes or 2.66 million pounds) without offering compensation.

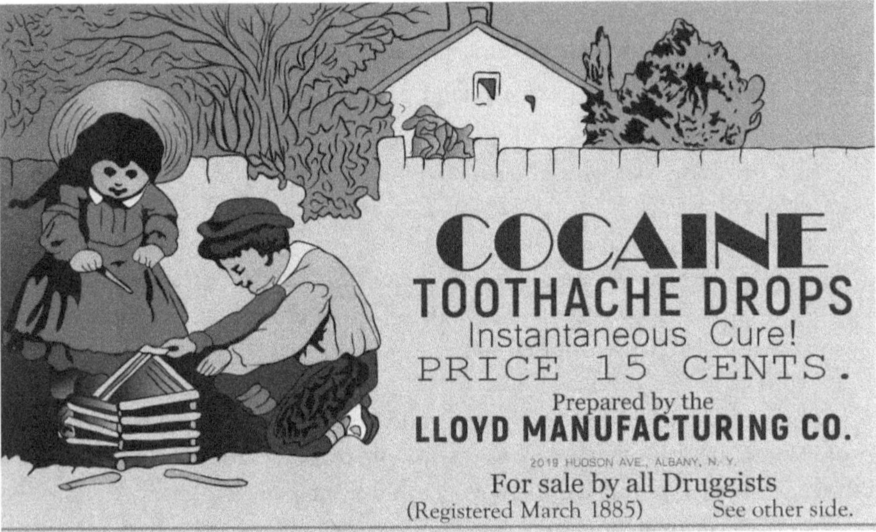

Be wary of solutions that end up being worse than the problems they attempt to solve. We should avoid legislating to enforce what is considered moral behaviour or to prevent what is viewed as deviant behaviour when no victims are involved. Legislation is seldom effective at stopping individuals from engaging in activities that do not directly harm others. As a result, it is an inefficient use of financial and human resources. Here are some simple solutions:

- The most effective way to discourage drug use is for governments to eliminate any perception of glamour or fun connected with it, and this must start with children. They need to see the harsh, gritty, sleazy, depraved, and devastating effects of hard drug use specifically. They should be informed about talented and famous individuals whose lives have been ruined or ended by drugs. A reasonable lesson can also be learned from how the government in the United Kingdom has taken action to reduce the use of one of society's legal 'soft drugs', cigarettes, which are known to kill millions each year. Despite its deadly history, the solution was not to ban it but, recognising that we can be manipulated into becoming 'volunteer victims'11, they have banned and reduced the means of manipulation – tobacco advertising.

- Providing comprehensive education about the effects of all drugs can be more helpful and effective than criminalising them. The real offence is not regulating them to enable safer use. Drug use and addiction are not criminal issues; they are matters of public health and education. The ultimate solution is not to 'fight a war' to eliminate the supply, because that approach is ineffective and will never succeed. The best approach is to nurture and educate people to reduce or eliminate demand. Those with a balanced philosophy and emotions learned through self-preservation are less likely to engage in self-destructive behaviour deliberately. The worst-case scenario is that education diminishes this behaviour.

Benefits of legalisation of all drugs – simple logic and facts

According to 2013 data from the United Nations Office on Drugs and Crime (UNODC) and the European crime-fighting agency Europol, the global drug trade was worth approximately **$435 billion** annually, with the cocaine trade alone valued at **$84 billion.** Such a substantial sum of money grants immense power to criminals and organised crime. There are eight fundamental issues that drug use and its illegality pose to society. They are:

- Criminality and organised crime.
- Hundreds of thousands of violent deaths per annum.
- Widespread corruption and destabilisation of governments.
- The underdevelopment of countries.
- Drug addictions and deaths due to dangerously concocted drugs.
- Crimes to fund the addiction.
- An increase in the number of criminals and prison populations.
- Many desperately poor families are destroyed when the primary breadwinner is tempted to smuggle drugs, gets caught, and faces a lengthy prison sentence or even the death penalty. Many have also died from smuggling drugs as a method of transport.

Some of the issues caused by the illegality of drugs include recent mass migrations from Central and South America due to interconnected factors: poverty, resulting from government destabilisation, and underdevelopment driven by organised crime and drug wars; the desire to escape the dangers posed by drug cartels, such as 'recruitment or death', and death as collateral damage during drug wars.

How would legalisation impact the problems caused by the illegalisation of drugs?

- If the drug market were organised similarly to cigarettes, at least four of the major problems mentioned earlier would disappear. Worst case, we would only face smuggling to avoid paying VAT, like with cigarettes. Nonetheless, this would be a minor issue since drugs, like cigarettes, would still be easily accessible.

- Criminality and organised crime would disappear just as they did after prohibition was repealed in America.

- The destabilisation of governments through the financial influence of crime syndicates would no longer be possible. The funds allocated to combat drug production and trafficking could be redirected to develop those countries at the forefront of these issues. No more Al Capones or drug lords of his kind.

- There would likely be a decrease in crimes linked to funding addiction, as drugs would become significantly cheaper.

- There would be a notable reduction in deaths caused by dangerously mixed drugs.

- We are now left with issues of drug use and addiction. Has the 'war on drugs' actually decreased drug use or addiction?

- According to *countthecost.org*: The global 'war on drugs' has been fought for 50 years, **without stopping the long-term trend of rising drug supply and use.** Beyond this failure, the UN Office on Drugs and Crime (UNODC) has also highlighted the many serious *'unintended negative consequences'* of the drug war. These costs come not from drug use itself, but from adopting a punitive enforcement-led approach that, by its nature, hands control of the trade to organised crime and criminalises many users. In doing so, this approach undermines development and security and fuels conflict in many poor and fragile countries.

- There is no evidence that legalisation would result in increased use of either hard or soft drugs. However, it is recognised that some individuals use them because of their taboo status.

- Even if addictions remain the same or increase due to higher drug use, we would still gain significant benefits by reducing or eliminating the other problems mentioned above. Is reducing to three problems better than having eight?

- A portion of the large sums spent on the 'war on drugs' and imprisonment could be diverted to treat those with addiction, similar to treatments for alcoholism, and to better inform the public about drug use beyond current efforts against cigarettes.

Switzerland's experience strengthens the common-sense suggestions on drugs

In the 1980s, Switzerland faced a health crisis related to HIV and AIDS, with the use of cannabis, heroin, and other opiates playing a central role. Zurich became recognised as a major centre for heroin addicts in Europe, and an area in the city centre was dubbed "Needle Park". The initial government response was to try to tackle the problem through law enforcement. They aimed to reduce drug use and trafficking through arrests and imprisonment. At one point, this led to the proportion of the prison population incarcerated for drug-related offences rising to 80 percent. As the desired results were not achieved and social problems grew, authorities eventually sought more effective ways to address the worst aspects of drug abuse and addiction faced by users.

In 1992, the government approved a trial of Heroin Assisted Treatment (HAT), also known as Heroin Maintenance Treatment. In this programme, addicts received medically-controlled doses of heroin daily at free heroin maintenance centres, where they also had access to showers, beds, and social workers to help them find housing and assistance with other life issues. The aim is to reintegrate into society after treatment eventually. An inspiring outcome for those on the programme was that two-thirds of them gained regular employment because they could concentrate on recovery rather than finding ways to fund their addiction.

The trial lasted until 1997 and was considered successful because it reduced some of the worst aspects of addiction, such as the spread of disease, criminal activity, prostitution to support the habit, and social exclusion. Other positive effects include:

- HIV infections have dropped significantly
- Deaths from heroin overdose have dropped by50%

    http://www.narconon.org/drug-information/switzerland-drug-addiction.html

In an article by Stephanie Nebehay, dated 25th October 2010, she wrote:

> "Switzerland's innovative policy of providing drug addicts with free methadone and clean needles has greatly reduced deaths while cutting crime rates and should serve as a global model, health experts said on Monday. Countries whose drug policy remains focused on punishing offenders, including Russia and much of Eastern Europe and Central Asia, [and the USA], should learn from a Swiss strategy based on "harm reduction" that protects both users and communities, they said."

http://www.reuters.com/article/us-swiss-drugs- idUSTRE69O3VI20101025

Portugal's common-sense approach to its drug problem

(Information from Michael Moore's 2015 documentary film, 'Where to Invade Next'):

They waged a war on drugs but were losing, so they decided to try something new.

In 2001, they decriminalised drug use. They no longer arrest people for using any drugs. This increased access to drug treatment.

By decriminalising drug use, the rate of drug consumption decreased. Policeman: "Human dignity is the backbone of our society. And all the laws have to be based on respecting and following that principle. And those principles are instilled in us, even in our training as policemen. A basic principle in our training is respect for the dignity of the human being, always." Do the following statistics suggest a rise in crime as a result of their 'radical' approach?

Portugal's murder rate (which is relatively low) per 100,000 of the population has had a steady decline between 2013 and 2016, with a spike in 2014.
2016 was 0.64, a 33.75% decline from 2015.
2015 was 0.96, a 9.24% increase from 2014.
2014 was 0.88, a 35.77% decline from 2013.
2013 was 1.37, an 18.64% increase from 2012.

Although legalising and regulating drugs could reduce the problems from eight to two (drug use and addiction), society's emotional stance towards hard drugs makes this change challenging. It would require a widespread educational campaign, similar to those in Switzerland and Portugal. Common sense suggests that this topic warrants serious debate—one based on facts, understanding human psychology, and recognising the failures of the 'war against drugs'. The inevitable scaremongering in this debate will require our most effective tool— logic—to take centre stage and emphasise the clear failure of current policies. The advantages of removing the seven harmful issues mentioned earlier, leaving only two problems to address instead of eight, should be a focus of this discussion. In a democracy, all strategies for tackling seemingly impossible problems must be reconsidered if progress is not made, especially after 59 years of the 'war on drugs' (1961–2020).

CHAPTER FOURTEEN

Common sense on some major life issues

The eleven major life issues discussed in this book are all characterised by one or a combination of the sciences of psychology, sociology, and biology. The closest aspect we have regarding how these sciences function is logic, not our emotions. It is the logical brain that we have used to discover these sciences. Science, in general, is defined by logic, and the science that governs our body is also logical. It makes sense that we utilise *the science of logic or common sense* to examine and explain our behaviour, as well as to guide the actions we should take concerning our life issues. This is essential because we have become far more complex than we were at the beginning of life.

The aim has been to demonstrate that, although our decision making is shaped by our thoughts and feelings, and this relationship benefits both, in our complex world, logical reasoning supported by accurate information should take precedence. Some major life challenges discussed in this book are deeply difficult and include illness, death, and upheaval in many lives. Applying common sense could significantly alleviate these issues.

This examination of common sense started with investigating how we first learnt to satisfy one of our basic needs, shelter. We discovered that more than one person was required to build more than a simple dwelling. This was our initial common-sense lesson in becoming competent and effective humans, through teamwork.

Our complex world is now, largely without conscious awareness, caught in a struggle between the logical and emotional minds. The emotional mind is prevailing. We have developed bombs capable of destroying everyone. As our world becomes more complicated, the need for logical thinking increases, and the knowledge we gain should become common sense.

As time passed, the inevitable happened. We became more complex individuals and created a more intricate world. However, our knowledge and understanding must keep pace with our increasingly complex nature. Otherwise, we risk falling prey to those who seek to deceive or harm us. At the very least, we will struggle to succeed in our current reality. Without a thorough understanding of the subtleties of modern human behaviour, we are vulnerable to making poor decisions.

Relationships have also been affected by living in a more complex world. Our desires and needs now go beyond food, clothes, and shelter, unlike when we led very simple lifestyles. It might seem that applying logic to such an emotional subject as relationships is unhelpful. However, if this reasoning includes an understanding of human behaviour, it shows us that, no matter how attracted we are to someone, a relationship will only succeed if there is compatibility. A lack of compatibility can be linked to many reasons for divorce listed by relationship counsellor Pooja Bedi. Her reasons, such as lack of intimacy, unrealistic expectations, not being ready for marriage, differences in background, inequality within the relationship, and poor communication, can all be described as 'not being on the same page.' These are all issues related to compatibility.

> The *logical mind* is the source of common sense, functioning much like a computer. Its responses develop as it encounters new facts. However, when our emotional mind takes over, it often obstructs new information and reasoning. Many of us have seen situations where individuals refuse to change or revise their beliefs despite new evidence. Similarly, they will not modify or reconsider their support for someone regardless of their behaviour. We often see this expression of the emotional mind within politics and religion.

This book has aimed to show that Aristotelian syllogistic reasoning, the product of our logical mind, is best suited for reaching accurate conclusions, which is highly desirable, especially in our complex world. In essence, it is much better and more effective at solving problems than our emotions are. All significant aspects of our lives discussed in this book can be improved by adopting a logical perspective. Logic states that, as nurturing children is essential, so is fostering the relationship between parents and their children. Logic suggests

that a broken relationship between parents can harm the well-being of children. Common sense can offer a happy balance between these two needs.

Our complex and emotional nature has also led to the widespread commercialisation of our food. This has caused our food and snack intake to extend far beyond what is natural and healthy. We now face a situation where the essential task of determining our proper diet has become a contentious issue, with many differing views. If we apply logic and science, this question can be easily settled. Logic shows us that what we put into our bodies should align with the scientific principles that govern them, not be based on opinions, culture, or traditions. However, mainly, our emotional mind has driven us to prioritise taste and cultural influences when deciding what to eat. The fact that we are still debating what we should or shouldn't eat after thousands of years of civilisation suggests we have not relied on a single guiding principle, such as science, to resolve the matter. Food has become a highly emotional issue. Some reasons include that it is no longer merely about satisfying hunger and providing nutrition; food now also serves as a source of comfort and entertainment.

Our dominant emotions have caused many to become addicted to drugs that kill, impair, and destroy lives. This sustains massive, powerful, and destructive criminal empires. Our logical mind tells us that their power only exists because drugs are illegal; yet, we fail to remove this power. The history of American prohibition should have taught us the folly of legislating against actions that both the supplier and the receiver are eager to pursue. Drug use is, in effect, a victimless crime; taking drugs is a consensual act, made illegal (unlike the equally dangerous cigarettes and alcohol) but does not directly violate or threaten the rights of others, and no one is forced to use it. This lesson was 'loudly' demonstrated by the fact that after prohibition was repealed, all the crime lords no longer had the basis on which to make their fortunes. They were, in effect, unemployed. And all the other destructive dynamics explored in chapter thirteen also vanished.

Only our emotions and false beliefs cause us to accept a 'non-curing' medicine. Logic shows that it is unwise to stick with a medicine that only alleviates symptoms without providing a cure. Yet, we continue because of a mix of self-interest (for those who profit from it), fear of illness, desperation for health, and a lack of accurate information.

Our complex nature has also contributed to the irrationality of polluting our world to the extent that life and health are often threatened and lost. As a result, caring for Mother Earth and our environment has become a major concern. We need to foster a shared understanding of the unspoken relationship we are supposed to have with Nature. How can we justify neglecting Mother Earth and our environment when it is the only home we have? Greed, driven by basic desires such as expecting the Earth to produce food unnaturally quickly and the willingness to amass wealth at any environmental cost, is usually the cause. Accurate knowledge, a balanced philosophy, and logical reasoning (common sense) would prevent us from following this destructive path.

A complex world filled with more desires than fulfilment has made stress a common experience and happiness a fleeting moment for many. Logic suggests that our thoughts and actions determine whether we experience happiness or unhappiness. Therefore, our minds must be nourished with ideas that encourage us to habitually engage in behaviours that lead to lasting happiness. Instead, our emotions often drive us towards short-term pleasures, like 'happy hour', which can result in long-term pain from neglecting ourselves and others.

A more complex world has rendered our formal education system even more inadequate than it was in simpler times. While our current education prepares us for employment, it fails to bridge the significant gap between being skilled at work and managing everyday life situations where common sense must prevail. To be consistently effective like animals, we need an education system that equips everyone to understand the major and minor life issues discussed in this book. However, simply acquiring detailed knowledge of these issues is not enough; we must also learn how to apply syllogistic logic to the information we gather. This is the most reliable way for people from different cultures to reach similar conclusions on many life issues that can lead to conflicts.

To minimise conflicts, syllogistic reasoning should be incorporated into formal education across all countries, thereby enhancing people's thinking skills globally. Syllogistic (or deductive) reasoning is akin to critical thinking and is defined as "The objective analysis and evaluation of an issue to form a judgement." Many conflicts stem from misunderstandings or poor analysis that lead to bad judgement. Therefore, critical thinking could help decrease conflicts by improving our judgement.

It is essential that a widespread, common understanding develops that many of our undesirable outcomes are not unavoidable and should not be regarded as normal or natural. For instance, dying from major illnesses like cancer and diabetes should not be called 'dying from natural causes' – because we are the cause. As human beings, responsible for shaping our lives and the world, we must observe, learn, and pass on this truth to each generation. We all need to grasp that cause-and-effect is the main principle governing our lives, and that we are accountable. Therefore, we are the only ones who can alter our undesirable outcomes. The logical mind must become the dominant force in all our affairs, as it is far more effective than our emotions at solving problems, especially in a complex world.

So, how do we enable syllogistic reasoning that fosters common sense and transforms our formal education system? Since this subject has rarely been explored in the modern context before this book, it could potentially be included as standard reading material and become **part** of this developmental process. An accurate understanding of the subjects covered in this book should be encouraged by our education system, so that they become common knowledge or common sense. But what are the essential subjects that schools should include in their curriculum which, if made compulsory, would act as a catalyst to nurture *a keen interest in life and people*, forming the very basis of common sense?

All seven of the recommended subjects below can help us develop this transformative common sense. They will provide us with relevant information to better understand many of our current life challenges. Once we understand these subjects, our mind-computer and emotional intelligence will determine which information is most relevant to extract and apply syllogistic reasoning to understand and resolve many of our significant life challenges.

1. **World history** involves understanding the sequence of human events, learning about various civilisations, and recognising their contributions to human progress. History, or a record or study of past events, is valuable for providing the context necessary to interpret and understand life issues accurately. We should teach students the importance of context and how to recognise it to better understand any given issue.

2. **A basic understanding of human psychology**—specifically how our minds function and how we think—enhances our ability to comprehend human behaviour.

3. **Sociology** – "*... the study of human social relationships and institutions. Sociology's subject matter is diverse, ranging from crime to religion, from the family to the state, from the divisions of race and social class to the shared beliefs of a common culture, and from social stability to radical change in whole societies. Unifying the study of these diverse subjects is sociology's purpose of understanding how human action and consciousness both shape and are shaped by surrounding cultural and social structures...*" – The University of North Carolina.

4. **Politics and the media – their influence is too crucial in shaping our reality for any of us to be unaware of them and the role we should play.**

Added to the above as part of a basic formula to inspire common sense, there should be three subjects that our ignorance of poses a clear and present danger.

5. **Nutrition** – A necessity to navigate the conflicting messages from both governments and the 'food' industry, motivated by profit.

6. **Human biology** – understanding this would help us better understand and analyse arguments about nutrition and medicine, which are often motivated by profit.

7. **At least a basic knowledge of our environment, how to look after it, and the dangers of neglecting it.**

Context is crucial for understanding many life issues and experiences. For example, love and hate can both be positive and negative. It is beneficial when we hate evil and harmful actions without just cause. However, it is harmful when we hate and harm those who are different but do us no harm. Giving love is good because it uplifts both the giver and the receiver. But it is problematic if loving a child means avoiding the discipline and values necessary for a balanced life, which could lead to the child growing up dysfunctional and unhappy.

If these subjects are made compulsory in schools, knowledge of them would be enough to act as a catalyst, inspiring post-school students to develop a deeper understanding of life and people. The result would be a population with greater awareness of knowledge that should be regarded as common sense. A society engaged in acquiring such knowledge would enhance our human experience and broaden understanding of life beyond what is covered in this book. Essentially, much more knowledge would become widespread common knowledge or common sense. We can conclude that many types of knowledge should become common sense but are not currently so. As a result, common sense is often perceived as 'not common' because many of us lack basic knowledge and simple logic. However, as we have seen, common sense involves much more than just logic. Therefore, we all lack some knowledge that ought to be considered common sense.

The end…or, our journey to a new level of understanding and insight that awaits us…